GENTLEMEN REVOLUTIONARIES

Gentlemen Revolutionaries

POWER AND JUSTICE IN THE
NEW AMERICAN REPUBLIC

Tom Cutterham

PRINCETON UNIVERSITY PRESS

PRINCETON & OXFORD

Published by Princeton University Press,
41 William Street, Princeton, New Jersey 08540

In the United Kingdom: Princeton University Press,
6 Oxford Street, Woodstock, Oxfordshire OX20 1TR

press.princeton.edu

Cover art: *Portrait of a Gentleman*, 1769 (oil on canvas), Nathaniel Hone (1718–84) /
Private Collection / Photo © Philip Mould Ltd, London / Bridgeman Images

First paperback printing, 2020
Paperback ISBN 978-0-691-21010-0

The Library of Congress has cataloged the cloth edition as follows:

Names: Cutterham, Tom, 1987– author.
Title: Gentlemen revolutionaries : power and justice in the new American republic /
    Tom Cutterham.
Description: Princeton : Princeton University Press, 2017. | Includes bibliographical
    references and index.
Identifiers: LCCN 2016047704| ISBN 9780691172668 (hardcover : alkaline paper) |
    ISBN 0691172668 (hardcover : alkaline paper)
Subjects: LCSH: United States—Politics and government—1775–1783. | United States—
    Politics and government—1783–1789. | Elite (Social sciences)—United States—History—
    18th century. | Power (Social sciences)—United States—History—18th century. | Upper
    class—United States—History—18th century. | Ideals (Philosophy)—Political aspects—
    United States—History—18th century. | Social justice—United States—History—18th
    century. | Social status—United States—History—18th century. | Social control—United
    States—History—18th century. | United States—Social conditions—To 1865. | BISAC:
    HISTORY / United States / Revolutionary Period (1775-1800). | HISTORY /
    Revolutionary. | HISTORY / United States / General. | PHILOSOPHY / Political.
Classification: LCC E303 .C87 2017 | DDC 303.3/72097309033—dc23
    LC record available at https://lccn.loc.gov/2016047704

British Library Cataloging-in-Publication Data is available

This book has been composed in Miller.

Printed in the United States of America

For Rob

CONTENTS

ACKNOWLEDGMENTS

THIS BOOK ABOUT ELITES was written at Oxford University, among wonderful friends and colleagues too numerous to list in full. I am grateful to Lizzy Emerson; to my fellow MSters of the Universe; and to the graduate student community at the Rothermere American Institute, especially Ken Owen, David Sim, Steve Tuffnell, Mandy Izadi, Paddy Andelic, Ursula Hackett, Kathryn Olivarius, Dan Rowe, and Louisa Hotson. Among the fellows of the Institute, I am indebted to Jay Sexton, Stephen Tuck, Gareth Davies, Pekka Hämäläinen, Don Ratcliffe, Sally Bailey, and especially Nigel Bowles. Nicholas Cole and Peter Thompson, my indefatigable supervisors, bore the brunt of failed ideas and off-kilter notions. Their inspiration and advice has been invaluable throughout.

Many librarians and archivists made this project possible. Most of all, of course, Jane Rawson and her team at the Vere Harmsworth Library. Rachel Jirka and Ellen Clark at Anderson House deserve a special mention for their warmth and solicitude towards an inexperienced researcher. Morgan Davies, Tom Nailor, Michael Moore, and Margaret Molloy kindly put me up during research travels. Funding for those travels came from the Rothermere American Institute, the Society of the Cincinnati, St Hugh's College, and the Royal Historical Society. My doctoral studies were funded by a scholarship from the Rothermere American Institute. I benefited immensely from attending the Global Dome program of the University of Notre Dame.

For the last three years of writing and rewriting this book, I was the Sir Christopher Cox Junior Fellow at New College. Caroline Thomas, Erica Longfellow, Michael Burden, Martin Pickup, Ryan Hanley, Jonathan Leader-Maynard, Anne Hanley, Aaron Graham, and many others made it an amazing home. Ben Tate of Princeton University Press, along with his colleagues Debbie Tegarden, Hannah Zuckerman, and Jay Boggis, helped me to navigate the excitement and frustration of publishing my first book. At the University of Birmingham, where I started working in September 2016, I have benefited from the support of many new friends and colleagues, whose names I expect to fill the acknowledgements of books to come.

One of the great delights of joining a profession is the opportunity to turn heroes into colleagues. Woody Holton and Patrick Griffin have been generous, unfailing, and indispensable friends both to me and to this project. Max Edling has provided inspiration and support since its beginning. Simon Middleton was a model external examiner, and has been an even better friend. Eliga Gould gave valuable encouragement and criticism in the final stages of writing this book. Saul Cornell, Lawrence Goldman, Joanna Innes, Colin Jones,

Sarah Pearsall, and Andrew O'Shaugnessy have each contributed to helping me become a professional historian, as have all the good folk of the British Group of Early American Historians.

I owe a great deal to the fellow young historians with whom both I and this book have grown up. Jonathan Gienapp and Mark Boonshoft bravely read and valuably commented on the entire manuscript. Through rituals I cannot detail here, Ben Park inducted me into the Junto. Michael Hattem, Rachel Herrmann, Michael Blaakman, Sara Georgini, Jonathan Wilson, Chris Minty, Joe Adelman, Christopher Jones, Jess Parr, Roy Rogers, and Nora Slonimsky, I salute you all. Finally, I offer thanks to those not yet named, without whose friendship and support none of this would be possible: Mike Smith, Jenny Oliver, Sam Ferguson, Dasha Luchinskaya, Stephanie Solywoda, Arthur Seymour, and my mother, Tina, who gave me both the gift of reading and the will to write.

GENTLEMEN REVOLUTIONARIES

Introduction

"AND FOR THE SUPPORT of this Declaration, with a firm reliance on the protection of divine Providence, we mutually pledge to each other our Lives, our Fortunes and our sacred Honor." So ends the document that began the United States on July 4, 1776. Its revolutionary authors were not only declaring a separation from the British empire. They were also making a personal commitment to each other, and to the new nation. They really were risking their fortunes and their lives. But what did they mean by "sacred Honor"? The American Revolution was led by men who set themselves above the ordinary, common man. They understood themselves as gentlemen. That status was a form of power, but it also relied on a set of rules that governed the actions of anyone who claimed it—a code of honor that helped draw the line between who was a gentleman and who was not. When the signers of the Declaration pledged their "sacred Honor" to the cause of independence, they were laying on the line one of their most valued possessions: their status as gentlemen.[1]

What exactly it meant to be a gentleman changed over time. It also depended on place and social context. A gentleman in Boston might not be one in London, and a gentleman out on the western frontier—where there were few if any to be found—might not be one in Philadelphia. The status of gentleman relied on being recognized by others. Rather than an innate quality, it was a kind of performance done in front of different, more or less discerning audiences.[2] At the same time, not everyone could act like a gentleman. By definition, gentility was restricted to an elite minority. In seventeenth-century England, gentlemen were landowners who got their income from rent. Doing any kind of work for money, even investing in commerce, was seen as beneath their dignity. Yet in the American colonies, almost nobody could fit that definition. By the middle of the eighteenth century, especially in the colonies, the requirements of gentility were beginning to adapt to different economic and social conditions.

Rather than disdaining work of any kind, the standards in place by the eve of the American Revolution separated manual work from work of the mind and the pen. Those who relied on the labor of their own hands, whether on farms, in workshops, or on board ships, could not be considered gentlemen. But merchants, lawyers, doctors, clergymen, and scholars could also lay claim to elite status. As the transatlantic consumer economy developed, even those who did not get their income from landed estates—or, like the gentlemen of the southern colonies, from slave plantations—could purchase the kinds of fashionable clothes, furniture, and accoutrements that were needed to make a performance of gentility. Using the advice in conduct books and the examples in English magazines like *The Spectator*, wealthy professionals learned how to behave, and how to recognize each other, as gentlemen. They could sometimes cement their status by marrying into the families of the landed gentry. Ambitious men signaled their rise by adopting, as much as they could, the markers and attitudes of gentility.

Before the revolution began, then, the idea of the gentleman was already in flux. American gentlemen could not rely on maintaining their status without effort. For southern planters, the need to signal their place in society through conspicuous consumption often meant getting deep in debt to the British merchants who sent them luxury goods in exchange for cash crops.[3] And the performance of gentility involved more than buying and wearing the right things. It also required adherence to the gentlemanly code of honor. While the expectations and behaviors that made up the code were slightly different in different parts of the colonies, there were some things that were supposed to characterize gentlemen everywhere. Most important, a gentleman was someone who could be trusted—who always dealt honestly and kept his word. If he was accused of breaking this code, it was expected that a gentleman would defend his honor, by fighting a duel if necessary. Maintaining the status of a gentleman could end up costing not just one's fortune, but one's life.[4]

There were some elements of the gentlemanly code of honor that fitted in particularly well with the new forms of wealth that came from commerce.[5] Merchants relied on building up a reputation for meeting their obligations— paying their debts and delivering goods according to agreement. The more solid their reputation, otherwise known as their credit or character, the more likely people were to deal with them, and the better terms they could secure. A merchant who possessed the character of a gentleman could use his respectability to gain a commercial advantage; and in turn, he could use the wealth he generated through trade to put on a convincing performance of gentility. When merchants began to be recognized as gentlemen in the American colonies, they also began to transform the meaning of the gentlemen's code of honor. The landed wealth of the old English gentlemen had set them above society because they never needed to depend on anyone. By contrast, merchants used gentility to secure mutually beneficial relationships with others. Where gentility had once implied independence, it could become a valuable element in the interdependent world of commerce.[6]

It was the revolution that finally gave American merchants access to the uppermost circles of society and power. Sweeping away royal officeholders and their loyalist allies, the revolution was the platform that launched a new national elite. Especially in the north, where there were few major landowners among the patriots, it was merchants and lawyers who made up this new cadre of gentlemen revolutionaries. Even in the south, elite planters were far from the old ideal of independent English gentry. They were intimately involved with the trade in their plantations' products, and with the organization of their local economies. Many had been trained as lawyers at London's Inns of Court. Up and down the new nation, the leaders of the revolution represented a new kind of gentleman. Eager to establish and keep hold of their elite status, these men saw the revolution as an opportunity to reconstruct the idea of gentility in their own image, replacing aristocratic traditions with their own conceptions of reason, merit, and justice.

This book argues that, in the wake of the Revolutionary War, a new national elite created itself through a process of debate and struggle over these gentlemanly ideals. They transformed the code of honor, and its demand for strict obedience to promises, into an ideology that animated political conflict and formed the basis of the new federal constitution. If we return to the Declaration of Independence, we find more than just an announcement to a candid world—we find a contract drawn up between a set of individuals, pledging their lives, fortunes, and sacred honor, and signing their names at the bottom. It was the sanctity of contract that defined the code of gentility Americans adopted during the 1780s, that they fought for in the political struggles of that decade, and that they sought to weave into the fabric of the new nation. For good and bad, their efforts helped determine the course of the United States and the emergence of an interdependent, commercial world. We owe the pattern of our modern lives, in part, to the eighteenth century's gentlemen revolutionaries.

The transformation of the American elite was deeply bound up with the creation of the new republic. Here, too, ideas about the gentlemanly code of honor played an important role. Once they had made the commitment to independence, the genteel revolutionary leaders linked their own reputations to that of the United States. They understood the republic as a metaphorical person, a child that was now coming of age, and taking its own separate place in the world. Their aim was to make sure it would become not just a man, but a gentleman. If the gentlemanly code of honor was meant to regulate the interactions between equal individuals, there was a similar set of rules to govern the relations between sovereign countries. The law of nations, like the code of honor, was unwritten, but it was the subject of a great deal of interpretative writing. It was a powerful tradition, but it was also contested and unstable, subject to the shifts of power and ideas.

In recent decades, as global and transnational connections in the modern world have come to seem more important than ever, historians have emphasized the role of international context and the law of nations in the founding of the United States. Some have argued that the relationships between the new United States and the other empires and nations of the world—and between the individual states that made up the union—were more important to the political struggles of the revolutionary era than social conflicts *within* the republic. The national elite that stood behind the federal constitution from 1787 were concerned first and foremost, these historians say, with creating a powerful central government that could prevent the union from breaking apart, secure the republic against external attack, and make the new nation respectable to its rivals. It was important to these men that the United States was recognized as an equal among nations, just as the code of honor depended on a similar recognition among gentlemen. Their own sense of identity was tied to the character of the republic.[7]

This book takes these insights in a different direction. Rather than giving the international context priority over questions of social order and conflict, I consider the international dimension of politics in the new republic as an extension of Americans' concerns about justice and power. Through commerce, almost all Americans belonged to an Atlantic and global economy that had enormous impact on their lives. International commodity prices affected the livelihood of even the smallest farmers, while the flows of goods and money through America's port cities and market hubs supported artisans and professionals as well as the merchants who directed those flows. The wealth and influence of the revolutionary elite was a product of this commercial economic order. After the enormous disruptions of the revolution, it was vital for them to reconstruct an international network of trade and investment. International law, and later the federal constitution, promised to do that by providing a stable environment where the sanctity of contract was enshrined. Securing the power and status of the United States also meant protecting their own long-term interests.

As the capitalist economy developed through the eighteenth century, people began to understand the forces of production, consumption, and trade in new ways. Adam Smith's *Inquiry into the Nature and Causes of the Wealth of Nations*, published in 1776, helped change the way they thought about competition between countries and individuals. Rather than sealing themselves off and keeping trade within imperial boundaries, Smith argued that all nations would benefit more from opening trade to each other. Like gentlemen, countries would have to become less independent, and more interdependent. At the same time, this international commercial system relied on a shared set of rules to be enforced by national governments. Free trade did not get rid of the need for powerful states. Most important, these states were needed to protect property rights. For commerce to work properly, merchants needed to be confident in keeping hold of their profits, wherever they were—and for that, they needed laws and courts that acted in their favor. These needs led to ideas about universal justice and natural law that became powerful ways of thinking about right and wrong.[8]

But these ideas were only some of the ways in which people conceived of justice in the late eighteenth century. In the wake of the American Revolution, struggles broke out across the new nation over the way republican society should be organized. As with the international context, our understanding of these struggles has benefited from recent work by historians. Elite ideas were shaped by Enlightenment cosmopolitanism, by the requirements of transnational commerce, and by gentlemen's own sense of hierarchical superiority. By the middle of the 1780s, however, they faced an important challenge from democratic and egalitarian movements that interpreted the principles of the revolution quite differently. Primarily based among rural communities in the middle and northern states, but also drawing on the urban and maritime working classes that had helped to drive the revolution, popular political movements made use of the expanded role given to many white men by the revolutionary state constitutions. At times, their activism also took the form of both violent and nonviolent resistance, for example shutting down courts and refusing to obey government officials. They demanded, in essence, that the power of the state be used to benefit all men equally, rather than prioritizing the property rights of the wealthy.[9]

The sense of justice that animated postrevolutionary popular movements was not based on the gentleman's code of honor, but on Christian and republican traditions of equity that had deep roots in communities across the English-speaking Atlantic world. They also drew on long-established race and gender divisions that generally excluded women, black people, Native Americans, and others from their notions of egalitarianism. Rather than disavowing hierarchy and property relations altogether, the populist movements of the 1780s rested on the equal rights of white men to possess the land on which they worked and to exercise dominion over their own families. On the frontier, this included a demand for government support in expropriating Indian land. Especially in the south, it went along with calls for the expansion of slave ownership. It was rarely these issues, however, that emerged as the principal contentions between the populists and their genteel opponents. What was central to the conflict was a struggle over the extent and limits of democracy.[10]

In the late eighteenth century, the word *democracy* still had primarily negative connotations. For gentlemen schooled in classical history and politics, democracy meant the rule of mobs and demagogues, an upturning of proper social and moral order. By the time of the Philadelphia Convention in 1787, such gentlemen were blaming their political failures on an "excess of democracy" in the state governments. What they opposed was not a clearly defined theory of democracy, but a set of practices and ideas that put the collective will of local communities above the universal laws of property and contract. This book is about how different, overlapping groups of gentlemen understood the danger of democracy, how they came up with ways to fight it, and how that affected their own ideas about justice and power. It looks at conflicts between groups of gentlemen, as they argued with each other about how best to respond to the democratic threat. And it argues that this process of formulating a collective response was central to the making of a national ruling class—a class that would be capable, in the years 1787–1789, of once more transforming America.[11]

Every gentleman who supported independence risked his fortune and his life—but not all did so in the same way. One division that arose between gentlemen in the early 1780s was between the army officers and their allies, and those who served the revolution in other capacities, as merchants, politicians, and diplomats. When the officers formed a national organization, the Society of the Cincinnati, in 1783, it sparked a heated controversy that played out in public debates, pamphlets, newspapers, and private letters. The tumult over the Cincinnati revealed differences between gentlemen's ideas that had previously gone unexamined. It also threatened to break apart friendships and political networks. At its heart was the question of how social order should be preserved and reproduced in a republican country. What role, for example, should inheritance play in the transmission of privilege and power? If almost all Americans agreed that the revolution had done away with monarchy and aristocracy, they still needed to work out what would replace those things as sources of stability and leadership. This debate is the subject of chapter 1.[12]

Other lines of thought were emerging at the same time about similar issues. How would the new nation distinguish itself from the old colonies without falling prey to licentiousness, a kind of social chaos that gentlemen thought of as the very opposite of freedom? For some, especially the representatives of New England's Congregationalist establishment, the colonies' religious and educational traditions could find a new and central role in the republic. Public schooling and public religion would teach Americans not to abuse their new independence. It would help maintain the sober order and hierarchy necessary for national greatness. But not every gentleman thought alike on matters of education or religion. For some young men, especially those who had come of age during the war, the revolution offered the chance to break out of the crushing embrace of old traditions. Chapter 2 tells the story of their attempts to develop new and revolutionary approaches to education and literature. Like the arguments over the Cincinnati, these debates were not about *whether* to impose new forms of hierarchical power, but just how that could be achieved. Both chapters, then, describe elite experiments in building a republican society that would accord with their own ideas about justice, status, and power.[13]

In the following three chapters, the focus shifts to American gentlemen's conflicts with alternative political movements and ideas. Chapter 3 looks at how they developed arguments against the confiscation of loyalist property after the war was over. The popularity of confiscation policies—which not only punished the enemy and those deemed to have been enemy sympathizers, but also helped replenish state coffers and redistribute land to those who had supported independence—posed an important challenge to the sanctity of property rights, one of commercial gentility's most fundamental principles. So when gentlemen came to the defense of their former enemies, against the will of ordinary citizens, it was an important moment in the formation of an American ruling class. Cosmopolitan ideas of natural law and universal rights came face to face with the democratic potential of the revolution. The result was a series of compromises and reverses that left gentlemen increasingly frustrated with the power of popular legislatures, especially when confiscation and related policies seemed to threaten the United States' diplomatic and commercial relationships.

By the middle of the decade, American trade was suffering as a result of exclusion from trade with the British empire. National leaders in and out of Congress looked to western lands expropriated from Native Americans as a source of future profit and the foundation of national credit. But they also argued over the specifics of sale and settlement, balancing the benefits of quick sales to speculators against the requirements of security and social order on the frontier. While thousands of would-be settlers demanded access to the land, and government aid in their war against the Indians, politicians and financiers in the east struggled over the creation of new property rights and the distribution of the spoils of conquest. Banking establishments were central to this process, especially the Bank of North America in Philadelphia, set up in 1781. When the bank came under attack from Pennsylvania's rural egalitarian movement, gentlemen were again put on the defensive. Capitalist economic development seemed to be incompatible with democratic power. Chapter 4 recounts how this conflict played out between 1784 and 1786—setting the stage for more violent and dramatic events soon to come.

Chapter 5 tells the story of the year that led up to the Constitutional Convention at Philadelphia in the summer of 1787. In western New England, rural unrest finally reached the point of armed rebellion by the autumn of 1786, leading American gentlemen to a new pitch of anxiety about the future of the republic. Meanwhile, in Rhode Island, the popular majority pursued an inflationary paper-money policy that quickly led to violent clashes between the regime and its opponents. Refusing to accept the rule of the state government, merchants and their allies pursued their struggle in print, in court, and in the streets. The two situations combined to create visions of complete social breakdown in the minds of anxious elites. A group of Connecticut poets produced *The Anarchiad*, a vicious satirical attack on rural insurgents and popular legislators alike. And in Massachusetts, Boston merchants combined with the Society of the Cincinnati to raise an army that would put down the rebellion. It was during these turbulent months that a network of leading gentlemen developed a radical strategy for reasserting control of the new nation, a last-ditch effort to establish the limits of American democracy.

By focusing on the years leading up to that summer in 1787, this book offers a quite different account from those that are dominated by the Constitutional Convention and the resulting ratification struggle. The men who gathered in Philadelphia had a unique perspective on what was going on in America, one that differed significantly from most of their countrymen. When they emerged from their sealed chamber to present their Constitution to the public, taking the name of Federalists, these gentlemen largely succeeded in reframing the political contest in their own terms. If we see only the battle between Federalists and Anti-Federalists, however, we miss a good deal of what really went on during the 1780s. We miss the democratic, egalitarian movements that so frightened American gentlemen. But we also miss the diverse ways those gentlemen tried to impose their own visions of justice before 1787. Removing the Convention from center stage allows us to uncover the social conflict that lay behind it, and to see the Constitution itself not as the product of a timeless wisdom, but as a move in that ongoing struggle. This book argues that the Constitution represented a dramatic tactical shift, a desperate gambit by which gentlemen hoped to turn the tables and restore their own authority.[14]

Through the story of these early years in the new republic, we may come to better understand what was at stake in that struggle. It was not a contest between progress and backwardness, a traditional society and its modern successor. Nor was it a battle between good and evil. Rather, it was a contest over different visions of the future. Was progress a matter of democracy, the triumph of popular will over the old rule of hierarchy and concentrated power? Or was it about the rise of the commercial economy and the legal order on which it depended—the sanctity of property and contract? Would progress bring greater equality, or less? Would it empower privileged elites, or undermine them? The United States began as a battleground between these different possibilities. That battle is not yet over. By giving an account of the historical formation of ideas and power, this book aspires to more than antiquarian interest. It aims to ask questions about justice, how it comes to be defined, and how it might be implemented, not only two hundred years ago, but in our own time. Many books about the founders create mirrors of the present. My hope for this one is to reflect not a motionless monument to imagined ideals, but a living struggle for the future of a revolution.

CHAPTER ONE

Inheritance

Such is the infirmity of human nature, that every appearance of
superiority (however necessary to the policy and government of a state)
naturally excites sullen suspicion in the breasts of the subordinate.

—STEPHEN MOYLAN, FORMER ARMY COLONEL, 1783

AMERICA'S REVOLUTIONARIES fought under the banner of equality. Deeply rooted in the language of the new republic was the notion that all citizens owed equal service, and were in turn owed equal respect and influence. This language had been passed down from the ancient Greeks and Romans, but it also bore the marks of Renaissance Italian city-republics, and of England's seventeenth-century revolutions. Long before they became rebels against the British crown, Americans had embraced this republican inheritance.[1] Yet however blunt the phrase seems, "all men are created equal," there was a great deal of complexity in how it could be understood.[2] The new United States remained a country of slaveholders. It was a republic built on inequality.[3]

However much they reveled in the symbols and the language of republican equality, those who called themselves gentlemen did not give up their sense of superiority. They did not give up their power over slaves or women, nor the status that set them apart from other men.[4] Struggles over how to understand that status and how to recast it in a revolutionary light began as soon as independence was declared, and they wore on long after it was won. As long as some men possessed what others did not, equality would remain a problematic ideal. And as long as those men desired to keep what they had, and pass it on to their children, there would always be the question of inheritance.

I. The Making of a Gentleman

If there has ever been a natural aristocrat, it was Alexander Hamilton. Everyone who knew him recognized it. He had not been born to wealth or privilege. But as a child growing up on Ste. Croix, a tiny Danish outpost in the Caribbean, those who came in contact with him seemed to know he was not destined to stay where he was. In 1772, the local gentlemen collected enough money and letters of recommendation to send the gifted orphan boy north to the mainland for his education. Five years later, at the age of twenty-two or thereabouts, he was serving at George Washington's right hand, at the heart of the American Revolution. It was there, at camp in the summer of 1777, that Hamilton first met John Laurens—a young man who had all the advantages that Hamilton had not. His father Henry, a slave trader and owner of rice-planting estates in South Carolina, was both rich and extremely influential. John had been trained as a lawyer at the Inns of Court in London, an education reserved for the sons of the most privileged and ambitious colonial families. There could hardly be two men more different in the circumstances of their birth. Yet within a few years, in the midst of revolutionary tumult, Hamilton and Laurens were devoted friends.[5]

They came to know one another in the unique environment of Washington's headquarters, among the staff officers whom the general called his "family." Hamilton and Laurens were particularly close, because they were both fluent French-speakers—one as a result of his elite education in Europe, the other his childhood in the Caribbean—and served together as translators. Hamilton had dropped out of college to become a captain of artillery before he was plucked by the general to serve on his staff. Laurens, on the other hand, took his place with the benefit of his father's influence in Congress. He joined Hamilton and two other aides at camp near Germantown, Philadelphia, in August 1777. It was not a promising moment for the Continental Army. By the end of September, they had suffered a defeat at the Battle of Brandywine— the first engagement in which the two aides served together—and the rebel capital of Pennsylvania had fallen to the British. It was through that winter at Valley Forge, and the following year of campaigning, that the two young men grew close. But it was only when Laurens left on a mission to his native South Carolina, in March 1779, that Alexander had a chance to express the depth of his feeling in writing.

"I wish, my Dear Laurens, it might be in my power, by action rather than words, to convince you that I love you," Hamilton wrote him soon after. "I shall only tell you that 'till you bade us Adieu, I hardly knew the value you had taught my heart to set upon you."[6] He was writing in a way that would have been familiar to any genteel and well-read young man in the late eighteenth century. It was part of what historians now call the culture of sensibility. Gentlemen, as well as ladies, were encouraged to show how sensitive they were to the ties of affection and sympathy. These concepts animated the moral philosophy of many Enlightenment thinkers, but they were also promoted and demonstrated in literature, especially in novels. For a literate and ambitious man like Hamilton, without a fortune or a family to support him, taking part in the culture of sensibility was a way to put himself on the same terms as his well-bred friend. Whatever differences there were between them, both were men of feeling, and that made them both better than ordinary men. "You should not have taken advantage of my sensibility to steal into my affections without my consent," Hamilton told Laurens. It was that sensibility that marked him as a gentleman.[7]

During the revolution, while many of the ties that bound society together seemed to be changing or under threat, friendship became an even more important bond. Especially in the army, where men were separated from their families and communities and often in grave danger, it is no surprise that such passionate friendships flourished. At the same time, sensibility was a culture and a language that only officers had access to. Their style of friendship served as just another distinction from the rank and file men—and this sense of separateness also reinforced the bonds between officers themselves. Washington's "family" was only the most prominent example. "All the family send their love," Hamilton would add at the bottom of his letters to Laurens. "All the lads embrace you. The General sends his love." "All the lads remember you as a friend and a brother." One of their number, James McHenry, even began to write "an heroic Poem of which the family are the subject."[8] Like other groups of friends, officers built up a mythology around themselves. Their heroic friendships helped them cope with war and social instability.

For men like Hamilton, it was a time of amazing opportunity. Only the tumultuous effects of the revolution could have allowed him to so quickly gain the responsibility and respectability he achieved as Washington's aide. The Continental Army needed officers, and men with the right talents and ambitions could rise quickly through the ranks. But such an atmosphere of rapid change was also bound to create tension and anxiety—feelings that echoed larger uncertainties about the role of commerce and the rise of mercantile gentlemen. Hamilton and his colleagues paid a great deal of attention to fine distinctions of status. Sometimes he struggled to reconcile his friendship for Laurens with the feelings of resentment and insecurity stirred up by his friend's powerful family. "Though we can all truly say, we love your character, and admire your military merit," Hamilton wrote, after Laurens was offered a promotion, any sign of unfair preference from Congress "cannot fail to give some of us uneasy sensations." Friendship among the family was given a sharp edge by the young men's competition for rank and glory.[9]

They also spent time wondering about their place in wider society. Would their success as officers be enough to secure their reputations and livelihood when the war was over? What was the real and reliable basis of social hierarchy? And what would be the effects of the revolution? "I am a stranger in this country," Hamilton once complained to Laurens. "I have no property here, no connexions. If I have talents and integrity, (as you say I have) these are justly deemed very spurious titles in these enlightened days, when unsupported by others more solid."[10] There was certainly some intended irony in these words.

Surely, a truly enlightened time would value personal qualities more than property. But the anxiety Hamilton expressed about his lack of a "more solid" claim to social status was real, too. He was questioning just how enlightened the new revolutionary world would really be. In a society where fortune and family continued to matter a great deal, his talents, integrity, and relationship with the Livingstons back in New York could only take him so far.

The same mixture of playful irony and anxiety about status suffused Hamilton's letters to Laurens, including the one that began the exchange in April 1779. "And Now my Dear as we are upon the subject of wife," Hamilton wrote, "I empower and command you to get me one in Carolina." In expressing his love for his friend, Hamilton had drawn on the literary culture of sensibility. When it came to his future wife, however, he affected a cynical attitude:

> She must be young, handsome (I lay most stress upon a good shape) sensible (a little learning will do), well bred (but she must have an aversion to the word *ton*) chaste and tender (I am an enthusiast in my notions of fidelity and fondness) of some good nature, a great deal of generosity (she must neither love money nor scolding, for I dislike equally a termagent and an œconomist). In politics, I am indifferent what side she may be of; I think I have arguments that will easily convert her to mine. As to religion a moderate stock will satisfy me. She must believe in god and hate a saint. But as to fortune, the larger stock of that the better.

However tongue-in-cheek the shopping list, there was a serious reality behind it. Perhaps the best way to secure the status Hamilton had earned as an officer was indeed to catch himself a "well-bred" wife with a large stock of fortune.[11]

After a while, the letters between Hamilton and Laurens became less playful, and more concerned with matters of military and political strategy. The truth was, Laurens had never found the time to join in with Hamilton's flights of fancy. He was too deeply engaged in the revolutionary struggle in South Carolina, and could spare little time to think about anything else. Laurens' political projects were inspired by his radical hope of abolishing slavery, in spite of his father's own slave-trading fortune—and they made him a deeply controversial figure in his own state. Back at Washington's headquarters, though, Hamilton remained bereft and downhearted. In early January 1780, he told Laurens that he had asked to be sent south, where he might take a more active role in the fighting. "In short Laurens I am disgusted with every thing in this world but yourself and very few more honest fellows and I have no other wish than as soon as possible to make a brilliant exit. 'Tis a weakness; but I feel I am not fit for this terrestreal Country."[12] Yet rather than go south to die gloriously on the battlefield, Hamilton soon fulfilled a quite different fantasy. That winter, he met Elizabeth Schuyler.

At twenty-two years old, Elizabeth was not much younger than Hamilton himself. It was in the company of her father that the two first met. Philip Schuyler was the general who had commanded the army's northern department before the Battle of Saratoga. In April 1779, the same month Laurens had gone to South Carolina, Schuyler resigned from the army and took up a seat in the Continental Congress, representing New York, where he owned some tens of thousands of acres. His wife Catherine, Elizabeth's mother, had been a Van Rensselaer; her mother had been a Van Cortland. Through these famous families, their names hearkening back to the state's Dutch origins, Elizabeth Schuyler was related to many of the leading patriots of New York. In short, she was certainly well-bred. Moreover, she and her sisters, along with her friend Catherine Livingston, enjoyed being the center of attention among the officers when they came to visit the army's winter encampment at Morristown, New Jersey. The social life of the camp, outside the season for military maneuvers, gave Hamilton ample opportunity to court the "black eyed" young lady from Albany.[13]

By March, when Hamilton went on a mission to negotiate with the British over military hostages, he was writing to Schuyler and addressing her as "my dearest girl." She was writing to him too, although we do not have the letter. "I cannot tell you what extacy I felt," he replied, "in casting my eye over the sweet effusions of tenderness it contains. My Betseys soul speaks in every line and bids me be the happiest of mortals. I am so and will be so." It was a transformation from the gloomy soldier who, months before, had declared himself "not fit for this terrestreal Country." In July he wrote to her again:

> I love you more and more every hour. The sweet softness and delicacy
> of your mind and manners, the elevation of your sentiments, the real
> goodness of your heart, its tenderness to me, the beauties of your face
> and person, your unpretending good sense and that innocent simplic-
> ity and frankness which pervade your actions; all these appear to me
> with increasing amiableness and place you in my estimation above all
> the rest of your sex.[14]

By then the couple were already engaged, and he felt entitled to give her instructions as well as compliments. She must spend more time reading and cultivating her accomplishments. Hamilton had definite ideas about the kind of lady he wanted to marry, not all of which he had expressed in his letter to Laurens.

Marrying Elizabeth Schuyler would certainly bring Hamilton into the new republican elite in a much more permanent way than his military rank. A friend in the French army, the Marquis de Fleury, wrote to congratulate him "heartyly on that conquest," which he had heard about from Schuyler's elder sister. Hamilton had two reasons to be pleased, said the Frenchman: "the first that you will get all that familly's interest, & that a man of your abilities wants a Little influence to do good to his country. The second that you will be in a very easy situation, & happin[es]s is not to be found without a Large estate."[15] Yet in spite of what he had said to Laurens, such talk made Hamilton uncomfortable. It was all very well for a marquis to be cynical, but for Hamilton the situation was a rather delicate one. His bride would not, in fact, bring with her a large inheritance—she had an elder brother as well as an elder sister. If he had felt anxiety before about his background and status, he now felt it all the more keenly as he stood on the threshold of genteel society.

"In spite of Schuyler's black eyes," Hamilton told Laurens, "I have still a part for the public and another for you."[16] He had not forgotten his friend, nor his responsibilities as an officer and a revolutionary. But the military and financial situation of the rebels had only worsened over the course of the year. Laurens himself was now a prisoner on parole in Philadelphia, having been captured at the fall of Charleston in May. In August, a force led by General Horatio Gates had suffered the Continental Army's worst defeat of the war at Camden, in which over a thousand of his men were killed. Severe shortages of money and supplies made it difficult for Washington to maintain morale among his men, or to respond to British victories. For Hamilton, the impending wedding made the shortfall in his pay all the more pressing. How would he support Elizabeth in the style she would expect? Letters like Fleury's offered little real encouragement. They only underlined the difficulties Hamilton still faced in fully establishing himself as a gentleman.

Four months before their wedding, Elizabeth received a long letter from her fiancé, a letter that must have told her a great deal about the paradoxical hopes and fears that crowded his mind. He began by telling her about a fellow officer who was thinking of quitting the army, and had written to his wife to ask her opinion. "You see what a fine opportunity she has to be enrolled in the catalogue of heroines," wrote Hamilton, "and I dare say she will set you an example of fortitude and patriotism. I know … that you will not be out done in this line by any of your sex, and that if you saw me inclined to quit the service of your country, you would dissuade me from it." He expected her to act like a "*Roman* wife," and help him to put the duties of patriotism above his personal desires—to maintain his sacred honor even in the face of temptations. He allowed himself to hope for peace that winter; but if it came, he teased her, she would have to "submit to the mortification of enjoying more domestic happiness and less fame." What would he be, after all, without the dash and glamour of an officer's uniform?[17]

Through his teasing, Hamilton tried to manage Elizabeth's expectations, and soften the pangs of his own insecurity. "Do you soberly relish the pleasure of being a poor man's wife?" he asked her. "Have you learned to think a home spun preferable to a brocade and the rumbling of a waggon wheel to the musical rattling of a coach and six?" Hamilton had good reason to put such questions to her. "Though they are asked with an air of levity, they merit a very serious consideration." His circumstances were "far from splendid," he wrote, and every day brought fresh proof of the "knavery" of army paymasters—and perhaps Congress itself. "They have already filed down what was in their hands more than one half, and I am told they go on diminishing it." The Continental currency was indeed practically worthless, the army's financial situation dire. Hamilton still played the role of gentleman, which required him to affect "an indifference to property," at least for his own sake. But thinking of his future bride gave him the chance to express his own fears. "Your future rank in life," he told her, "is a perfect lottery."[18]

These anxieties, of course, were not purely personal. It was not only Hamilton and Schuyler who felt uncertain about the future in the difficult year of 1780. The question of the nation's fate tinged everything with a sense of exceptional purpose. When Elizabeth Schuyler met Martha Washington at Morristown, the same winter she first met Hamilton, she was impressed not only by the older lady's handsomeness, but by her "plain, brown gown of homespun stuff.... She was always," wrote Schuyler, "my ideal of a true woman." To be a frugal, republican wife was the counterpart to Hamilton's masculine patriotic ideal.[19] When they married at last that December, in the southeast parlor of her father's Albany mansion, it was a small, simple ceremony in the old Dutch style of Elizabeth's ancestors. Hamilton wore his lieutenant's uniform and brought one guest—James McHenry, the poet of Washington's "family." This was a wedding in the very midst of revolutionary war. But like all weddings, it also invoked a sense of continuity and propriety, a sense of the order of things. The noon light, reflecting from the snow outside, gave the room an austere brightness. It must have shone in Elizabeth's black eyes.[20]

While the celebrating couple stayed at Philip Schuyler's mansion, soldiers back at the barracks near Morristown continued to freeze and starve. The situation was growing increasingly desperate, and Washington knew it. In May, there had been a mutiny in the Connecticut line, and the general wrote to the state's governor Jonathan Trumbull to explain the reasons for it. "It is with infinite pain that I inform you," he wrote, "that we are reduced to an extremity for want of meat.... There are certain bounds, beyond which it is impossible for human nature to go. We are arrived at these." In the end, he had managed to keep the men under control, "but this without relief can only be momentary." By the end of the year, the situation had still not improved. "It would be well for the troops," Washington wrote to the New Jersey gentleman Gouverneur Morris, "if like chameleons, they could live upon air, or like the bear, suck their paws for sustenance during the rigour of the approaching season."[21] If it was not defeated by the British, there was every possibility his army would be beaten by lack of supplies.[22]

In their desperation, Congress sent Hamilton's friend John Laurens—who had once shared the task of translating Washington's correspondence with the

Americans' French allies—on an urgent mission to Europe in search of resources to keep up the war. Since the fall of Charleston, Laurens had spent most of the year as a prisoner, living at the seat of Congress in Philadelphia but unable to break the terms of his parole by going anywhere else. Now freed by an exchange with the British, his mission was to convince the French to step up their financial support for the revolution, and to negotiate loans from the Dutch. It was the silver coin brought back from France by Laurens that would become the capital of the new nation's first bank. Before he set off, though, Laurens had first to get Washington's account of the state of the war effort. His visit to army headquarters was the first time he had seen Hamilton for nearly two years. It was a brief and bitter-sweet reunion, under the circumstances. It was clear to all three men just how bad things had become.

"The efforts we have been compelled to make for carrying on the war," Washington told Laurens, "have exceeded the natural abilities of this country and by degrees brought it to a crisis, which renders immediate and efficacious succours from abroad indispensable to its safety." In short, Congress was out of money—and not only as a result of "errors ... in the administration of our finances," but much more fundamentally because of "the want of a sufficient stock of wealth." With commerce cut off, few Americans were making any money. Nor were they much accustomed to paying taxes. If Congress and the states tried to raise more taxes, the people may start to think "they have only exchanged one tyranny for another." In the long term, there were reasons for confidence. Washington expected rapid "advancement in population and prosperity" once independence was achieved, and the "vast and valuable tracts of unlocated lands" could be sold off. Americans remained "firmly attached" to independence, and "affectionate to the alliance with France." Yet in wartime, the general wrote, such feelings were no substitute for money.[23]

This letter was specifically designed to elicit more financial help from the French government. To help the scheme along, the Marquis de Lafayette wrote to his contacts in Paris mentioning the letter, so that they would ask to see it without Laurens needing to offer—the idea was that it would have more weight if it was not seen as written deliberately for French eyes. Nonetheless, what Washington had said about the lack of funds was no exaggeration. There were mutinies in the Pennsylvania and New Jersey lines the very same month. One week, Washington was describing "the distressed condition of the troops at West Point" to the president of Congress; the next week he was sending those same West Point troops to New Jersey "to compel the mutineers to submission." A British force under Benedict Arnold—the turncoat who had almost succeeded in giving away West Point the year before—landed in Virginia to prepare the way for Lord Cornwallis's army; and as General Nathanael Greene reported, American troops in the south were likewise "destitute of everything."[24]

It was in these troubling circumstances that Congress set about handing over control of its finances to a single individual, the superintendent of finance, Robert Morris. Born in Liverpool, the son of a tobacco trader, Morris was by the outbreak of the revolution one of Philadelphia's most prominent merchants. During the war, while the United States made itself poor fighting the empire, Morris grew richer still by helping to supply its armies. Congress needed merchants and their networks just as much as it needed soldiers, and for those prepared to take the risk, war could be much more lucrative than peace. Morris had the credentials of a gentleman in Philadelphia society—he had money, and he moved in the highest circles. But he was a controversial and suspicious figure, even among the city's elite. Among his enemies was the president of Pennsylvania's Executive Council, Joseph Reed, a lawyer educated at the College of New Jersey and London's Middle Temple. According to Reed, Morris was "a pecuniary dictator," appointed "in wretched extremity."[25] None could deny the extremity, yet the measures Morris planned to implement were startling.[26]

"I take to be the most essential part of the duty of the Superintendent of Finance," Morris told Congress in March, "to reduce the expenditures as nearly as possible to what in reason and justice they ought to be." Before he would agree to take on the appointment, Morris wanted the power to dismiss officers he deemed superfluous. He made it clear that, while the long-term goal may be to raise money and win the war, his immediate plan was drastic cuts. Austerity, he reasoned, would control the inflation of Continental currency and restore an impression of fiscal responsibility to the Congressional government. That, in turn, would help them raise new loans, on better terms, from the Dutch, French, and Spanish. In the meantime, the army would have to get by on even less. Morris's strategy was for a war of financial attrition. As his supporter Hamilton put it, "'Tis by introducing order into our finances—by restoreing public credit—not by gaining battles, that we are finally to gain our object."[27]

How would Washington's men, already demoralized and weakened to the point of mutiny, have responded to Morris's cost-cutting plan? In the end, luckily, nobody had to find out. Before it could be implemented, Lord Cornwallis moved his army into Yorktown, following orders to take up a fortified coastal position—and Washington, making use of a temporary naval superiority provided by his French allies, decided to strike. To take advantage of the moment, a combined French and American force marched from Newport, Rhode Island, into the Chesapeake area, through late August and early September, beginning the siege of Yorktown in early October. Crucially, Washington convinced Morris to support the campaign by putting his own wealth on the line. To pay for supplies and cover the soldiers' pay, Morris issued notes backed by his personal credit, which was by then worth more than the notes issued by Congress itself. It was an enormous risk for all involved. But when it paid off with Cornwallis' surrender, it made Morris's reputation as a patriot and a gentleman.[28]

It was also an important moment for Hamilton. He finally got the chance to command on the front line, alongside his friend John Laurens. "Two nights ago, my Eliza, my duty and my honor obliged me to take a step in which your happiness was too much risked," he told his new bride. "I commanded an attack upon one of the enemy's redoubts; we carried it in an instant, and with little loss." The action had involved not a little recklessness. But its success gave the young colonel the glory he sought. "You will see the particulars in the Philadelphia papers," he told his new wife. "There will be, certainly, nothing more of this kind; all the rest will be by approach; and if there should be another occasion, it will not fall to my turn to execute it."[29] The next day, Cornwallis' officers began negotiations for surrender, with Laurens serving as the American representative. That November, with the Yorktown victory complete, Hamilton left the army, and Washington's "family," and entered a new phase of his life.

II. A Union of Officers

Victory at Yorktown did not immediately end the war, but it dramatically altered the balance of expectations. "The consequences will be extensively beneficial," wrote Washington's artillery commander, Henry Knox, to John Jay, then Congress's ambassador to Spain. "The enemy will immediately be confined to Charleston and New York and reduced to a defensive war of these two posts, for which they have not more troops in America than to form adequate garrisons."[30] Within months, Lord North resigned as prime minister and a new ministry, favoring peace, took over the British government. Still, the victory had not solved all of the Americans' problems. Among the most pressing remained the situation of Congressional finance, and especially the state of army pay. As the end of the war came into view, soldiers and officers grew increasingly concerned with making sure that they were properly rewarded for their service. They knew that once the army was disbanded, they would lose much of their power to negotiate with Congress. If there was anything to be done, it would have to be done before peace was definitively made.

For officers, the issue of pay was just one element in a mesh of factors that also had to do with honor, status, and respect. To many of them, the army was an imagined community that felt more real than the United States. With some reason, they claimed they had been through a quite different experience of the war; and they expected the sacrifices they had made, and the risks they had taken, to be recognized and rewarded by the nation as a whole. As officers, they had been raised above the ranks of ordinary men. They had become accustomed to a certain level of respect and obedience.[31] What would become of this once the army was disbanded, and the officers dispersed back to their old homes and communities? If Congress could not keep its promises over pay, what kind of treatment could officers expect from civilian society at large? In the wake of the victory at Yorktown, these questions began to seem increasingly important and troubling. They reflected a shift of focus from winning the war against Britain, to building a new, independent society.

Henry Knox was to play an important role in this transition for the army and its officer corps. At thirty-one, Knox became the youngest major general in the Continental Army when Washington promoted him soon after Yorktown. Placed in command of West Point the following summer, Knox was effectively in charge of the day-to-day running of the army in the final year of the war. Yet when the revolution broke out, Knox had been a Boston bookseller on the edge of polite society, barely qualified to call himself a gentleman. In 1759, Knox's father lost his shipbuilding business and fled to the Caribbean, leaving his wife and his young sons to look after themselves. Nine-year-old Henry, ensconced at the expensive Boston Latin School, had been on a path to Harvard and the colonial elite. Now everything changed. He became an apprentice bookseller, and in time had his own successful shop. He courted and married Lucy Flucker, the daughter of one of the town's leading merchants, a Tory who opposed his daughter's match with someone so low in the social scale. For the rest of his life, Knox struggled to prove himself to Lucy, her family, and the world. The vicissitudes of fortune and gentility haunted him, as they did many others.[32]

While the struggle over empire grew in Boston, Knox became increasingly radical in his politics—which only increased the antagonism of his wife's family. He joined the militia, learned how to handle artillery, and pored over the military books in his shop. By the time war came, he was ready to serve Washington's army, encamped outside his native city. Quickly, Knox was commissioned a colonel, and he continued to rise. The war changed Knox's life, just as it changed Hamilton's. It gave him the chance to show the value of his learning and the strength of his character: in short, to be a gentleman. But it did not make him rich. For Knox, and many other men in similar circumstances, the end of the war was a worrying prospect, in spite of the American victory. As the peace negotiations moved forward, and Congress continued to drag its feet in the matter of army pay, the atmosphere at West Point and the nearby camp at Newburgh grew bitter and confrontational. More and more, Knox found his loyalty caught between the nation's civilian leaders, and an army that distrusted them.

By December 1782, Knox and a group of senior officers decided to do something. They commissioned a delegation to go to Philadelphia and present a memorial to Congress. Their tone was deferential, but full of anguish. The army had suffered "hardships exceedingly disproportionate to any other citizens in America. . . . We have struggled with our difficulties, year after year, hoping that each would be the last," they wrote; "but we have been disappointed.... Shadows have been offered us while the substance has been gleaned by others." Many citizens believed the existing arrangement—where officers were entitled to half pay for life as a reward for their service—was corrupt and undeserved. In the past, standing armies and military pensions had been seen as tools of royal tyranny. The officers were anxious both to secure their money and to prevent "disharmony" from arising in postwar society. So they proposed a compromise: "we are willing," they declared, to give up half pay in exchange for several years' full pay or a single lump sum. It was a solution cash-strapped Congress would find hard to accept. Yet as Knox's memorial warned them, testing the army's patience too far "may have fatal effects."[33]

One of the congressmen who received the officers' memorial that winter was Alexander Hamilton. Appointed that July to represent New York in the new session, he had arrived in Philadelphia late in November. "Remember your promise," he had told Elizabeth, as he left her and his newborn son to travel south; "don't fail to write me by every post." He also asked her to send along his ceremonial sword.[34] When the officers' proposal was presented a month later, Hamilton saw it as an opportunity to bring about a major political change. Along with Robert Morris and a few other allies, Hamilton wanted to establish a much stronger fiscal power in Congress, which could provide for the payment of public creditors—including the army. Most congressmen, representing the views of their state governments, were reluctant to grant themselves any such powers. Congress was in many ways more like an alliance between separate states than a national government. The army's discontent, however, made Hamilton's reforms seem much more urgent. Over the next few months, he and Morris worked to put a new system in place that would establish Congress's authority and finances independent of state governments.[35]

By trying to manipulate the pressure from the army, though, they were playing a dangerous game. Just how far would the leading officers be prepared to go to see their pay claims satisfied? That problem related to the deeper issue of honor and reputation. What men like Knox wanted more than anything was to secure their status as gentlemen. Money was part of that, but so were many other things. Part of the substance of gentility was an obedience to unwritten rules of conduct, rules that concerned honesty and trustworthiness, founded in the free agreement between equal individuals. For an officer to disobey his commander, or the army's civilian leadership, would be a betrayal of that code, a forfeiture of virtue. "I consider the reputation of the American Army as one of the most immaculate things on earth," Knox told Alexander McDougall, the leader of the army's delegation to Congress. "We should even suffer wrongs and injuries to the utmost verge of toleration rather than sully it to the least degree." He would not risk his reputation by acting against Congress.[36]

Not all the officers at Newburgh, or all those in Philadelphia, felt the same way. By March 10, with the pay issue still unresolved, an anonymous address was published in camp, urging the officers to consider their position. "Faith has its limits," wrote the author. "To be tame and unprovoked when injuries press hard upon you, is more than weakness." He urged his readers to seek redress while they still had power. After all,

> what have you to expect from peace, when your voice shall sink, and your strength dissipate by division? When those very swords, the instruments and companions of your glory, shall be taken from your sides, and no remaining mark of military distinction left but your wants, infirmities and scars? Can you then consent to be the only sufferers from this revolution, and retiring from the field, grow old in poverty, wretchedness and contempt?[37]

These were precisely the fears that had animated discontent in camp for at least a year, fears that went beyond the issue of money to encompass the nature of the revolution itself, and the future of the men who had fought to achieve it. What world could they hope for when their role as officers was over?

Behind the anonymous address stood a cabal of officers led by Washington's old rival, Horatio Gates. In it, they had proposed a mass meeting in camp the next day to decide on the officers' next move—in all likelihood, a move against Congress. Only Washington's personal intervention could rescue the situation. He first issued orders forbidding the meeting as "disorderly" and "irregular." But he had to do more than that. He set a new meeting for five days hence, a Saturday, at which the officers' grievances were to be discussed. He let the conspirators think he would not be attending himself. Then, when the day came, Washington appeared. Denouncing the address, he asked the officers, "as you value your own sacred honor ... to express your utmost horror and detestation of the man, who wishes ... to overturn the liberties of our country, and who wickedly attempts to open the flood-gates of civil discord, and deluge our rising empire in blood."[38] In the face of their revered commander, all enthusiasm for the conflict collapsed. Knox introduced resolutions confirming the officers' confidence in Congress, which were agreed unanimously by those present. Once again, Washington had triumphed over Gates.[39]

As the news spread over the following weeks, the event was transformed into a heroic moment for the army—a common pledge of obedience in the face of great hardship, a confirmation of the officers' republican virtue and their gentlemanly honor. In Congress, the drama had the double effect of confirming the army's loyalty, while demonstrating the strain it was under. Within weeks, the faction led by Morris and Hamilton managed to push through first a deal on officers' pay—giving them full pay for five years instead of a lifetime's half pay—and then their larger plan, the federal taxing power known as the "impost," which would finally give Congress a source of revenue independent from state governments. It was not just the army that was intended to benefit. Indeed, some thought the army was "to be made use of as mere Puppits to establish Continental funds." By concentrating fiscal strength in Congress, the aim was to secure the interests of public creditors and the American merchant elite, not the least of whom was "the Financier" himself, Robert Morris.[40]

With the arrival of spring, 1783, Henry Knox and his fellow officers had reason to be optimistic. It had been a struggle, but they had won their compromise with Congress over half pay, and there were signs the financial situation might soon be resolved. Meanwhile, the British garrison at Charleston had been evacuated, leaving only New York under enemy occupation. Peace was surely just around the corner. Nonetheless, it was still uncertain just what that would mean for the officers. Once the army was disbanded, they would no longer pose any danger to Congress. They would no longer have any influence over the civilian leadership. And though the officers had not taken the fatal step over the brink of mutiny and civil war, their trust in the government was utterly threadbare. Who would protect the independence they had fought for? Who would bring the revolution to fulfillment—and what would that look like? It was not long after the events at Newburgh that Knox's mind turned to a scheme that would maintain a role for the army in the future of the new nation.

Alongside Friedrich von Steuben, the Prussian-born major general who had drilled Washington's army at Valley Forge, Knox began drawing up plans for an association of officers that would persist after demobilization, independent of either Congress or the army itself. It was to be called the Society of the Cincinnati.[41] This name, which referred to a Roman senator of the fifth century BCE, had a sort of double meaning. Cincinnatus was called upon to leave his farm and family to rescue the Roman republic in a time of war, but he was also famous for relinquishing power as soon as the republic was safe. Knox wrote that the officers were "resolved to follow his example, by returning to their citizenship." The emblem he and von Steuben designed, though, did not focus on that aspect of the story. It showed Cincinnatus taking up his sword and the insignia of office, with the motto, "Omnia reliquit servare Rempublicam," *He gives up everything to serve the Republic*. On the reverse, the badge showed a rising sun, a flourishing port city, and Cincinnatus being crowned by the goddess of Fame, with the words "Virtutis Praemium," *the Reward of Virtue*.[42]

In the Society's founding document, known as the Institution, Knox wrote that its purpose was "to perpetuate the mutual friendships which have been formed under the pressure of common danger, and, in many instances, cemented by the blood of the parties." But there was also a distinctively political element in the Society's initial formulation. Among its principles, as listed by Knox, was "an unalterable determination to promote and cherish, between the respective States, that union and national honor so essentially necessary to their happiness, and the future dignity of the American Empire." In their annual meetings, the state branches of the Society were also to discuss matters concerning "the general union of the states," and pass on their observations to the other branches. And the Society could admit as honorary members "men in the respective States eminent for their abilities and patriotism, whose views may be directed to the same laudable objects with those of the Cincinnati." Clearly, Knox intended the Society's members to share a vision for the new republic.[43]

From one point of view, the Cincinnati was a radically egalitarian project. At its heart was the ideal of gentlemanly friendship between equals that the experience of war and army life had done much to promote. Through regular meetings, and through its very existence, the Society would "render permanent the cordial affections subsisting among the officers," even after they returned to their own communities and families. Its spirit would "dictate brotherly kindness in all things" among the members, including "the most substantial acts of beneficence ... towards those Officers and their Families who unfortunately may be under the necessity of receiving it."[44] Regardless of previous differences in rank, or their fortunes either before or after the war, the officers would help each other and their families. This aspect of the Society celebrated the kind of friendship that had grown between Alexander Hamilton and John Laurens, a friendship that would have been unlikely in ordinary circumstances. It envisaged the new republic as an extension of that kind of egalitarian friendship into the civil and political sphere.[45]

At the same time, though, Knox himself envisaged the Society as a hierarchical force in American society. As a result of their sacrifice and leadership during the war, he implied, the officers of the Continental Army had a right, and perhaps a duty, to guide the new republic as they saw fit. Those who had served in the rank and file were of course excluded from membership. Just as it had been in the army itself, officers would continue to be superior to ordinary men. As Hamilton had once put it to his friend John Jay, "Let officers be men of sense and sentiment, and the nearer the soldiers approach to machines perhaps the better."[46] Was this the ideal that the Cincinnati wanted to extend to the postwar life of the new nation? Throughout the events of Newburgh and the negotiations with Congress over pay, the officers had acted as though they were the whole army, and as if they deserved all the credit for winning the war. Through the Cincinnati, they would exert even more control over "the remembrance of this vast event." The organization would maintain the officers' social distinction, and thus also their power.

Knox drafted the Society's Institution on April 15, the day before news of the peace treaty reached camp. Over the following month he, von Steuben, and other senior officers—including Hamilton—worked to establish the Cincinnati. They formally signed the Institution on May 13, and sent copies to every regiment, seeking members. Joining required officers to sign away one month's salary as a contribution to the Society's charitable fund, so it was not a step to take lightly. But of the 5,795 men eligible to join, almost half did so: 2,403.[47] One thing they may have hoped is that the Cincinnati would help keep up pressure on Congress to deliver on its promises of pay. The Society also offered a measure of security for members if they were to fall on hard times—and for their wives and children, if they died. In fact, membership was to be inherited by members' eldest sons, perpetuating the Society down the generations. For many Americans, both members and critics of the Society, that promise to future generations was a key part of the meaning of the project.

With the war finally at an end, the Cincinnati represented an attempt to help shape the new republic's independent future. For men like Knox and Hamilton, it embodied much of the achievement of the revolution, especially in its emphasis on the bonds of friendship and the equal status of brother officers. The Society was a response to the fear that dissolution of the army would also dissolve those bonds, and reduce former officers back to their prewar social status. As such, it was also an embodiment of certain ideas about republican society and politics. Cincinnati officers expected to be treated with respect in the public life of the new nation. They also expected that their military sacrifice and heroism would set them, rightfully, above ordinary citizens. In this vision, a republic was not defined by political or social equality, even among white men. Some sort of hierarchy was crucial to the officers' sense of order and propriety—and to their idea of leadership. The problem was that army officers were not the only ones thinking along such lines. It soon became clear that other American gentlemen had different ideas about how to achieve a social order appropriate for the United States.

Even within the Society, there was uncertainty from the beginning about its aims and motives, and about how it would be received by Americans in general. Major General William Heath told Knox, as early as May, that he had worries about how the public would react when news of the Cincinnati spread. "With a sagacity peculiar to himself," Knox wrote to another Massachusetts general, Benjamin Lincoln, "he thinks through the mist he sees spirits and hobgoblins of hideous forms and no popularity." Still, the inaugural meeting of the Massachusetts branch went ahead in June, with Heath in attendance, and Lincoln elected president. The worst, and earliest, controversy took place in South Carolina, where British troops had until recently been occupying the capital, and civil government was in the process of being restored. Here, tensions over authority and leadership left over from the war created heightened suspicions around the organization of the Cincinnati. In August, to assuage such feelings, the group chose to publicly disavow "all intention of Interfering in any Degree with the Constitutional Powers of Congress or the Civil authority of this State." The cracks in Knox's vision were already beginning to appear.[48]

At several meetings over the following months, the South Carolina Cincinnati adopted a set of by-laws that included a provision exempting them from any mandate of the national society that interfered "in any shape what soever, with the Civil Policy of this, any other of the United States, or the United States in general ... they prizing too highly the CIVIL LIBERTIES of their country, and their own RIGHTS AS CITIZENS, to consent that a Military Society should in any sense dictate to Civil Authority."[49] This was a pre-emptive move, meant to soften public opinion and avert any hostility to the Society. But South Carolina was already fraught with division over the post-war settlement, including debates about the disenfranchisement of alleged British loyalists, and the confiscation of their property. The state government had yet to fully establish its authority and legitimacy. The introduction of a new factor, the Cincinnati, only confused matters further. As for the concilia-tory by-laws, the effort seems to have backfired. For in the same month they were published, along with the Society's Institution, a pamphlet came out in Charleston that not only attacked the organization, but launched the debate into the national public sphere.

This pamphlet, titled *Considerations on the Society or Order of the Cincin-nati*, was published under the inflammatory pseudonym "Cassius," one of the men who had assassinated Julius Caesar in order to save the Roman republic from tyranny. Its message was that the Cincinnati, regardless of what its lead-ers said, would in short order lead the country down the path of oligarchy and monarchism. The pamphlet argued that the Society and its Institution were bound to create, in the words of its title page, "a race of hereditary patricians, or nobility." Its elision between the title of "society" and "order" was perfectly deliberate: it emphasized the comparison with European orders of nobility and knighthood. "This Order," wrote Cassius, "is planted in a fiery, hot ambi-tion, and thirst for power; and its branches will end in tyranny."[50] Within a few months, the *Considerations* were reprinted in Philadelphia, and in Hart-ford, Connecticut; and it ran serially in Boston's *Independent Chronicle* from January to April 1784. William Heath's hobgoblins were well and truly let loose. Suddenly, everyone was talking about the dangerous and tyrannical Cincinnati.

Cassius was in fact Aedanus Burke, one of South Carolina's most senior judges—a fact that quickly became common knowledge, and gave his pamphlet even more legitimacy. Burke was a friend of several of the state Cincinnati leaders, including the Society branch president and former governor, William Moultrie. Burke had been captured along with the military leadership—and John Laurens—at the fall of Charleston in 1780, and spent time with them on parole in Philadelphia. He had even served briefly in the army himself, though not quite for long enough to be eligible for membership in the Cincinnati.

Burke was an Irish-born lawyer who had trained in Virginia before moving south. Like both Hamilton and Knox, he had not grown up as part of the colonial establishment, and had established himself as a gentleman during the course of the war through service to the state. His pamphlet was not an attack on the Cincinnati from below, but rather from a rival quarter of the new nation's emerging elite. Burke's argument would soon find echoes among others in similar positions.[51]

One of the Cincinnati's staunchest critics was the Massachusetts merchant and congressman Elbridge Gerry. In November 1783, Gerry wrote a long letter to his close friend John Adams, in which he enclosed the Society's "Institution and Strictures thereon" (probably Burke's pamphlet) for Adams's perusal. Gerry was no enemy to the army or its officers. On the matter of pay, he wrote that "such a vertuous Army claims the Generosity of their Country." He disapproved, however, of "the Superiority which the officers, on their Return Home, naturally assumed over their fellow Citizens, who were at least their Equals, & in many Instances Superiors before the War." It was their claims to social status, more than their demands for money, that generated resentment towards the officers. Moreover, Gerry implied that the Cincinnati itself was in fact a "Species of Influence supposed to have had its Birth in a foreign climate & to have been innocently fostered by the worthy officers of our Army." He seems to have meant Prussia, but there were also rumors that the Cincinnati was a project of the French court to retain its influence over America. For Gerry, the Cincinnati only made sense as part of a larger framework of conspiracy.[52]

Like all gentlemen, Gerry was committed to the importance of maintaining the public credit, and what he considered an orderly fiscal system. Debts had to be paid, and contracts abided by. But he was deeply suspicious of the superintendent of finance, Robert Morris, and the faction that surrounded him in Congress. Morris's powers were considered by some, he wrote, as "dangerous and unconstitutional." Gerry's republicanism was in the old British mode. He hated the idea of centralizing power in a court that would control both the national finances and a powerful standing army, especially if that court was situated in one city, where "an oligarchical Influence" could take root. If such a system were to be implemented, and at the same time "should We consent to an order of Cincinnati consisting of all the Officers of the Army & Citizens of Consiquence in the united States," then, Gerry predicted, "how easy the Transition from a Republican to any other Form of Government, however despotic!" Combined with Morris's clique in Congress, the Cincinnati would reduce the new nation to an oligarchy.[53]

Over the ensuing winter, speculation about the dangerous influence of the new Society spread through the ranks of America's diplomatic and political elites. One member from North Carolina reported to Knox that Burke's pamphlet "has created opponents to the Cincinnati" in that state. As a topic of conversation, it was widespread enough that nobody had to read the pamphlet to know what it said. "His objections, I am told, are founded upon a surmise that the Cincinnati mean to establish a numerous peerage in direct contradiction to the federal union of the states," wrote Knox's correspondent. "This he has tortured out of the 'hereditary succession.'" For many of the Cincinnati's members, Burke's critique seemed completely unjustified and "altogether chimerical."[54] Yet it was being taken seriously by those outside the organization. It seemed likely that the North Carolina assembly, "in their April sessions, will be moved to suppress the Society." In Massachusetts, the legislature even set up a special committee to look into its "tendency to create a race of hereditary nobility." The *Considerations* had not only spurred public discussion of the Cincinnati—they completely shaped it.[55]

Hereditary membership was the central issue of most criticism. It was there that Burke and others saw the potential for a gradual evolution of the Society into a kind of aristocratic caste. Even if the officers could claim special credit for their wartime service, surely that could not apply to their sons, grandsons, and so on? From Paris in January 1784, Benjamin Franklin wrote to his daughter Sarah expressing his surprise that "a Number of private Persons should think proper to distinguish themselves and their Posterity, from their fellow Citizens, and form an Order of *hereditary Knights*, in direct Opposition to the solemnly declared Sense of their Country!" The notion of "*descending Honour*, to Posterity who could have no Share in obtaining it, is not only groundless and absurd," Franklin continued, "but often hurtful to that Posterity, since it is apt to make them proud." In Europe such pride made many noble families indolent and poor because they would not work. To Franklin, and to generations of Americans since, his own life offered a model of the true American gentleman, one whose status was the result of personal merit and effort.[56]

At the same time, though, Franklin acknowledged that parents almost always had a hand in making their children into who they were. If honor was to extend in any direction, Franklin wrote, then it should move upwards, as it supposedly did in China, where parents were entitled to "all the same Ceremonies of Respect from the People" that their children may be granted.[57] Family remained deeply important to the structure of American life. Wives, children, and even slaves were often understood as dependants of individual white men—a republic of political equals was really one of hierarchical households, each one's interests represented by the man at its head. To provide for his family, even after death, was part of the duty of any gentleman, and it was a central part of the rationale behind the Society of the Cincinnati in the first place. Like Franklin, Henry Knox had worked hard to achieve rank and status. He sought to turn that achievement into something permanent. In doing so, he sparked a debate that helped reveal the contradictory assumptions behind America's republican vision.

III. Imagining Republican Elites

The growing controversy over the Cincinnati threatened to tear apart the fabric of the new nation's elite, and in a much more public way than the New-burgh conspiracy had done. In order to present a powerful and respectable image to the rest of the world, the United States needed a unified establish-ment that could demonstrate its control of the country and its resources. If European empires were going to sign treaties with American diplomats, they needed to be sure that those diplomats were speaking with authority, backed up by legal, military, and financial power. One of the most important roles of Congress was to present this impression of united central government. But now that the war seemed all but over, the mask was beginning to slip. The new republic remained deeply vulnerable to the machinations of European powers, especially as it sought to adjust to exclusion from the British empire's commercial network. That vulnerability was underlined by the belief, among some of its opponents, that the Society itself was part of a foreign plot. Of course, the very public controversy only served to weaken the image of Amer-ican leadership.

The situation was also a personal embarrassment to Washington. He was the Society's nominal president and a close friend of its leading figures, but he had played no role in its establishment. His attitude had been lukewarm from the start. When his friends and political allies from outside the army began to weigh in on the debate, echoing the critique in Burke's pamphlet, Washington found himself in a difficult position. He faced a particular problem with the French branch of the Society, where several French officers had enthusiasti-cally petitioned for membership, only to find the organization subject to attack from both American diplomats and French radicals. "Most of the Americans Here are indecently Violent Against our Assossiation," the Marquis de Lafay-ette told Washington in March. "You easely guess I am not Remiss in opposing them.... However if it is found that the Heredity Endangers the Free Princi-ples of democrasy, I am as Ready as Any Man to Renounce it." Lafayette urged Washington to take control of the matter and make a judgment about the hereditary provision.[58] By intervening, he risked alienating one side or the other. But how long could he stay silent?

Before he made up his mind, Washington consulted Thomas Jefferson, someone whom he could trust to give an honest and considered opinion "with frankness, and the fullest latitude of a friend." Writing in early April, Wash-ington wanted to know both Jefferson's own thoughts on the Society, and as far as possible, the mind of Congress in general on the subject. "The Pamphlet ascribed to Mr Burke, has I am told had its effect," Washington wrote. "People are alarmed, especially in the Eastern States. How justly, or how contrary to the avowed principles of the Society and the purity of their motives, I will not declare, least it should appear that I wanted to biass your judgment rather

INHERITANCE [29]

than to obtain an opinion." He also invited Jefferson to give an opinion of what should be done to resolve the public controversy.[59] The Society's first national meeting was to take place in Philadelphia the next month. That would be the opportunity to take action.

In his reply, Jefferson shrewdly picked up on one of Washington's principal concerns: the effect of the Cincinnati on his own reputation. Burke himself had written that "the discretion of the Commander in Chief, which I take to be his distinguishing characteristic, is signal on this occasion; for he has appeared quite neutral in this business." Neutral, that is, "if we except his becoming an honorary member of it." Washington was eager to maintain this reputation for discretion and neutrality, and Jefferson's letter reflected that concern. "The character which will be handed to future ages at the head of our revolution," wrote Jefferson, should not be allowed to be compromised. As for the Cincinnati itself, Jefferson's condemnation was severe. Like Burke, he carefully exempted the officers from any malicious intent. But the organization itself was "against the spirit" of republican society, he wrote. It would promote privilege, tyranny, and the "influence of foreign courts." Among his fellow Congressmen, moreover, Jefferson had "found but one who is not opposed to the institution." Their recommendation, he predicted, would be "total discontinuance."[60]

By the time he reached Philadelphia in May, with Jefferson's words settling in his mind, Washington had decided how to act. The meeting was conducted in secret, behind the closed doors of the City Tavern—but one delegate, Winthrop Sargent, recorded the events and speeches in a coded diary. Washington took charge from the beginning. "Opposition," he announced in his opening speech, "had become violent and formidable, and call'd for serious consideration." The Society must "strike out every word, sentence, and clause which has a political tendency." It must "discontinue the hereditary part in all its connexions, *absolutely*." It must "admit no more honorary members," place its funds "in the hands of the [state] Legislatures for the *express purposes* for which they were intended," and "abolish General Meetings altogether." All these changes were absolutely necessary. "No alterations short of what is enumerated here will, in my opinion, reconcile the Society to the Community— whether these will do it, is questionable." As Winthrop Sargent put it, he spoke "with much warmth and agitation." If the officers would not agree to his proposals, he threatened to withdraw himself from the Society altogether.[61]

Washington's reform program would mean a complete overhaul of the Institution. As Sargent recorded, he "seemed desirous to expunge all the essentials with which the Society was endowed by those from whom it had its origin." Many of the members, including Sargent himself, had serious doubts about what Washington was asking for. But they could do little to resist the general's force, charisma, and political skill. Before his proposals were passed on to working committees, on the third day of the proceedings, he had it "resolved that the President General [would] have a right *ex officio* to attend all committees, debate and vote."[62] Washington was thus able to shepherd his program personally through each stage of the process. By the end of the meeting, he had achieved a comprehensive victory. The revised Institution, he hoped, would satisfy the critics and put an end to the public controversy.

For the reforms to become effective, however, they had to be adopted by individual meetings of the state branches. These Washington could not bully and manipulate directly. Instead he wrote a circular letter to accompany the proposals, which put the case for reform at length. "The original Institution appeared, in the Opinion of many respectable Characters, to have comprehended Objects which are deemed incompatible with the Genius and Spirit of the Confederation," the letter read. "Therefore, to remove every Cause of Inquietude, to annihilate every Source of Jealousy ... we have agreed that the following material Alterations and Amendments should take place." Signed by Washington as president of the Society, the letter closed with an invocation of Cincinnatus himself, and the tranquil pleasures of civilian life: "Let us leave a Lesson to Posterity, That the Glory of Soldiers cannot be completed, without acting well the Part of Citizens." In effect, he was asking officers to give up their hopes of achieving, through the Cincinnati, a measure of collective status and power.[63]

Not everyone in the Society was willing to go along with Washington's reforms. His acceptance of its critics' position seemed, to some, like a surrender, even a betrayal. Just as he had done at Newburgh, Washington was using his influence over the officers on behalf of the civilian leadership, demonstrating more trust in men like Jefferson than in those who had loyally served him during the war. From the beginning, the Society of Cincinnati was a matter of pride, and Washington's heavy-handed approach at the general meeting was not well-calculated to win over members in the long term. News of the proposed reforms did have the desired effect on public debate, which by the summer of 1784 had largely moved on from the issue of the Cincinnati. But dissent against Washington's program continued to create tensions among the former officers. In his farewell letter to the army a year earlier, Washington had urged them to add their "best endeavours" to the support of federal union and the strength of the central government.[64] As the Cincinnati delegates left Philadelphia that May, however, a unified national elite seemed further away than ever.

Defenders of the Society as originally designed had begun to develop their arguments as soon as the first public criticism appeared. In November 1783, the month after Aedanus Burke's pamphlet was published in Charleston, a Philadelphia Cincinnatus called Stephen Moylan wrote and published a rebuttal. Like Burke, Moylan was born in Ireland—in fact, he was the founding president of the Friendly Sons of St Patrick, a fraternal organization of Irish

Pennsylvanians that counted Washington among its honorary members. After serving briefly as quartermaster general and as an aide to Washington, before the arrival of Hamilton or Laurens, Moylan became a commander of cavalry and dragoons. By the end of the war, he was a brigadier general, having returned home due to ill health following the victory at Yorktown.[65] Moylan's pamphlet defense of the Cincinnati was made up of three elements that each contradicted Burke's position, but also tended to contradict each other. He argued that distinctions were inevitable and equality impossible; that superior rank gave no real benefit or happiness to those who held it; and that only property, not rank or honor, constituted power.

"I dare say," wrote Moylan, under the moniker An Obscure Individual, "that even Cassius will not contend that absolute, perfect, equality is possible to the government of any state. As the mind must govern the hands, so the man of intelligence must direct the man of labour." Drawing on recent ideas about the progress of history, developed by Scottish Enlightenment authors like Adam Ferguson and Adam Smith, Moylan remarked that inequality increases as societies improve. Indeed, distinctions of rank and status "have seldom failed to benefit the country that bestowed them," not least because they generate "a spirit of emulation ... which when diffused among a people, gives vigour to every spring of government and vibration to the heart of every member of the community." Yet at the same time, "the advantages of nature or of fortune ... contribute little to the promotion of happiness," Moylan argued. "Those who look up ... from a lower station" seldom have any "just occasion to envy" those above them. High status was not a pleasure, but a burden and a responsibility. To emulate the socially superior was good; to envy them, misplaced.[66]

Nonetheless, resentment was bound to arise, Moylan admitted. "Such is the infirmity of human nature, that every *appearance* of superiority (however necessary to the policy and government of a state) naturally excites sullen suspicion in the breasts of the subordinate." That suspicion, he implied, was what lay behind criticism of the Cincinnati. It was only natural for those excluded from the Society to believe that it had a sinister purpose. But, Moylan claimed, in reality there was no particular power or real superiority to be gained from membership in a society. Honors create an *"appearance"* of value, like the image stamped on a coin, but it is the metal beneath that really matters. *"Property alone constitutes power,"* he wrote, *"and power is conferred by Congress and the representatives of the people."*[67] What did he mean? The sentence seems to balance between two visions of power at the same time, one based on property, and the other on popular representation and consent. But if these two principles came into conflict, which would trump the other? That question lay right at the heart of political conflict in the new republic. It would be some time yet, however, before it was fully uncovered, let alone answered.

In Moylan's defense of the Cincinnati, strong ideological continuities met the disruptive shock of revolutionary discourse. He found it difficult to reconcile his understanding of the just social hierarchy—"the man of intelligence must direct the man of labour"—with the egalitarianism of some republican and revolutionary rhetoric. In the beginning of the revolution, the notion of popular consent had been a way of drawing the American people together in a condemnation of the British king and Parliament. When government began to interfere with property rights, the withdrawal of consent was the appropriate reaction, as John Locke had argued a century earlier. But what did that mean for the construction of society *after* the revolution? Americans continued to speak in the idiom of popular, republican radicalism that had inspired action against the British empire. But how could a language of *opposition* be transformed into one of creation and development? Finding themselves on the receiving end of virulent republican rhetoric, defenders of the Cincinnati were forced to look for new ways to understand the dynamics of power and justice.

After the general meeting of 1784, debate over the future of the Society moved out of the public sphere to become a conversation among members themselves. The visible products of this discussion behind the scenes was a series of circular letters on behalf of various state branches. The reforms Washington had pushed through in Philadelphia would not become effective until they were ratified by the delegates at the next general meeting, to be held three years later, in 1787. During that three-year window, several factions emerged within the Society, advocating quite different approaches to reform, and different ways of responding to public criticism. Neither Henry Knox nor Friedrich von Steuben, the original architects of the Institution, raised their voices in opposition to Washington. Both men were close friends of the general, with political ambitions of their own. They were understandably reluctant to risk the most important connection they had by openly opposing Washington's plans. It was, instead, from the state society of New Hampshire that a voice of conservative, antireform leadership emerged.

"We view with grief and astonishment the uneasiness which the establishment of our Society gave to some of our Fellow-Citizens," began the letter, drafted by a committee headed by General John Sullivan over the winter of 1784–1785. They were shocked by the accusations leveled at the Cincinnati by its critics. "Nothing could afford us more pleasure, than to quiet the minds and remove the fears of our fellow-citizens," they wrote. But they refused "to yield to Arguments that have no force, to acknowledge dangers that do not exist, to recede from a Plan founded on the most laudable Principles thereby stamping the mark of suspicion on the most virtuous actions."[68] If the Society reformed its charter in accordance with the critics' demands, it would seem like an admission that the criticism was justified—and that was a step the New Hampshire officers were unwilling to take. As to the charge that the Society was an attempt to raise officers to a superior status, Sullivan's letter asserted the contrary. They should be allowed the same rights to assembly and incorporation as anyone else, including the right to administer their own funds.

Like Moylan's pamphlet, the New Hampshire letter argued that the Cincinnati could create a distinction of *status* without creating a real difference of *power*. Contrary to the critics, the Cincinnati was by no means an order of nobility. If the officers had chosen "to have their Garments cut differently from other Persons and that their Children should follow their Example, we believe few persons would seriously pronounce this a creation of an Order of Nobility." Nobility, or aristocracy, implied something more than a mere inherited difference—it implied a position of privilege in the eyes of the state. Burke had argued that the one would inevitably lead to the other. But that was a conjecture the New Hampshire Cincinnati could not entertain. If wearing a medal counted as being ennobled, then Congress had already granted the privilege to many. "If it should be said," on the other hand, " the difference lies in the descent," then that must mean that a medal ennobles a descendant while having no such effect upon the ancestor to whom it was originally granted. That, they declared, "is an Argument too feeble and absurd to deserve a serious refutation."[69]

By taking a stand against the Cincinnati's critics, the New Hampshire branch members also stood up to Washington and his reform agenda. Clearly, the aim of the reforms had been to quiet the public outcry against the Society. "But if every Jealousy however founded is to be removed and the tongue of envy silenced at all events would not this have been more effectually & more honorably [achieved] by laying the ax to the root of the tree and abolishing the society at once ... ?" The attempt at revising the Institution was a slight against the friendships on which the Society was based. It would be better to get rid of it altogether than allow it to go on in neutered form. This had, indeed, been Jefferson's recommendation to Washington. Now it served as an expression of the members' anger and resistance. In closing, the New Hampshire letter returned to an old republican theme, one that had animated the cause of the revolution itself. "We never shall accede," they wrote, "to any plan which permits any man or body of men to dispose of or even direct us in the disposition of our property." [70] It was property, more than any other principle, that continued to define American gentlemen's political values.

At their meeting on July 4, 1786, the New York branch of the Cincinnati elected five honorary members: James Duane, the mayor of the city; John Hobart, a judge of the state supreme court; William Duer, secretary to the Board of Treasury; Chancellor Robert Livingston, a senior judge; and Richard Morris (no relation to Robert the financier), chief secretary of the state.[71] Thus they moved further toward fulfilling Elbridge Gerry's great fear, that the Cincinnati would eventually include not only all the officers but all the "Citizens of

Consiquence in the united States." The Pennsylvania society had practiced a similar policy: John Dickinson, the state's president, was an honorary member; and so was the financier, Robert Morris. Philadelphia and New York City were the de facto capitals of the United States—Congress had sat at New York's City Hall since the beginning of 1785, while some of the most important banking and commercial operations remained based in Philadelphia. It was these cities, then, that best fostered a new national elite. Through their inclusive policies, the local Cincinnati branches undermined the idea of a distinction based on military service. Instead, they served to strengthen class boundaries, knitting together all the new nation's gentlemen of influence.

When the New York branch appointed a committee to consider Washington's reform program, the newly elected honorary member, Richard Morris, was included. Duer and Duane were both part of the group that authored a circular letter expressing the branch's response to the rest of the Society. Both committees were dominated, however, by Alexander Hamilton. Leaving Congress in June 1783, Hamilton and his young family had lived briefly with the Schuylers near Albany, before moving to the city shortly after the British evacuation. In New York, Hamilton began a career as a lawyer. From its beginning, he was also an active member of the Cincinnati. By 1786, he was well-established among the city's leading gentlemen, and he was certainly the leading thinker in the New York branch of the Society—it was Hamilton who gave the oration that opened the meeting on July 4th. He masterminded a response to Washington's plan that had little in common with the conservative vision expressed in the New Hampshire branch's letter. Yet it was far from a simple acquiescence. Hamilton's view of the Society represented a new way of thinking about postrevolutionary America, and especially the role of elites within a republican system.

Two days after the July 4th meeting, Hamilton's committee made its report on the proposed changes to the Institution. "Though they highly approve the motives which dictated those alterations," the committee wrote, "they are of opinion it would be inexpedient to adopt them." Like the New Hampshire society before them, the New Yorkers strenuously objected to the idea that the money they had raised for charitable purposes should be handed over for safekeeping to the legislature of the state. For all their collective political power, members of the Cincinnati knew they could not trust the people's elected representatives to look after their money. In Philadelphia that same year, Robert Morris's bank was under attack by populist legislators. Giving them power over the society was unthinkable. Likewise, of course, the New York Cincinnati had no intention to stop admitting honorary members. But Hamilton's committee did not reject the idea that the Society needed some major changes in order to align with proper republican principles. They proposed alterations both "in deference to the sense of many of our fellow citizens," and "in conformity to the true spirit of the Institution itself."[72]

Hamilton's proposed reforms had two related elements. The first was also the central plank of Washington's own platform: the abolition of hereditary membership. "As far as it may intend an hereditary succession, by right of primogeniture," wrote the committee, the original Institution "is liable to this objection, that it *refers to birth* what ought to belong *to merit only*, a principle inconsistent with the genius of a Society founded on friendship and patriotism."[73] Unlike the New Hampshire members, unlike Moylan, and unlike the original designers of the Society, the New Yorkers understood the hereditary principle as inconsistent with America's revolutionary and patriotic values. The war had tied officers together by bonds of friendship and mutual struggle. To propagate the Society into the future on the basis of blood seemed, to Hamilton and his colleagues, inappropriate. For Hamilton himself, service in the army had been a way of rising above his family background. While he now faced the difficulty of securing a future for his own family, he also recognized that merit and birth were independent qualities.[74]

The second element of the New Yorkers' proposed reforms to the Society involved completely removing the distinction between regular and honorary members. Such a distinction, they wrote, "holds up an odious difference between men who have served their country in one way, and those who have served it in another."[75] Men like James Duane and William Duer, not to mention Robert Morris himself, had worked in private and government capacities during the war, supporting—and profiting from—the struggle with Britain. Did they not also have a stake in the remembrance of the war, and the direction of the new nation? Did they not also deserve to share the status of the victorious officers? Hamilton's reforms would allow each branch simply to elect who it pleased, making its own judgments about the merit and suitability of candidates. In one sense, it would mean critics could no longer charge the Cincinnati with giving an unfair distinction to military officers. But it would consolidate the idea that the Society represented all the men of consequence. By removing the hereditary provision along with the specific link to army service, Hamilton's proposals would transform the Cincinnati into a self-selected meritocracy: an organized national elite.

When the critical reaction to the Society first emerged in late 1783 and early 1784, it was often remarked in defense of the organizers that they had written the Institution hastily, in the last days before the army's demobilization, and that perhaps its provisions had not been deeply considered. Even Aedanus Burke, the Society's most outspoken critic, suggested that the officers had not properly understood the effects they were setting in motion. The response of Washington, who had both his own reputation and the stability of the federal government on his mind, was equally hasty—by pushing through his package of reforms, he sought to bury the controversy by rendering the Society impermanent and ineffectual. Yet in the wake of the general meeting in May 1784, the members in their state branches had the opportunity to reflect on the questions and assumptions that lay behind the formation of the Society and the charges of its critics. Although most branches did not publish their results, both the New Hampshire and New York branches offered substantive visions of the Cincinnati that embodied their own understandings of the new, republican political order. The differences between them reflected the depth of uncertainty, in the minds of American gentlemen, about just what the new, postrevolutionary world should look like.

By the time the New York branch of the Cincinnati sent their circular letter to the other branches in November 1786, anxiety about the future of the republic had reached fever pitch. During the years of debate over the Cincinnati, other struggles had developed that posed much greater threats to American gentlemen's political values and expectations. While the Cincinnati question saw suspicion and mistrust cast among a divided elite, that division faded in the face of challenges from below. That September, Hamilton had joined James Madison and other leading politicians at a convention in Annapolis, Maryland, where they had agreed on the necessity of a new convention to discuss the federal government, to be held in Philadelphia the following year. Those gathered at Annapolis agreed that "the Situation of the United States [was] delicate and critical." The circular letter Hamilton drafted for the New York Cincinnati emphasized the need to reach a consensus on the future of the Society, and to redirect attention to the future of the Union itself. "The members of the Cincinnati," he wrote, "always actuated by the same virtuous and generous motives, which have hitherto directed their conduct, will pride themselves in being, thro every vicissitude of her future fate, the steady and faithful supporters of her Liberty, her Laws and her Government."[76]

CHAPTER TWO

Obedience

*The people, having emancipated themselves from the British government
... have, in some places at least, forgotten that they could never be
emancipated from the bonds of justice.*

—PETER THACKER, BOSTON MINISTER, 1783

THE AMERICAN REVOLUTION was an act of disobedience. In committees
and town meetings, on the streets and in the countryside, up and down the
colonies, Americans defied their Parliament and their king.[1] They withdrew
consent from powers that claimed to rule over them, and they fought to keep
those powers from regaining control. That momentous, revolutionary process
had a powerful effect on those who acted in it. It led some of them to rethink
the bonds of obedience and power that shaped their everyday lives. "We have
been told that our Struggle has loosened the bands of Government every
where," wrote John Adams to his wife Abigail in 1776. "That Children and Ap-
prentices were disobedient—that schools and Colledges were grown turbulent
—that Indians slighted their Guardians and Negroes grew insolent to their
Masters."[2] From the very start, gentlemen like Adams feared what would happen if the revolution reached down deep into society itself.

As soon as the war with Britain had been won and the immediate external
danger seemed to have passed, those gentlemen began a new campaign to put
an end to disobedience. Restoring order in the new republic meant making
sure all Americans knew their places, and acted their parts. It meant teaching
people how to live properly. Being free from British rule did not mean being
free from obligations, expectations, and the power of social superiors.[3] That
kind of unruly freedom had its own name among gentlemen—licentiousness.
And the licentiousness of ordinary people, many gentlemen believed, was the
single greatest threat to the success and safety of the new republic.

I. The Bonds of Establishment

On the day of his graduation from Yale College, in September 1778, Joel Barlow recited a poem of his own composition about what the United States would be like after the war against Britain had been won.[4] In the midst of war, "The Prospect of Peace" was an idyllic vision. It foresaw a harmonious society where all Americans contentedly fulfilled the roles laid down for them:

> Along these shores, amid these flowery vales,
> The woodland shout the joyous ear assails;
> Industrious crouds in different labours toil,
> Those ply the arts and these improve the soil.
> Here the fond merchant counts his rising gain,
> There strides the rustic o'er the furrow'd plain,
> Here walks the statesman, pensive and serene,
> And there the school boys gambol round the green.[5]

This orderly world of joyous rustics and serene statesmen was a soothing fantasy for a class of graduates who left Yale at a moment of real turmoil, with victory in the war far from certain. Yet Barlow at least affected optimism, in spite of his lack of funds and connections. "We are not the first men in the world to have broke loose from college without fortune to puff us into public notice," he wrote to his friend and classmate, Noah Webster. "If ever virtue and merit are to be rewarded, it is in America."[6] The world they entered, and the expectations they brought to it, were shaped not only by the revolution, but just as much by the deeply entrenched patterns of the New England establishment.[7]

Like Alexander Hamilton, Barlow had volunteered in the patriot militia while he was a college student. He served in the ranks during Washington's defeat at Long Island in 1776. But unlike Hamilton, he did not distinguish himself as a leader, or see active service in the battle. That autumn, he returned to Yale. Two years later, it was through the patronage of a fellow poet and a former tutor, Timothy Dwight, that Barlow got his first job. Dwight had set up an academy in Northampton, Massachusetts, and he invited Barlow to come and teach there. It was, after all, an offer Barlow might have been expecting. For generations of ambitious but less-wealthy college-educated New England men, school-teaching was the first step in professional life. Often, it was a disappointing one. As John Adams had put it twenty-three years earlier during his own time as a teacher, "the school is indeed a school of affliction, a large number of little runtlings, just capable of lisping A.B.C. and troubling the Master." Adams used his teaching job as a way to pay his way through his studies in law. Barlow saw it as a way to earn a living while he worked on his poetry. Like Adams, he didn't stay there long.[8]

Abraham Baldwin, another Yale classmate, had taken a post as a chaplain in the Continental Army. In the spring of 1780, he wrote to Barlow: "The plan is for you to come and be a chaplain to our other Brigade, for I have them both to preach to.... [T]here is not a situation in the army more agreeable to your turn," Baldwin assured his friend. "You would be happy in it." Barlow agreed. Thus he skipped rapidly from one rung to the next on a well-established career trajectory that led from college to the schoolhouse and then to the ministry.[9] This pattern was so drearily predictable that John Trumbull had written a poem about in 1772, called *The Progress of Dullness*:

> Few months now past, he sees with pain
> His purse as empty as his brain;
> His father leaves him then to fate,
> And throws him off, as useless weight;
> But gives him good advice, to teach
> A school at first, and then to preach.
> Thou reason'st well; it must be so;
> For nothing else thy son can do. [10]

But the war gave a novel complexion to Barlow's move from teaching to preaching. The life of an army chaplain need not be all dull. Within a month of his arrival in camp, Barlow dined with Washington himself. "How do you think I felt," he wrote, "when the greatest man upon Earth placed me at His right hand ... at table?"[11]

In 1778, when Barlow graduated, the condition of the established clergy in New England seemed worryingly shaky. A draft constitution for the state of Massachusetts proposed to the people that year had not included provisions for supporting either churches or schools—and the assemblymen had to dismiss their own chaplain when he published a series of articles opposing its ratification. The people rejected the draft constitution in a referendum, and the state remained mired in debate over its republican future. Meanwhile, in September 1778, the venerable minister of Boston's First Church, Charles Chauncy, preached and published a sermon noting the "sad case of salary-men, and particularly the clergy," whose income had been drastically reduced in real terms because of wartime currency inflation. "Surely the pastors of the churches in this state are not so inconsiderable and contemptible an order of men as not to be worth the notice of government?" Without support for the religious establishment, the revolution would forfeit its providential favor, leading to defeat on the battlefield. "Was [our land] ever in a more corrupt and degenerate state?" Chauncy asked. "Was it ever in a more unhappy situation, *morally* speaking, to engage in war?"[12]

With the costs of war to bear, New Englanders were reluctant to keep up their spending on religious and educational establishments. As early as 1775,

Samuel Adams had reported that "some of our towns have dismissed their school masters, alleging that the extraordinary expense of defending the country renders them unable to support them." Struggles over public finance and the role of establishment went on throughout the war and continued after it was over. The debates over the constitution were a particular flashpoint. In a new draft written largely by John Adams, and debated in 1779, the provision for support of the clergy sparked heated controversy—so much that it required the suspension of a procedural rule which limited delegates to two speeches on any one issue. The inclusion of some kind of public support for religion was never really in doubt. "The happiness of the people and the good order and preservation of civil government essentially depend upon piety, religion, and morality," spelled out the Declaration of Rights. But the Congregational Church proved unable to defend its special status against, on one hand, the strong delegation of Baptists led by Isaac Backus and, on the other, the growing number of nonchurchgoers in Massachusetts society.[13]

The new constitution, therefore, continued taxation for religious support, but gave local communities the power to hire and fire ministers as they saw fit, regardless of denomination. "The people," complained one minister in 1783, were determined to keep clergymen "in the closest dependence on them," and "may, at any time, dismiss them from their service."[14] So the war, and the larger revolution, disrupted the clerical and educational establishment in a significant way. The army chaplaincy had an important role in offsetting the effects of that disruption, providing an avenue of employment to college graduates who continued to emerge from Yale and Harvard throughout the war. That in turn was important to maintaining the status and power of the colleges themselves. In eighteenth-century New England, the colleges were crucial elements of the established social order. They were not only centers of orthodox learning, but also—perhaps more important—gateways to elite networks. They relied on the continuing ability to offer social and professional as well as educational advantages, just as society and the professions relied on the colleges to provide the right sort of people to fill their ranks, and to bestow validation on the sons of the establishment.

This network of power and status was the foundation of New England gentility. As it shifted and changed in response to the pressures of the revolution, new fault lines opened up over just what it meant to be a gentleman, and to belong to the establishment. For young men like Barlow and his friend Noah Webster, the revolution and its rhetoric of freedom opened a new vista of opportunity that stood out clearly against the stultifying predictability and limited prospects of the established path, the "Progress of Dullness." From their position somewhere near the bottom of the old elite, they found it easy to cast a critical eye on their own world, to adopt the stance of innovators and iconoclasts. But they were by no means representatives of the downtrodden. Their visions of social order, like Barlow's "Prospect of Peace," remained strictly hierarchical. The new republic demanded obedience and discipline, as well as leadership. In that sense, they remained embedded in the old patterns of established order. The question was just how much those patterns could adapt to accommodate the effects of the revolution.

When Joel Barlow arrived at camp to join the Continental Army in September, 1780, his friend Abraham Baldwin was not the only chaplain there to meet him. Enos Hitchcock had been serving in the army since 1776. Educated at Harvard in the mid-1760s, he represented an older generation of New England ministers, one that had come of age not during the Revolutionary War, but in the first stirrings of the imperial crisis. When the war eventually broke out, Hitchcock left his post as minister to the parish of Beverly, Massachusetts, to become a chaplain. "I have stept aside, a little space, in the great emergencies of our bleeding country," he wrote to his parishioners in 1778, "that, if possible, I might have some influence with my fellow-countrymen, either by precept or example, to remain firm & steadfast in the Defence & support of their dear & Heavenborn Liberties; on which depends the happiness of ages to come—of generations yet unborn." By aligning itself with the patriot cause, New England's church establishment worked to maintain a position of moral leadership. Yet from the beginning, men like Hitchcock recognized the social disruption that might be caused by war.[15]

That was the other reason he had decided to become a chaplain. "I might, by my presence & admonitions," he wrote, "give some check to the dangerous growth of Vice among our young people; who, I hope, will before long, return to dwell with the multitude of their brethren in civil life, & form no small part of the commonwealth." War would transform not only those who fought, but the communities they would return to, Hitchcock recognized. "How unhappy must it have been for such a number of promising men to have lived amidst the many Temptations of an Army, for several years, without any public appearance or form of Religion? This would have rendered their return dangerous," he concluded, "lest they infect the whole flock." One side of Hitchcock's role as a spiritual shepherd was to encourage in his countrymen a revolutionary zeal in defense of their "Heavenborn Liberties."[16] But the other was to make sure those same countrymen did not depart from the traditional morality and ideology of previous generations. He recognized that the revolution was not just a war against the British Empire. It would also involve the reshaping of society. That was a process the church hoped to guide and control.

Ezra Stiles, the new president of Yale, wrote to Hitchcock in 1780 to inform him of Barlow's arrival and talents. "He is a young gentleman of Learning, Sobriety, and ten thousand Excellencies," wrote Stiles. "His merit in Poetry and belles Lettres and in the Sciences in general is great. So great I fear that the World will never do him justice. How he may succeed in preaching I don't Know, but his Sensibility and Amiableness of Manners certainly recommend him." Barlow was indeed an amiable and well-educated young gentleman, a poet and a wit—but not by training, or by inclination, a preacher. He made as much as he could of his time away from camp on furlough. In stolen moments, avoiding the watchful eye of her suspicious and disapproving father, Barlow wooed and soon married Ruth Baldwin, the sister of his friend Abraham. Meanwhile, he devoted himself whenever he could to the composition of an epic poem, *The Vision of Columbus*, that celebrated the triumph of American civilization on a hemispheric scale. It would finally be published in 1787, but already in 1782 Barlow was seeking subscriptions to the work. In the summer of 1782, he rode south in the company of General Benjamin Lincoln, "as amiable as he is great," to seek patronage from high society in Philadelphia.[17]

When they were finally discharged from the army in June 1783, Barlow and Hitchcock followed predictably different paths—though both men participated in the founding of their local Cincinnati branches. For the younger man, the chaplaincy had been an opportunity to escape the dullness of school teaching, a chance for adventure and to see the world outside New England, to gain inspiration for his poetry and to take a more active part in revolution. Barlow did not return to teaching, nor did he find a position as a minister. Instead, he went into business as a printer, with an already established partner, Elisha Babcock. It was an unorthodox decision. Printing was hard, manual work that required both strength and dexterity. It was not a genteel pursuit. Yet it did represent a particularly American approach to progress through the diffusion of knowledge and literature. Benjamin Franklin had appeared in Barlow's "Prospect of Peace" as a representative of American genius.[18] Like Franklin, Barlow the printer would be able to pursue his literary ambitions alongside his role as trader and artisan. "This new-born Empire should my voice employ," he had written back in 1779, "The Muse's transport and the Patriot's joy."[19]

If printing helped turn literature into a business, the revolution turned it into a national project of this "new-born Empire." With the fashionable, patriotic reading public now facing the problem of whether to continue reading and importing British works, educated New Englanders like Barlow saw a new role for themselves. America's glorious cause was the spur New England gentlemen needed to revitalize their flagging cultural authority. If Trumbull's *Progress of Dullness* serves as an illustration of the lack of confidence and purpose in the teaching-and-preaching classes of late colonial New England, Barlow's *Vision of Columbus* projected a newly optimistic spirit. American poets could work for the glory of their country, and win themselves respect as well. They had to create a new literature for the new nation, one that was just as civilized as Britain's, but also reflected the new-found freedom of the republic. Like the Augustans of early eighteenth-century Britain, Barlow and his colleagues—the Connecticut Wits, as they were later known—aimed to construct a commercial literary culture: a network of publishers and booksellers that would print and promote their work, and a system of copyright protection and establishment patronage. Barlow did not envisage himself as a solitary scribbler, but as part of a literary movement that would help secure independence and cultivate the new American society.

Hitchcock, on the other hand, proposed to contribute to the construction of the new republic in a different way. During his own furloughs from the army, the older man had neither been writing poetry nor falling in love. He had been preaching at the First Congregational Church of Providence, Rhode Island, and it was there that he returned at the end of the war to take up the post of minister. Hitchcock was already well connected with the leading figures of the New England establishment: with Stiles, of course, but also with Joseph Willard, the recently appointed president of Harvard, and with James Manning, president of the College of Rhode Island, later Brown University. When Manning died in 1785, Hitchcock preached the funeral sermon, and he received his doctorate in divinity from the college in 1788. So it was as an integral member of the Congregationalist establishment in that most unorthodox of New England states, Rhode Island, that Hitchcock spent his life after the army. Most of all, he committed his attention and energy to promoting education. As he had foreseen, the revolution destabilized social order in New England just as it had done elsewhere. Like many of his fellow ministers, he came to believe that education was the key to restoring the virtue of the people and the proper authority of the establishment.[20]

"It is generally allowed at the present day, that the choice of the people is the only source of power," declared Harvard graduate and minister Zabdiel Adams on election day in Boston, 1782. Nobody could deny the centrality of popular sovereignty – embodied in the processes of elected, representative government – to the new republican state. Yet men like Adams were quick to point out the danger that such ideas posed to an orderly and just society. The Constitution of 1780, drafted primarily by Adams's cousins John and Samuel, included qualifications that meant only men with "the annual income of three pounds, or any estate of the value of sixty pounds" could vote for representatives.[21] This provision helped keep the government in the hands of those who the establishment elite believed would behave responsibly, those who could make judgments on the basis of their own independent interests. Make government too democratic, too responsive to the ideas of the people, and you would end up with chaos, thought the Adams cousins and their allies. "Very popular governments have sometimes been found too weak to prevent tumults, insurrections and factions," Zabdiel told his audience. What Massachusetts needed was "a union of all the most enlightened and virtuous people," whose rule "makes it the interest of the people to obey."[22]

Public schooling was a crucial support for this kind of enlightened leadership. Schools taught their pupils "the *nature* [and] the *value* of that liberty, for which we are now so justly contending." Without them, "an ignorant people," who did not know the true nature of liberty, "will soon become slaves, or run into anarchy." As Zabdiel Adams made clear in another sermon he preached the following year, the proper role of popular sovereignty lay in "electing wise men and true, and then submitting cheerfully to their commands." Clearly, the people of Boston—and New England more generally—needed to be reminded of this lesson. In the same year, 1783, Peter Thacker condemned the effects of the revolution on the public attitude to politics. "The people," wrote Thacker, "having emancipated themselves from the British government, and felt their competence to carry every point they chose, have, in some places at least, forgotten that they could never be emancipated from the bonds of justice." The wartime experience of committee rule had been carried too far. "They have been ready to suppose that their declaration and authority were sufficient to dissolve the most solemn engagements, and that *the people could do no wrong*."[23]

From the moment the war ended, Massachusetts clergy and the leaders of its establishment began their campaign against the excesses of popular sovereignty, placing education and obedience at the center of their vision for an orderly and well-governed republic. And establishment representatives elsewhere in New England followed suit. Celebrating the adoption of New Hampshire's new constitution, modeled on Massachusetts', in 1784 the minister Samuel McClintock insisted that "a wise and knowing people will think it no less their interest than their duty to support government and yield obedience to laws." Moreover, since "virtue is the basis of republics," wrote McClintock, "the education of the youth in useful knowledge and the principles of virtue" was essential. In Connecticut, the Yale professor Samuel Wales likewise wrote that "no state can long be happy . . . unless government be revered and the law obeyed." Now that the war was over, New Englanders everywhere had to forget about revolution and return to obedience. Hence "the education of youth," Wales went on, "is of the utmost importance." Nor would Joel Barlow have disagreed—he and Elisha Babcock published Wales's sermon.[24]

From his new position in Rhode Island, Enos Hitchcock made his own contribution to this burgeoning defense of the traditional establishment. Whereas most of his colleagues had referred to education relatively briefly, as one element connected to their larger social and political themes, it was Hitchcock who approached the subject most directly and comprehensively. On a Wednesday evening in November, 1785, he gave an address to the board of trustees of the schoolhouse in Providence, which they commissioned to be published shortly afterwards under the title, *A Discourse on Education*. "Much credit," he told the local worthies, "is due to everyone who steps forth in so good a cause, and distinguishes himself by his exertions for the establishment and support of schools upon such principles, and in such manner as shall be most subservient to general good."[25] Those principles Hitchcock endeavoured to set out. His discourse was a learned performance, quoting and reflecting many of the most established European authorities on republican education.[26] At its center, though, was a paradox no one had managed to solve: the nature of the state and society depended on the character of its individual citizens, yet those characters were formed by the education they received from the state and society.

Men and women possessed "latent powers and qualities," Hitchcock pointed out, innate "faculties of the human soul" that were "in themselves noble and excellent, and capable of continual enlargement." But drawing out and shaping those innate qualities was the work of education. Like a plant, "the form, size, and qualities of the mind depend upon the means of education being employed during the season of its growth and improvement." Putting it in the words of Richard Price, the radical British Unitarian minister and friend of the American Revolution, Hitchcock went on, "as the chisel works the rude block into shape, so does education form the human soul." Echoing John Locke's much-read handbook on genteel education, he wrote, "it is the judgement of the most accurate writers upon this subject that of the men we meet, nine parts out of ten are what they are, good or bad, according to their education." In other words, schooling mattered. Bad education caused social discord just as good education created harmony. That was why Hitchcock had been so concerned about the experience New England's young men would get in the Continental Army. As a chaplain, he had tried to counteract the corrupting effects of army life. Now he took the same approach to society as a whole.[27]

The "very existence" of the republican state, Hitchcock argued, "depends on the wisdom and virtue of the people at large; and these must depend of the education and habits of mind acquired whilst young." As Jean-Jacques Burlamaqui once wrote—one of "the best writers on government," according to Hitchcock—"those who have a bad education make no scruple to violate the best constitutions in the world." Political transformation could not be accomplished by constitutional means alone, then, or by writing good laws. The people themselves had to be made virtuous by education. That was especially the case in a republic, Hitchcock argued, where without hereditary leaders "we have little else than the understanding and virtue of the people to combine them together in society, and gain their consent and subjection to necessary and just government." Like his fellow ministers, Hitchcock had little trust in the people to define liberty for themselves. "If the means of education be neglected, the rising generation would grow up unformed and without principle," he wrote. "Their ideas of freedom would degenerate into licentious independence; and they would fall prey to their own animosities and contentions." For all their innate noble faculties, human beings had a "depraved nature," Hitchcock warned, against which only the right education held the balance.[28]

At the end of what he called "our promiscuous discourse," Hitchock presented a vignette that served to summarize his vision of power: a sketch "taken from real life" of an ideal woman and her education. "Convinced of the countless evils which attend the female sex from their passion for dress and show," her parents tell us, "we endeavoured to give her a low, that is a true opinion of these things." Still, "she always wore such apparel in her young days as became her rank and station." Class or rank, as well as gender, were integral aspects of Hitchcock's patriarchal vision. Clothing was an important matter, because it made visible the distinctions between people according to the shared rules of the community. The unnamed woman in Hitchcock's tale was "sensible, but not assuming; humble, but not mean ... the most dutiful child, the most affectionate wife .... Her lot is among the saints." This image of obedience in the form of a woman was a bold rhetorical touch, meant to help the listeners and readers of *A Discourse on Education* see that submission within a proper hierarchy was natural, divinely ordained, and beautiful. It used New Englanders' assumptions about family, gender, and fatherhood to recalibrate their ideas about republican obedience.[29]

The religious and patriarchal themes of Hitchcock's discourse betrayed his allegiance to the traditional establishment, in spite of his quotations from republican authors. Like many other ministers during the revolution, he aimed to accommodate the rhetoric of liberty and republicanism to the needs of a conservative social order. As a Harvard man in Rhode Island, Hitchcock represented a larger regional hegemony within that region's most heterodox part. Even as he gave his speech to the proprietors of the local schoolhouse in Providence, that evening in 1785, political turmoil over commerce, tax burdens, and paper money was beginning to take hold of the state. Within a year, a radical new government elected by the people would begin to shake the foundations of the local merchant elite, and with it the larger establishment network. So Hitchcock's concerns over public order and justice, over the natural "licentiousness" of the people, were born out of very real anxieties. The future of the new republic was in question. There was only so far that the old regime could stretch to accommodate new men and their new ideas—and if education was meant to roll back the tide, well, it was already too late for that.

II. The Education of Youth in America

Of all the young men who graduated alongside Joel Barlow in September 1778, Noah Webster was to be perhaps the most famous—the founding father of the American dictionary. Yet leaving Yale, Webster had among the bleakest prospects. Unlike his friend, he had no great poetic ambition, and he had achieved no particular distinction in college. His education had cost his family almost all of what they could spare. When Webster arrived home from Yale that fall, "his father put into his hands an eight-dollar bill of continental money, then worth three or four dollars, saying to him 'take this, you must now seek your living; I can do no more for you.'" He was, he later recalled bitterly, "cast upon the world, at the age of twenty, without property, without patrons, and in the midst of a war which had disturbed all occupations; had impoverished the country; and the termination of which could not be foreseen." For Webster, there seemed to be no optimistic "prospect of peace." Rather his future, like that of his country, lay gravely in doubt.[30]

Webster did not find shelter with his friends in the ranks of the army chaplaincy. Instead, he intended to take up the genteel profession of the law. As a young John Adams had done a generation earlier, Webster took up teaching in order to pay for his legal education; and like Adams, he longed to escape. In the summer of 1780, while Barlow was preparing for his oral exam before the Association of Ministers, which would qualify him to become a chaplain, Webster went to Litchfield. There he worked in the law office of Jedediah Strong, and attended the lectures of Tapping Reeve, who would within a few years establish Litchfield Law School.[31] Among Webster's cohort in Litchfield was a Yale classmate, Oliver Wolcott, Jr., the son of a Connecticut congressman. Both father and son would go on to become governors of the state. The law was just as much an element of the elite establishment as the colleges and the clergy. It gave its gentlemen practitioners access to power, specialist knowledge, and an income independent of manual labor. Moreover, unlike ministers, lawyers were not beholden to particular congregations, and because they were not salarymen, they did not suffer so much from the problem of wartime inflation. No wonder the Litchfield establishment attracted many young trainees.

But like other establishment circles, the legal profession depended on close self-regulation. If there were too many qualified lawyers, the value of legal expertise would be diminished. Gentlemen like Oliver Wolcott and Alexander Hamilton, who could draw on influential connections, might do nicely. But obscurities like Webster faced much greater challenges to building a legal career. In the spring of 1781, he and twenty other candidates sat the examination for the Litchfield bar—all twenty were rejected. Wolcott had already passed, a few months earlier. The rebuff was a symptom of strain in the Connecticut establishment, a sign that the numbers of new men seeking to gain entry were beginning to overwhelm the systems of self-regulation. After his failure, Webster went straight to Hartford and passed the bar there, but when he began to look for work as a lawyer, he could find none. Webster treasured his legal qualifications, and he always signed himself "Noah Webster, Esquire," but neither Yale nor the bar exam were enough to secure him the status and livelihood he was seeking. Dejectedly, he returned to teaching. For the summer of 1781, he set up a school in Sharon, just northwest of Litchfield, the town that had rejected him.[32]

The next year, after a fruitless search for "mercantile employment" that winter, Webster finally decided to get out of Connecticut. He established a new school across the border in Goshen, New York, only twenty miles west of where Washington's victorious army lay encamped at Newburgh. As the young army officers began to wonder when they would receive the rewards of their hard work, and what the new republic really had to offer them, Webster must have shared some of their feelings. He knew, at least, that he did not want to be a teacher. In his memoir, he recalled in the third person, "He knew not by what means he could find business better suited to his inclinations.... He was without money and without friends to afford him any particular aid." Money and friends seemed to be a necessary prerequisite for entry into the establishment. Barlow had got his jobs through his friends from Yale, first at Timothy Dwight's academy, and then in the chaplaincy with Abraham Baldwin. If only Webster could figure out a way to make his college connections useful. It was in this state of mind, one of "extreme depression and gloomy forebodings," that he finally hit on a new project. He drily described it in the memoir as "composing elementary books for the instruction of children." This was to be the project that would change his life.[33]

When he was a child, Webster himself had learned to read and write with a textbook first printed in London in 1740, and reprinted many, many times since, including by Benjamin Franklin in Philadelphia in 1747. It was written by an Englishman called Thomas Dilworth, and was entitled *A New Guide to the English Tongue*. By 1782, though, Dilworth's book was no longer very new. Webster, drawing on his experience as a teacher, planned to write his own version, one "better adapted to assist the learner." He was not yet, as he would later become, an advocate of wholesale spelling reform. But he did have ideas about how English grammar worked, and how children could best be brought to learn it. If he had to be a schoolteacher, then why shouldn't he be teacher to the whole country? Webster wrote to his friend Barlow about his idea, and the poet wrote back at the end of August, 1782. "I like your plan about Dilworth. It will be useful and successful in the world at large if you can make it useful to yourself." Perhaps Barlow was thinking of his own poetic endeavors when he added, "It is a work of labour and you ought to make something by it."[34]

Barlow's letter was encouraging, but he did have a caveat to add. "You know our country is prejudiced in favour of old Dilworth, the nurse of us all," he told Webster. Generations of Americans had learned their grammar from *A New Guide to the English Tongue*. "It will be difficult to turn their attention from it." This was a problem Webster took seriously. It helped make clearer in his mind exactly why now was the moment to make the attempt. The biggest strength of his new work over Dilworth's, Webster realized, would be its homegrown American quality. Like the writing of Barlow and the other Connecticut Wits, Webster's textbooks would be contributions to a new American literature, and a new national culture, that both relied upon and helped to bolster Americans' feelings of independence. That was the case Webster made clear in the introduction to his first textbook, the 1783 spelling book that would later become known as the blue-backed speller. Sometimes, he argued, a people had to throw out what was old and erroneous, and bring in something new. A revolution in politics was only the beginning of the larger changes that were made possible by the onset of independence.[35]

"It commonly requires lengths of time and favourable circumstances," he wrote in the introduction to the speller, "to diffuse and establish a sentiment among the body of the people." But as soon as it has "acquired the stamp of time and the authority of general custom . . . even error becomes too sacred to be violated by the assaults of innovation." Dilworth's spelling book, full as it was with English place-names and the names of English monarchs, became a sort of metaphor for the whole British empire—and Webster's new textbook became a tool for building the new republic. "The present period," he wrote, "is an era of wonders; greater changes have been wrought in the minds of men, in the short compass of eight years past, than are commonly effected in a century." There had been a "concurrence of those powerful causes that effect almost instantaneous revolutions in states," great shifts in sentiment that put the whole world in a new light. Independence had opened America's eyes to the reality of her British heritage. "She now sees a mixture of profound wisdom and consummate folly in the British constitution," Webster claimed, and "a ridiculous compound of freedom and tyranny in their laws. . . . She views the vices of that nation with abhorrence, their errors with pity, and their follies with contempt."[36]

There was something personal in Webster's rhetoric, in his strident rejection of the mother country and his embrace of independence. He remembered the humiliating moment when his own father had told him to go out and seek a living, and the moment the Litchfield bar association had denied him. Anger toward his parents, and toward the Connecticut establishment that had failed to provide for him in spite of his qualifications, animated the fiery prose of his introduction. Webster was still only twenty-three years old when he wrote it in the fall of 1782. The final peace treaty with Britain had yet to be agreed by the diplomats in Paris, but the young man was determined to establish his own independence and self-sufficiency. His own situation and that of his youthful country reacted with each other in his imagination, and merged in the pages of his speller, just as they did in the rhyming couplets of Joel Barlow's still-unfinished epic. For the young generation that had come of age during the war, the revolution was a symbol they could use to guide and validate their own choices—a symbol of freedom. "The Americans stand astonished at their former delusion," Webster wrote, "and enjoy the pleasure of their final separation from their insolent sovereigns."[37]

For gentlemen who identified themselves with the revolution, as Webster did, it was common to think of the new nation as a kind of metaphorical person, an infant or a man just lately come of age. This had a particular resonance for educators like Webster, who believed that the shaping of a young man's life early on would determine his character later. America's childhood under its "insolent" British sovereign had taught it "erroneous maxims in politics and religion," which the revolution had revealed and tried to abolish. But the young country had been brought up with other bad habits too. "Europe is grown old in folly, corruption and tyranny," wrote Webster. "Laws are perverted, manners are licentious, literature is declining and human nature debased." That inheritance of corruption and licentiousness had to be rooted out. "For America in her infancy to adopt the present maxims of the old world, would be to stamp the wrinkles of decrepit old age upon the bloom of youth and to plant the seeds of decay in a vigorous constitution." Webster wanted to implant new and rational principles to take the place of the old. And in keeping with New England's grammar school tradition, he was especially interested in the role of language in the formation of character. Reform American language, his textbooks implied, and everything else would follow.[38]

The problem was a lack of regularity. Out of the former British colonies had come the seed of a single nation, America. But in order to achieve that promise, ways of speaking and writing across the new states had to be made properly uniform. The goal of Webster's textbooks was to take American language and "reduce it to order," so that a unified American nationhood, culture, and politics could emerge. New England and Virginia were both home, Webster complained, to "a peculiar pronunciation which affords much diversion to their neighbors," while the middle states were "tinctured with a variety of Irish, Scotch, and German dialects which are justly censured as deviations from propriety and the standards of elegant pronunciation." As a result, "the dialect of one State is as ridiculous as that of another; each is authorised by local custom; and neither is supported by any superior excellence." All this had to be rationalized, "reduced to rules," its "corruptions" cleared away, and "one uniform standard of elegant pronunciation" established. Without such measures, the new nation would never make itself respectable. "It is the business of *Americans*," the introduction to the spelling-book concluded, "to diffuse an uniformity and purity of *language*,—to add superior dignity to this infant Empire and to human nature."[39]

Webster believed there was an unwritten truth to language—a kind of natural law—that could only be accessed by expert knowledge. It was the job of the grammarian and instructor to create an "accurate" guide to that hidden reality. In that sense, he was much like the authors who wrote guides to gentlemanly behavior, or even to justice itself. He was not *setting* the standards, but simply providing a means for anyone to follow them. His book would give "the rules for ascertaining the just pronunciation," which the users of the language might follow, in the same way that lawyers and judges used commentaries and treatises to ascertain justice in the law. Like them, his qualifications came from expertise. "I have devoted nine years to the acquisition of knowledge," he told his readers. "The criticism of those who know more, will be received with gratitude." But there was no final, objective arbiter for these standards, just as there was no definitive text of the natural law. Rather, the true "standard of pronunciation," wrote Webster, "is nothing less than the customary pronunciation of the most accurate scholars and literary Gentlemen." Everything came back to the authority of hierarchy. Justice was defined by the customs of the powerful.[40]

Clearly, then, Webster's project did not entail a complete declaration of independence from the New England establishment. His authority as an educator in fact relied on his own education, and his success depended on the support of connections in the establishment structure. Through the winter of 1782 to 1783, Webster traipsed around the colleges and educational institutions of the north seeking endorsements for the first of three projected books, the whole thing to be titled *The American Instructor*. Samuel Smith, a professor of moral philosophy and the future president of Princeton, wrote him a kind letter, as did his former law tutor, Tapping Reeve. He also visited Ezra Stiles, the Yale President who had written to Enos Hitchcock praising Joel Barlow's literary talents. Stiles took Webster's plan to heart, and provided a strong endorsement. He also suggested a new title: the rather cumbersome, *A Grammatical Institute of the English Language*. Perhaps out of politeness, and eager to secure the recommendation, Webster adopted the change. His relationship to the senior members of the educational establishment remained one of deference, in spite of his disappointments. But Webster was also setting out on a new path, that would take him far beyond the world of New England and its colleges.

That path necessarily involved a pragmatic attitude to the commercial aspects of literature. While he was preparing to publish his first volume, Webster was also concerned with another vital aspect of his project, the copyright laws that would secure his profit from the venture. Many New England authors associated with the new nationalist literary movement had begun to mount a concerted campaign for legal protections for their work, and their campaign produced rapid results. Joel Barlow wrote to Elias Boudinot, the president of Congress, in January 1783 to request congressional action on the matter. A committee was appointed, and in May a resolution recommended that the states should pass laws granting copyright to all authors of new works in the United States for a minimum of fourteen years. Webster wrote his own petitions to the Connecticut legislature, but by the time he came to present them an act had already been passed. "Several literary gentlemen" had petitioned for the act, to clamp down especially on a pirated edition of John Trumbull's *M'Fingal*. Likewise, the Yale poet Timothy Dwight helped pass a copyright law in Massachusetts, where he sat in the assembly. In New England, the rise of the new nationalist literature went hand in hand with the rise of copyright—and the same men stood behind both.[41]

While Dwight, Trumbull, Barlow, and the other Connecticut Wits seemed content to remain tightly ensconced in their own regional networks, however, it was Webster who did the most to spread the new nationalist message through the entire United States. Importantly, his ideological vision of the revolutionary American republic was matched by his commercial ambition. With Barlow's financial help, and John Trumbull's encouragement, Webster contracted with the Hartford firm of Hudson & Goodwin to publish the first installment of the *Grammatical Institute*, the speller, in October 1783. The second part, the grammar book, came out in March 1784. The third and final part was a reader—a compilation of texts for use in schoolroom exercises. While the speller had listed American place-names instead of English ones, it was in the reader that Webster could really fly his nationalist colors. He used extracts from the literary productions of his friends, including Barlow's still-unpublished epic, *The Vision of Columbus*. This third volume was published in early 1785, not by Hudson & Goodwin but by none other than Barlow & Babcock. The old network had come through for Webster in the end. But he intended to reach out beyond the confines of New England. That spring, 1785, he embarked on a national tour.[42]

Setting off by boat from New Haven, Webster had two purposes in traveling. One was to continue his campaign for copyright laws throughout the states. New England, with its established literary culture, had responded quickly to the demands of its authors, but the other states lagged behind. The second purpose was to sell his books. If Webster was to achieve the nationwide success of Dilworth's speller, he needed to take an active role in marketing. Of course, if he wanted to profit in the long term, he would need to have the copyright laws in place. Webster's mission to unify the American language thus matched up closely with the general project of creating an integrated national marketplace, which in turn would rely on a reciprocity and uniformity of law and government. He visited New York, Philadelphia, Baltimore, and Charleston, as well as Mount Vernon, where he was received with fastidious politeness by George and Martha Washington. Shipping boxes of his books to each city he visited, he gave free copies to schools in the hope they would be taken up for regular use. In Charleston, he gave two-hundred copies of the speller to a local college the day after the Fourth of July. Patriotism, Webster found, could be a valuable tool of commerce.[43]

For the moment, nonetheless, teaching remained Webster's primary source of income. On his way south through Baltimore, he placed an advertisement declaring that he would open a school, "for the Instruction of young Gentlemen and Ladies in Reading, Speaking and Writing the English language with Propriety and Correctness." When he returned to the city in August, following July in Charleston, he did indeed open a school—but for the teaching of choral music. He made up a choir of his ten students to sing at church services, in exchange for the use of the church as a venue for his school. Within a few weeks, he had hit on a new idea: he would give lectures on the English language, based on the principles he had developed in the *Grammatical Institute*. This plan would not only provide a stream of income from tickets, it would also help promote his books, and bolster his own expert credentials. So it was that Noah Webster found himself in a Baltimore church on a rainy Wednesday in October, lecturing "to a small audience" and, in a way, completing the trajectory that the New England establishment had set out for him—"first to teach a school, and then to preach."[44]

Over the next year, Webster continued his journeying around the country, giving lectures and selling textbooks wherever he went, on a sort of perpetual book tour. He also developed his ideas about education beyond the realm of language and pronunciation. Webster's primary expertise, after all, was not as a linguist or philologist, but as a teacher. His political and cultural vision of the new American nation had first taken form in his writing on dialect in the introduction to the blue-backed speller. Even then, he had had strong opinions about how American children should be educated, and the problems with existing educational culture in the new republic. By the end of April, 1786, Webster added a new lecture to his series, which he titled, "General Remarks on Education." This was to be much more overtly political than his more technical linguistic papers. As he described it in an advertisement printed that July, the new lecture would analyze "the influence of education on morals, and of morals on government," as well as the "connection between the mode of education and the form of government." In other words, he would be dealing with the very same questions that troubled Enos Hitchcock, the paradoxical relationship between the state and individuals.[45]

Webster delivered his lecture on education for the first time in Wilmington, Delaware, "to a crowded audience, whose applause is flattering." It was quite different from the reception he had received for his first lecture on linguistics. Certainly his delivery had improved, but the content might have had something to do with it as well. He published a serialized version of the lecture in the newspaper he set up in New York in December 1787, and then a slightly amended version, called "On the Education of Youth in America," in his 1790 *Collection of Essays and Fugitiv Writings*—by that time, he was getting more involved in spelling reform. The vision Webster presented in these essays shared plenty of similarities with Hitchcock's *Discourse on Education*, and with the era's commonplace attitudes towards education. Yet in certain points, it asserted a radical break, especially from the assumptions of the New England establishment. Whereas clergymen like Hitchcock often seemed to adapt republican rhetoric to their own needs, Webster took the idea of revolution seriously. In constructing his program for proper education, he drew on the sense of anger and the desire for renewal he had expressed in the blue-backed speller's introduction. Rather than writing in support of existing practices, he wrote as a critic and reformer.[46]

By elaborating his ideas about the proper education for American children, Webster was making an implicit argument about the kind of gentlemanly ideals that were suitable for the new nation. This argument was closely linked to a theory of historical change. "Education," he wrote, "proceeds by gradual advances, from simplicity to corruption." In decadent European nations, superficial manners had become the most important objects of schooling. Advancing from safety, through utility, the education of gentlemen "among the opulent part of civilized nations" was now devoted "principally to show and amusement." In contrast, Webster argued that it was much better to seek "an uncorrupted heart and an improved head" than to prioritize "a genteel address" and an easy manner. Education should be pursued outside the cities, in order to avoid their corrupting influence. "The goodness of a heart is of infinitely more consequence to society than an elegance of manners," he wrote. "Nor will any superficial accomplishments repair the want of principle in the mind. It is always better to be *vulgarly right* than *politely wrong*." Where genteel European education had become debased by the pursuit of correct manners, Americans should pursue more substantial aims.[47]

In terms of the knowledge students should acquire, Webster was an advocate of utility and specialization. "Young gentlemen are not all designed for the same line of business, and why should they pursue the same studies?" he asked. "Why should a merchant trouble himself with the rules of Greek and Roman syntax or a planter puzzle his head with conic sections?" There should be different courses for those intending different careers, Webster argued. Merchants might usefully learn living foreign languages rather than dead ones, and farmers should learn "practical husbandry" and agriculture. "Indeed it appears to me," wrote Webster, thinking of his own time at Yale and his failed attempt to find work as a merchant and a lawyer, "that what is now called a *liberal education* disqualifies a man for business." A college education gave a man "a fondness for ease, for pleasure or for books, which no efforts can overcome." It was "better calculated to fit youth for the learned professions than for business." What young gentlemen needed most of all was useful training in the fields of their future endeavor. American gentlemen, according to Webster's vision, would not be men of ease and leisure. They would be businessmen.[48]

If these standards of morality and useful knowledge were to be properly inculcated in the youth of America, though, another character would need to be considered—that of the teachers themselves. "The principal defect in our plan of education in America," wrote Webster, "is the want of good teachers in the academies and common schools." It was this defect that occupied the core of his essay. "The instructors of youth ought, of all men, to be the most prudent, accomplished, agreeable, and respectable," he went on. They should be men of "good breeding and good manners." Lessons were best received "from a man who is loved and respected." Yet the reality was that "the most important business in civil society," the education of its youth, "is in many parts of America committed to the most worthless characters." Below the level of the great colleges, most teachers were "men of no breeding," and many of them were "men infamous for the most detestable vices." If Americans were to take education seriously, they had to take account of the kind of person who conducted it. If it was schooling that formed the citizens and future character of the state, then teachers were among the most important statesmen.[49]

"The practice of employing low and vicious characters to direct the studies of youth is in the highest degree criminal," wrote Webster. It was also "glaringly absurd." Parents want their children to be "well-bred," obedient, and respectful, yet they "place them under the care of clowns ... men of the most profligate lives," whom "both parents and children despise." Did these parents not realize, Webster asked, that "children always imitate those with whom they live or associate?" As we have seen, the role of teacher in New England tended to be seen as a form of short-term employment for college graduates on their way to better things. Schools were often organized informally, and teachers were treated as little more than the servants of their charges' parents. Institutions like Timothy Dwight's academy, where Joel Barlow taught briefly before joining the army chaplaincy, tried to formalize schooling and improve the conditions of teachers. Webster wanted to universalize that model and turn teaching into a respectable profession. "Respect for an instructor" was far better than corporal punishment for maintaining discipline in the classroom. Teachers should be "judicious and reasonable" enough to command a parent's confidence. In order to turn children into gentlemen, in short, it made sense that teachers should be gentlemen themselves.[50]

Like his friend Joel Barlow, the poet and printer, Webster had followed a path that did not accord with the established notions of gentility and respectability in eighteenth-century New England. Rejected by the legal profession, unable to make his way in business, and without the support of powerful family connections, he had turned his years of teaching into a career in itself, through his textbooks and lectures. So when Webster sought to establish the credibility of teachers, to "make it respectable for the first and best of men to superintend the education of youth," it was part of a process of self-creation that resonated with all the possibilities of revolution. These central passages in his essay were a diatribe against neglectful parents, and by extension, against the entire established system in which he had grown up. Within his essay was an anxious demand for recognition and status that was very similar to that of the army officers at Newburgh in 1783. "Americans," he wrote in the closing lines of his essay,

> unshackle your minds and act like independent beings. You have been children long enough, subject to the control and subservient to a haughty parent. You have now an interest of your own to augment and defend: you have an empire to raise and support by your exertions and a national character to establish and extend by your wisdom and virtues.

For Webster, the promise of education was tied up with the struggle for independence—not just America's but his own as well. In setting out to shape the character of the nation, young men like Webster were creating new characters for themselves.[51]

III. The Politics of Education

Noah Webster was not alone in seeing the American Revolution as an opportunity for radical educational reform. In 1778, the same year Webster and Barlow graduated from Yale, none other than Thomas Jefferson proposed a new plan of public education for the state of Virginia—and over the following decades, he continued to fight for the ideas and principles contained in it. Where the representatives of the New England establishment, men like Hitchcock, were campaigning to defend and bolster an existing system, Jefferson's plan for Virginia involved the creation of something entirely new. In that state, schooling was organized on a private and ad hoc basis. Aside from the very richest, whose parents could afford to employ private tutors, Virginian children were sent either to a few philanthropic academies, or to private "field schools" much like the schools set up by Webster in New York and Baltimore. There was no way for the state to regulate the kind of education provided by these institutions. What Jefferson proposed in his *Bill for the More General Diffusion of Knowledge* was a completely new system: a secular establishment for the republic of Virginia.[52]

Some forms of government were better than others when it came to protecting "individuals in the free exercise of their natural rights," Jefferson wrote in the Bill's preface. But "even under the best forms, those entrusted with power have, in time, and by slow operations, perverted it into tyranny." This gradual corruption would affect any government, under any constitution. How could Virginia, and America, avoid that fate? "It is believed that the most effectual means of preventing this would be, to illuminate, as far as practicable, the minds of the people at large," he continued. Education would give ordinary Virginian voters the tools to root out "ambition" and corruption. Without it, Jefferson assumed, they would be too easily duped by demagogues seeking to turn themselves into tyrants. In a republic, the people at large were "entrusted with power," but they could not actually be *trusted* to protect that power and use it wisely. Their minds had to be illuminated, to enable them to see as clearly as gentlemen like Jefferson. And, of course, it would be such gentlemen who would establish and control the system of illumination. For republican theorists like him, education was a crucial means of bypassing the threat of genuine popular power.[53]

Jefferson's bill proposed to build new schools throughout the state, where "all the free children, male and female ... shall be intitled to receive tuition gratis, for the term of three years," or longer if their parents were willing to pay for it. But it did not end there. As much as he wanted to illuminate the minds of the ordinary, Jefferson's plan was also to select and elevate the extraordinary. "Those persons, whom nature hath endowed with genius and virtue," were to be picked out and groomed for leadership in the republic. Rising from the local schools to grammar schools, and then to the College of William and Mary, this natural aristocracy was to be "rendered by liberal education worthy to receive, and able to guard the sacred deposit of the rights and liberties of their fellow citizens." Crucially, the process of selecting this republican elite would occur "without regard to wealth, birth or other accidental condition or circumstance"—except, of course, their supposed natural endowments of genius and virtue. Jefferson's proposal, then, was much more than a system of education. It was a plan to reconstruct Virginia's class system, to undermine hereditary privilege and create a new cadre of republican gentlemen to rule the republic.[54]

"The people will be happiest whose laws are best, and best administered," wrote Jefferson, and "laws will be wisely formed, and honestly administered, in proportion as those who form and administer them are wise and honest." What mattered most to Jefferson was not creating a system of equality, but ensuring that those on top were the most suitable, the wisest and most honest. Those who reached high stations due to birth and fortune, he implied, were just as likely to be "weak or wicked" as wise or honest.[55] Like Alexander Hamilton in the debate over the Cincinnati, Jefferson argued that leadership in a republic should be meritocratic, not hereditary. Of course, that left open the question of how merit could be determined, and who was to be in charge of the system. What made someone "worthy to receive" the blessings of liberty, in Thomas Jefferson's eyes? Left unspoken were the standards of justice that determined what actions were wicked, and what were wise. Behind every scheme of education in the new republic lay the same need to make people conform to a set of principles that was still being developed.

Jefferson's bill was defeated in 1778. In the midst of war, and facing invasion by the British army, Virginians had more pressing concerns, and few resources to spare. But Jefferson did not abandon hope. Two years later, in his *Notes on the State of Virginia*, he wrote at some length about the vision that lay behind the bill. The general education of the public would, he wrote, lay "the principle foundations of future order." It would instill in the minds of ordinary Virginians "the first elements of morality." As their judgment developed, Jefferson projected, this moral understanding would "teach them how to work out their own greatest happiness, by shewing them that it does not depend on the condition of life in which chance has placed them, but is always the result of a good conscience, good health, occupation, and freedom in all just pursuits." In other words, education would make people accept their place in society without complaining—it would teach them what pursuits and ambitions were *just*, and what were not. That way, they would be made "the safe, as they are the ultimate, guardians of their own liberty," ready to protect the existing social order and its natural, meritocratic rulers.[56]

Jefferson did not give up on getting his scheme passed. Writing from Paris in 1786, the same year Webster first gave his lecture on education, Jefferson told George Washington that the bill might eventually be passed—and that would mean the two charity schools Washington had proposed to set up would be obsolete. "It is an axiom in my mind," he told Washington, "that our liberty can never be safe but in the hands of the people themselves, & that too of the people with a certain degree of instruction." Because education was so vital to liberty and proper government, it was "the business of the state to effect, and on a general plan," not the role of private enterprise or ad hoc charity.[57] This was also the opinion of John Adams, who had written the year before that "the whole people must take upon themselves the education of the whole people, and must be willing to bear the expenses of it. There should not be a district of one mile square without a school in it," Adams went on, "not founded by a charitable individual, but maintained at the expense of the people themselves."[58]

For both men, as for many other republican thinkers in the ancient world and the eighteenth century alike, education was fundamentally a part of the political constitution of the state—a public, not a private matter. Yet as the 1780s wore on, the prospect of radical educational reform grew no closer. By the time he wrote his *Defense of the Constitutions of the United States*, Adams was expressing a more cynical position. "Such is the miserable blindness of mankind," he wrote, "it is very doubtful that the pitiful motive of saving the expense would not wholly extinguish public education," unless it were protected by some superior law, or perhaps superior lawmakers. "General public education never can exist in a simple democracy," Adams now declared. Without guidance from a higher chamber of wise and honest men, the people were too unenlightened even to provide for their own enlightenment.[59] By calling attention to the need for education, republicans like Jefferson and Adams were really emphasizing how unfit for rule the people were. Their arguments were the same as those of Enos Hitchcock and his fellow clergymen. Popular sovereignty was one thing, but it would only be legitimate in their eyes if the people were willing and able to follow deeper principles of justice. To do so, they had to submit to being educated.

In Pennsylvania, too, the idea of republican education was embroiled with refined gentlemen's doubts and fears about democracy—and especially the kinds of democratic culture and ideas that were emanating from the west. From the end of the war, increased economic pressure brought to bear by merchants and creditors in the east led communities in the west to organize in defense of their land and freedom. The postwar contraction of the money supply, and the collapse of rural credit networks, caused an economic depression that saw a wave of foreclosures sweep western Pennsylvania. Many families, facing the seizure of their homes and farms, picked up what property they could move and fled further west. But others rallied around local politicians like William Findley and John Smilie, both Irish immigrants who had been in western Pennsylvania since the end of the Seven Years War, had served in the Revolutionary War, and came to Westmoreland County early in the 1780s. Such men took the lead in a popular campaign to resist the new economic power being exerted by Philadelphia gentlemen like Robert Morris. As we shall see, they came close to succeeding. From the beginning of the decade, their embrace of revolutionary popular politics pressed eastern elites to come up with new forms of control, and new ways to maintain their vision of justice.[60]

Among the allies of the gentlemen's cause was Benjamin Rush, a physician who had earned his medical degree at the University of Edinburgh, and a signer of the Declaration of Independence.[61] As a man of science and a believer in rational reform, trained in one of the hotbeds of European enlightenment, Rush did not restrict himself to thinking about questions of medicine and public health. His expertise, prestige, and friendships made him an influential character in the Pennsylvania capital. Thus it was that in 1782, he came to be sitting on the porch of one of Robert Morris's closest business associates, William Bingham, discussing the future of education in the new nation. Sitting with Rush on Bingham's elegant porch was the elderly John Montgomery, a congressman from Westmoreland County who was seeking legislative backing for a project of his own—to expand the local grammar school in Carlisle into an academy. In Rush, who had already once before the revolution sought to involve himself in the creation of a new college, Montgomery's proposal sparked a decade of thinking and writing about education that went far beyond an academy for Carlisle. Education, he came to believe, could help solve the new republic's problems of obedience and social order.[62]

What was needed in Carlisle, Rush told Montgomery, was not an academy but a full-blown college. The University of Pennsylvania, though it was no longer dominated by Episcopalians, remained associated with eastern elites. Its influence did not extend into the distant western part of the state. Rush envisaged a new college in the west as a way to organize the growing Presbyterian church and make it both powerful and respectable. It was, moreover, a way to introduce order to the backcountry, turning educated Presbyterian "prophets" into the agents of genteel values. A college would work, Rush wrote, to "soften the tempers of our turbulent brethren, to inspire them with liberal sentiments in government and religion, to teach them moderation in their conduct to other sects, and to rescue them from the charges of bigotry and persecution that are so often brought against them." Rush was serious about the importance of religion, but he also saw the college as a political tool to pacify turbulent western communities.[63]

If new leaders could be educated with eastern backing, they might take the place of men like Findley who lacked the moderation and "liberal sentiments" Rush sought to inculcate. Montgomery, an older westerner who was no ally of either Findley or Morris, found his project gradually taken over by Rush's designs. Rush proposed to name the college after John Dickinson, the wealthy planter and politician who had become president of Pennsylvania's supreme executive council in November 1782. Dickinson, an honorary member of the Cincinnati, was a friend of the conservative Republican faction in Philadelphia, and Rush had to reassure Montgomery that he was a suitable patron. "His conduct is highly approved of by all classes and parties," Rush insisted. Soon enough, however, opposition began to mount. The planned college was being called "a *Tory scheme.*" No epithet could have been more distasteful to backcountry radicals. They understood all too well the intentions of Rush and his elite backers. Montgomery tried to pull back and return to his plan for an academy. But Rush pressed on. Despite the opposition of western legislators from Carlisle's own county, he managed to win over the conservative-dominated assembly. In September, 1783, a year after the meeting on Bingham's porch, Dickinson College was chartered by the state of Pennsylvania.[64]

The first full meeting of the new college's board of trustees was to be held in Carlisle in April 1784. In the months preceding the meeting, Rush spent his time reading and gathering his ideas about education, and setting them down in an essay, "Thoughts Upon the Mode of Education Proper in a Republic." This work went beyond the question of the west per se, to address the larger issue that so concerned his fellow educationalists up and down the country: in a country where the people were the sovereigns, how were they to be made fit for self-rule? As Rush put it in the opening lines of his essay, "the business of education has acquired a new complexion by the independence of our country. The form of government we have assumed has created a new class of duties to every American." Participation in a republic was a *duty*, not just a right, and it had to be performed properly. America needed to take advantage of the revolutionary moment to reform its practices of education, Rush wrote, and to lay the foundations for "nurseries of wise and good men," which would stamp right impressions of justice and virtue in the "yielding texture" of the people's minds.[65]

Like the educationalists of the New England clerical establishment, Rush held that "the only foundation for a useful education in a republic is to be laid in RELIGION. Without this, there can be no virtue, and without virtue there can be no liberty, and liberty is the object and life of all republican governments." In this, he departed from what he called the "paradoxical ... modern" view, "that it is improper to fill the minds of youth with religious prejudices of any kind," but there were few Americans who wanted to remove religion from education altogether. For Rush, instilling the doctrines of religion contributed to the goal of civilizing schoolchildren and making them useful members of society. "Man is naturally an ungovernable animal," but "when we add the restraints of ecclesiastical to those of domestic and civil government, we produce in him the highest degrees of order and virtue." Obedience to government of all kinds was the first aim of education for Rush, as it was for men like Enos Hitchcock and Zabdiel Adams. "In the education of youth," Rush wrote, "let the authority of our masters be as absolute as possible.... By this mode of education, we prepare our youth for the subordination of laws and thereby qualify them for becoming good citizens of the republic."[66]

At the same time, Rush saw education as a way of making people more alike. "Our schools of learning, by producing one general and uniform system of education, will render the mass of the people more homogenous," he wrote. This homogeneity, in turn, would "fit them more easily for uniform and peaceable government." In short, Rush considered it both possible and necessary to "convert men into republican machines," uniform cogs that could properly perform their parts in the "great machine of the government of the state." Like Webster, he was concerned with the "propriety and elegance" of the American language. In Pennsylvania, in particular, "while our citizens are composed of the natives of so many different kingdoms in Europe," education was all the more important, to instill homogeneous American and republican principles. Yet even this could only go so far—Rush appended to his essay a call for restrictions on immigration. In all this, he had his eyes on the backcountry and its democrats, many of their leaders Irish-born. Such people were not truly civilised republicans, but "artful pedagogues" who opposed useful new establishments like Dickinson College. For Rush, "aristocratic or democratic juntos" were equally dangerous, and both may be born out of "the prevalence of ignorance and vice."[67]

Rush's ideal republican citizen "must watch for the state as if its liberties depended on his vigilance alone, but he must do this in such a manner as not to defraud his creditors or neglect his family." The ties of patriarchal hierarchy and contractual justice were to be embedded in the idea of the republic itself, and taught in schools across the state. Likewise, it was important to inculcate women with the proper "principles of liberty and government," since it was from their mothers that male children received their first impressions. It was vital, therefore, that women be taught to think "justly" on such "great subjects." Rush sought to turn women into republican mothers just as he would turn men into republican machines. In both cases, his vision of education was not framed around the acquisition of a knowledge that would allow citizens to participate fully in governing the republic. Instead, it was a program designed to secure subordination and obedience through discipline and uniformity—a plan inspired by the ancient Spartans, and designed to counteract the threat to the republic that Rush saw emerging from the heterogeneous, turbulent, and democratic people of the Appalachian west.[68]

When Noah Webster gave his lecture on education in Philadelphia, on March 11, 1786, Benjamin Rush was almost certainly in the audience. The two men had met for the first time only a few weeks earlier, when Rush played host to their mutual acquaintance, "the celebrated Scotch Lecturer or Natural Philosopher," Henry Moyes. It was Moyes's lectures on optics a year earlier that had inspired Webster's own turn on the public stage. Now, in Rush's Philadelphia parlor, the younger man listened to the two doctors "converse of *harmony of tastes*."[69] It was a topic well-suited to two men with such broad scientific and philosophical interests. Moyes himself, the blind son of a dissenting minister in Kirkcaldy, had been a student of David Hume in Edinburgh and Thomas Reid in Glasgow, earning a doctorate himself before becoming a popular lecturer in England and America. Moyes's greatest advocate was Adam Smith, who had taken the boy as "his constant companion" while he composed *The Wealth of Nations* and afterwards directed his education and provided letters of introduction.[70] In short, Moyes was a true representative of the Scottish enlightenment—an intellectual tradition that made a deep mark on both Rush and Webster's thought.[71]

The night after Webster's lecture, three weeks after the meeting with Moyes, Webster and Rush dined together in Philadelphia. Spurred by Webster's talk, education must have been the leading topic of their conversation. Clearly, both men shared similar ideas about the need for educational reform. But as yet, neither had put their thoughts down in print. Rush had circulated his essay "On the Mode of Education Proper in a Republic" among a few friends, and he must have discussed its contents with the trustees of Dickinson College soon after he wrote it, but it was not until almost two months after he dined with Webster that it appeared in published form. Webster's own lecture did not make its way into print until late the following year, in his own *American Magazine*. It seems likely, then, that the two men influenced each other's work before it reached publication. When Rush included a paragraph in his essay calling for teachers to be "distinguished for their abilities and knowledge ... grave in their manners, gentle in their tempers, exemplary in their morals, and of sound principles in religion and government," was he taking a cue from Webster's favorite argument?[72] The two had disagreements—about the use of the Bible in teaching, for one thing—but their essays bear the marks of each other's ideas.

Most important, they both understood education as a means to the creation of a modern, commercial republic. Far more than Jefferson or Adams, Webster and Rush believed that the future of America was business, and that their programs for schooling should meet the needs of future businessmen. Rush's curriculum may have been more conservative than Webster's—preserving ancient languages, for example—but he was clear that he meant it not just for "young men intended for the learned professions of law, physic, or divinity," but also for the men "intended for the counting house, for many such, I hope, will be educated in our colleges." If merchants were to be gentlemen in America, then they should have the education to match their status, argued Rush. "The time is past when an academical education was thought to be unnecessary to qualify a young man for merchandise. I conceive no profession is capable of receiving more embellishments from it." Not only that, but commerce was itself an essential foundation of the new republican state. "I consider its effects next to those of religion in humanizing mankind," Rush wrote, "and lastly, I view it as the means of uniting the different nations of the world together by the ties of mutual wants and obligations."[73]

This vision of an interdependent commercial world was central to the emerging set of ideas that most American gentlemen shared. They saw not just the relations between nations, but the whole of human society, as a complex web of "mutual wants and obligations," interests and contracts. Navigating and conducting that world was the business of gentlemen. But it was also important that ordinary people understood its rules and principles, at least enough that they would not interfere with its operations. As Adam Smith had remarked, "an instructed and intelligent people are always more decent and orderly than a stupid one" (just as Rush once pointed out that "a weak and ignorant woman will always be governed with the greatest difficulty").[74] So American educationalists had to design school systems that would teach ordinary people the rules of justice that governed the world of commerce, the unwritten code that tied together the community of mercantile gentlemen. In a sense, then, the new education would turn all Americans into gentlemen, by subjecting them all to the same code. This was the only appropriate response to the republican problem of popular sovereignty. As Jefferson put it, the people had to be made fit to rule themselves.

"There are some acts of the American legislatures," Webster wrote, "which astonish men of information." He was thinking of the kinds of acts pushed through by popular, democratic movements in states up and down the country, especially in Pennsylvania and Rhode Island in the middle of the 1780s: laws that aimed to ease the burden on indebted rural communities by delaying taxes, making obligations payable in kind, ensuring goods were valued by a third party rather than by creditors, and worst of all in the eyes of many merchants, emissions of paper money. Paper money printed by state governments, laid out to their creditors, and then collected back in as taxes, increased the volume of circulating currency and thus gave rural debtors something with which to pay their own creditors, to avoid having their property seized. But it also caused inflation, which reduced the value of debts, damaging the assets of creditors. Policies like paper money were popular with rural majorities, but they were hated by the metropolitan mercantile elites, including Benjamin Rush and his friends in Philadelphia. James Madison named them "improper and wicked projects" and held them among the worst vices of the American political system of the 1780s.[75]

To gentlemen, such policies were based on a combination of ignorance and a willful struggle for power by democratic leaders. Webster preferred to believe that they should not be "ascribed to bad intentions," but to "ignorance either in the men themselves," that is, the legislators, "or their constituents. They often mistake their own interest, because they do not foresee the remote consequences of a measure." In the short term, paper money and other such measures seemed like good ideas, but to men like Webster it was obvious that in the long term they would destroy the basis of commerce and the prosperity of the new nation. What the people did not understand was that modern commerce had developed its own very specific set of rules, which allowed little room for alternative concepts of fairness and equity. The conditions of trade had to be consistent, and that meant contracts had to be honored and inflation avoided. For Webster, the solution was to use schooling to give the people "an acquaintance with ethics and with the general principles of law, commerce, money, and government." Public education was a process of subordinating the people to those principles.[76]

Most American gentlemen were deeply sympathetic to the goals of educationalists like Webster and Rush. They shared the two men's understanding of the problems posed by popular sovereignty, and the need for new ways of creating an obedient public within a republican system. Many gentlemen had benefited from schooling and college themselves, and they were often involved with philanthropic projects to support their own local academies and colleges. Yet their shared goals were not enough to see plans for massive reforms of public education succeed. Jefferson's proposals had failed when he put them forward during the war, and there was little sign of their being revived in the Virginia legislature of the 1780s. Though Rush was successful in helping establish Dickinson College, his broader proposals in Pennsylvania were likewise marred by the enormous public expense they would incur, at a time when governments were already struggling to raise revenue to pay their wartime debts. Webster's ideas included no systematic plan of institutional reform at all. So the real effect of all this talk about schooling was not to spur action by state governments or Congress. Rather, it was to raise concerns about the nature and direction of the new republic, and to reinforce gentlemen's own beliefs about the fundamental principles of justice.

Through their projects for a new national literature and a uniform, purified American English language, men like Joel Barlow and Noah Webster set out to form the Confederation of thirteen states into a single, homogeneous community—a great machine in which all the parts interlocked and worked together, in Benjamin Rush's memorable image. They saw the revolution as a moment in which outmoded systems, including the old educational establishments of New England, should be reformed according to new and better principles. But hidden behind their rhetoric of revolutionary optimism was a pervasive fear about the possibilities that same revolution had opened up for other kinds of American people: those who had no claim to the status of gentlemen. In this respect, the reformers were still very much on the same side as the older generation: men like Enos Hitchcock, Peter Thacker, and the Adams cousins, who sought to preserve structures of power formed under British rule. The appeal of throwing off old shackles only went so far. Even the most precarious gentlemen preferred that boundaries of class and status remain in place. Education, in their hands, was just as much a tool to reconstruct those boundaries as to break them down.

CHAPTER THREE

Justice

I will ask you one political question. Can property be secure under a
numerous democratic assembly which undertakes to dispose of the
property of a citizen?

—AEDANUS BURKE, SOUTH CAROLINA JUDGE, 1782

WHEN THE AMERICAN REVOLUTION took sovereign power away from the
Crown and Parliament of Britain, it placed it where every revolutionary agreed
it ought to be—in the people. It was not so easy to agree what this popular sovereignty actually meant.[1] During the revolutionary years, many states wrote
new constitutions, placing enhanced powers in the hands of elected assemblies and expanding the group of people who could vote in those elections. It
was these democratic institutions that for many Americans embodied the
promise of popular sovereignty. Voting rights were still restricted. Almost
nowhere could women or African-Americans participate in democratic processes. But after the revolution, more people than ever before could exercise
sovereign power through their state assemblies.[2]

Democracy exercised through the assemblies, though, was not the only
way popular sovereignty was understood. To gentlemen of wealth and privilege, granting supreme power to the representatives of popular majorities
seemed extremely dangerous. What would happen to accumulated property
if the many held unlimited sway over the few? Such gentlemen preferred to
see the new republic as a set of rules—a system of justice—that bound every-
body equally, including the assemblies themselves. With property and contract rights at its core, the gentlemanly ideal of justice offered a strong line of
defense for inequalities of wealth and power.[3] In debates that flared up even
as the war was ending, gentlemen revolutionaries fought hard to restrict the
mandate of democracy, and to entrench their own idea of justice at the heart
of the republic.

I. Uneasy Settlements

On May 12, 1780, John Laurens was with the Continental Army in Charleston when Benjamin Lincoln surrendered the town to the British. He spent the next six months on parole, languishing among civilians in Philadelphia. His capture was "the greatest and most humiliating misfortune of my life," he told George Washington.[4] It must have been with a pleasant irony, then, that he accepted the general's appointment to negotiate the British surrender at Yorktown a year and a half later. Laurens, along with his friend Hamilton, had commanded Continental and French forces in the assault on British lines, after nightfall on October 14, 1781. Three days later, Laurens met with the British commissioners, and on the 19th, Lord Cornwallis effected the British surrender. "This is an illustrious day my dear friend," Laurens wrote to an old member of Washington's military family.[5] If there was any bitterness to sharpen the taste of victory, it was that Laurens and Hamilton would once again part ways—the latter bound for Albany, where he hoped to embrace Elizabeth within three weeks; the former for his native South Carolina, where the war was not yet over.

Since the fall of Charleston, the republican government of South Carolina led by Governor John Rutledge had been in exile. A bitter partisan war raged across the state, especially in the backcountry, spilling into Georgia and North Carolina. After the defeat of General Horatio Gates at the Battle of Camden in August, 1780, Nathanael Greene had been put in charge of the campaign. His victories in the backcountry, including at Cowpens, King's Mountain, and Guildford Courthouse, had restored a large part of the state to the patriots, but their position was far from secure. British forces controlled only the coast—but that meant the capital, the shipping, and any hope of return to a normal life. After Yorktown neither Washington nor Congress could persuade the French, with their victorious navy, to continue the campaign in the south. Without this support, Greene and Rutledge held out little hope of retaking Charleston until a general peace was declared and the British withdrew voluntarily. The task facing them, then, by the time John Laurens joined them in December 1781, was to construct some semblance of a civil order in the shadow of an occupied capital, while containing a still-dangerous enemy force.[6]

There was one measure to bolster South Carolina's military resources that Laurens had already tried, and failed, to have his fellow revolutionaries adopt—the arming of enslaved men to fight for the republican state on the promise of their freedom. In the eyes of Laurens' countrymen, this was a truly radical proposal. While Rhode Islanders had enlisted enslaved men in its so-called black regiment since 1778, and some of those men had fought at Yorktown, the use of black troops had remained anathema in the south. In a slave society with a plantation economy set up to depend on forced African and

African-American labor, the idea that some of those men could be given guns, trained for war, and set free was almost unthinkable. It certainly horrified the gentlemen planters in the governor's council when Laurens first publicly proposed it in 1779. What was more, they surely suspected something of the sympathies that lay behind his plan.[7]

Laurens, the son of a slave trader, was an avowed abolitionist, haunted since his youth by "the groans of despairing multitudes, toiling for the luxuries of merciless tyrants."[8] As early as 1777, he had put to his father Henry the idea of emancipating the family's slaves for military service. Such a plan would, he believed, "advance those who are unjustly deprived of the Rights of Mankind to a State which would be a proper Gradation between abject Slavery and perfect Liberty."[9] Habits of subordination would make them good soldiers, and what was more, the patriots needed them. Henry Laurens rejected the plan, but two years later John was back pursuing it on a much grander scale, enlisting his friend Hamilton to help get congressional support. Unless some such measure was adopted, Laurens and Hamilton argued, British forces threatened to overwhelm the south. Practical and strategic reasons alone made the "black project" an urgent necessity. Yet it was always intended to be more than that as well.

"An essential part of the plan," Hamilton told his friend John Jay, then president of Congress, "is to give them their freedom with their muskets. This will secure their fidelity, animate their courage, and I believe will have a good influence upon those who remain, by opening a door to their emancipation." Such a prospect was, Hamilton explained, just as important as the plan's practical merits. "The dictates of humanity and true policy equally interest me in favour of this unfortunate class of men."[10] This time, Henry Laurens took his son's side, and added his voice to those in Congress who were prepared to recommend the raising of black troops in the south. John Laurens was to take command of them personally. "It will be my duty and my pride," he told his father, "to transform the timid Slave into a firm defender of Liberty and render him worthy to enjoy it himself."[11] It was an attitude full of gentlemanly condescension, but it was also one that repulsed most of the Laurens's fellow southern slaveholders.

In spite of Congress's recommendation, the "black project" got nowhere with South Carolina's legislators in 1779—and then the dire predictions made by its backers, that without these troops the south would fall to Clinton and Cornwallis, were borne out in fact. When he returned to his state in the wake of Yorktown, Laurens may have thought that his proposal would meet at least a more humble, if not a more sympathetic reception. This time he also had a crucial ally in General Greene, the former Quaker, who had both the qualification of military command and the gratitude of a state he had helped rescue. Greene looked at South Carolina with the eye of a northerner, but also an experienced and successful strategist. The British, it appeared, had "farther designs upon this country," and they would need to be met with an enhanced force, Greene told Governor Rutledge in December, 1781. "The natural strength of this country in point of numbers appears to me to consist much more of the blacks than the whites. Could they be incorporated, and employed for its defense," he wrote, "it would afford you double security."[12]

Rutledge was not likely to be convinced by this line of argument. It was more than simply the expense of freeing his enslaved laborers that bothered him. More important was the fear of general rebellion instilled by the idea of armed black men. Security against the British was one thing, but to raise such an army seemed to put at risk the security of the entire social and economic order in the south. Even the British, in spite of Clinton's extension of the offer of freedom to all slaves who fought for the king in June 1779, had not used such troops on the front lines in their southern campaign. Instead the British kept the self-emancipated men who joined their ranks at work on ancillary duties. They had no wish to upend the slave society that had once proved so profitable to the empire. There were men in the British ranks who were driven, like Laurens, by moral conviction. But abolitionism was by no means the official strategy. Likewise, Rutledge's aim was to protect that society under republican rule—not to revolutionize it.

Rutledge was also eager, perhaps partly in light of Greene's unorthodox ideas, to restore the civil government as soon as possible. To that end, he ordered elections in November for a session of the legislature, which had not met since the fall of Charleston. The assembly was to be held in Jacksonborough, thirty-five miles from the occupied capital. Using his emergency powers, Rutledge altered the terms of the franchise for the new election. Those who had lived under the protection of the British and had not declared their allegiance to Rutledge's revolutionary government would have no vote. "The Tory interest is entirely excluded," wrote Judge Aedanus Burke. "For my part I would think it madness to allow men to influence our elections who had borne arms against us without giving some test of their attachment to us—for ought we know it would be giving away our country, and the resources of it."[13] The assembly at Jacksonborough would consider the plan for arming enslaved men, Rutledge decided; it would also draw the outlines of South Carolina's postwar settlement, and declare the fate of those who found themselves on the wrong side.

Calling such an assembly before the war was really over, and with British troops still at large raiding beyond the boundaries of Charleston, was a dangerous maneuver. Even with the restricted suffrage, it was difficult to predict the character of the meeting. Would John Laurens and his "black project," with Greene's help, finally succeed? And how would a people riven for two years by a bitter civil war deal with the opportunity to rearrange society and settle old scores? Of the revolutionary struggles in the thirteen states, South Carolina's had been one of the hardest. Who could say what effect that had had upon its population? "Between friends," wrote the Governor's brother Edward to a correspondent in Congress at Philadelphia, "I fear there will be damned strange works when once the assembly get together."[14]

John Rutledge's opening speech was not well calculated to calm simmering resentments. "Since the last meeting of the General Assembly," he began, "the good people of this state have not only felt the common calamities of war, but, from the wanton and savage manner in which it has been prosecuted, they have experienced such severities as are unpractised, and will scarcely be credited by civilized nations."[15] In fact Rutledge's speech revealed a pressing concern beyond questions of loyalty to the republican regime: the public purse and public credit. The war had not only been expensive for the people of South Carolina, but also for the state. Any postwar settlement would also be a matter of restoring economic order by repealing paper money laws and paying off the state's debt. "It is just and reasonable," Rutledge declared, that "satisfactory assurances of payment be given to the public creditors." Restoring the state's revenue was a critical concern, but with the port of Charleston occupied, how was it supposed to be achieved?

Since raising new taxes "would be difficult if not impracticable," there was just one obvious place to look for funds: to the so-called Tory interest, the men who had declared loyalty to the king in exchange for the protection of royal forces, and who had failed to take advantage of Rutledge's offer of conditional amnesty. Up until now, he remarked, "the extraordinary lenity of this state has been conspicuous" towards such people. "It is with you to determine," Rutledge told the assembly, "whether the forfeiture and appropriation of their property should now take place."[16] It was certainly true that South Carolina would not be the first state to expropriate the property of British loyalists. In 1777, when Henry Laurens was its president, Congress had "earnestly recommended to the several states to confiscate and make sale of all real and personal estate therein, of such of their inhabitants and other persons who have forfeited the same, and the right to the protection of their respective states."[17] Many states enthusiastically heeded the call.[18]

Such measures were deemed to be justified not only by the financial necessity of the war, but also by its brutality. "Pursued by the injustice and the vengeance of Great Britain," Congress had explained in 1777, "these United States have been compelled to engage in a bloody and expensive war." They invoked the "boundless rapine" and "more than savage barbarity" of the British army, aided by "venal foreigners" like the Hessians, and "domestic traitors"— that is, loyalists. Confiscation was not an act to be undertaken lightly, nor was it merely an act of revenge. American gentlemen pointed to British atrocities to show that the basic civil contract of what Rutledge called "civilized nations" had been broken. Only in those circumstances would they violate the sacred right of property. By the end of the war, the assembly at Jacksonborough could claim that it was "inconsistent with public justice and policy to afford protection any longer to the property of British subjects."[19]

Still, advocating the seizure of property made most American gentlemen deeply uneasy. "I hope they will be lenient," Rutledge's brother Edward worried during the assembly, "but as I said before, I fear. Though I am for some confiscation, yet I have done everything in my power to restrain the tempers of the impetuous."[20] John Laurens—who chaired the committee on confiscation— did his best to advocate restraint.[21] "I will ask you one political question," wrote Aedanus Burke to Congressman Arthur Middleton, the same man with whom Edward Rutledge shared his misgivings: "Can property be secure under a numerous democratic assembly which undertakes to dispose of the property of a citizen? The men of property in our house join heartily in this measure, but they do not reflect the time may come when the precedent may be execrated by their posterity."[22]

The initial list drawn up for confiscation featured "about seven hundred" names.[23] In the end, somewhat fewer than 500 people were affected by a combination of outright confiscation and a 12 percent property tax called an "amercement."[24] Around the same number had been saved by friends in the assembly who attested their loyalty. There was a fine balance to be struck between the gentlemanly sensibility towards property rights, and the public spirit that manifested itself at Jacksonborough. After years of brutal warfare, the idea of leniency towards the republic's enemies was noxious to many. "The lower and rougher class," observed the German botanist and traveler Johann David Schoepf, "breathed nothing but the bitterness of vengeance." In the fragile political circumstances in which they found themselves, the state's political leadership could not avoid taking such popular passions into account. Their aim at Jacksonborough was to establish the legitimacy of the republican state in the eyes of the people at large.[25]

Adding to this atmosphere of tension was the return of Laurens's "black project," in a proposal to recruit and arm 2,500 enslaved men from the confiscated plantations.[26] Outside the assembly, Laurens had the support of General Greene; within it, of Pennsylvania-born David Ramsay and a handful of others. Naturally, the argument rested not on the justice of emancipation, but on the state's dire military and financial situation. "We have not the Ability to raise a Tax, our Lads would not be drafted, and we were obliged to turn our thoughts to recruiting—with Negroes," Edward Rutledge recalled. Yet many believed the project had deeper motives, and the involvement of Greene and Ramsay helped to raise suspicions on that count. "The northern people," observed Aedanus Burke, "regard the condition in which we hold our slaves in a light different from us. I am much deceived indeed, if they do not secretly wish for a general emancipation, if the present struggle was over."[27] Southern identity, as well as South Carolina's economic system, was already deeply entangled with slavery. Any attack on the institution was seen as an attack on the south.

Laurens and his allies "pushed the matter as far as it could well go" before, as Edward Rutledge put it, "people in general returned to their senses" and the measure was defeated.[28] Recounting his struggle to Alexander Hamilton a few months later, Laurens wrote that he "urged the matter very strenuously ... but I was out-voted, having only reason on my side, and being opposed by a triple-headed monster that shed the baneful influence of Avarice, prejudice, and pusillanimity in all our Assemblies."[29] In truth, though, the revolution had only made slavery stronger in South Carolina. Though it decimated the enslaved population, with thousands escaping behind British lines, the war gave way to a major boom in new slave imports as planters rushed to replace their labor force. Crucially, the postwar period also saw the extension of slaveholding into the backcountry and among a more middling class of men. In their rush to restore unity and prosperity to the state, South Carolina's genteel leadership had no time at all for John Laurens's idea of "reason."[30]

Yet in the wake of the assembly at Jacksonborough, slaveholders still could not rest fully secure in the enjoyment of their property. The Confiscation Act's attack on loyalists precipitated retaliation from General Leslie, the British commander in Charleston, who threatened plundering raids into the city's hinterland. Enslaved people were the most realistic target for any such action. The new governor, John Mathews, elected by the assembly to replace John Rutledge, responded to Leslie with the counterthreat of further confiscations, namely of the debts owed to loyalists and British merchants. "There is a considerable value in English debts which we have in our power," as John Laurens pointed out.[31] Did the seizure of enslaved people owned by some South Carolinians justify others breaking their contracts with British creditors? The state's leaders were reluctant to make any such argument. Instead, Mathews negotiated a quid pro quo with the British garrison: slave property would be restored "as far as is practicable" to its purported owners; debts would be enforced regardless of the creditor's loyalty. As Christopher Gadsden commented, it was a deal that most benefited "the great negro holders ... near the sea."[32]

In the summer of 1782, before this short-lived treaty was made, John Laurens was killed in a British raid. He had fallen, his dear friend Alexander Hamilton put it bitterly, "a sacrifice to his ardor in a trifling skirmish."[33] He died with his dreams of emancipation just as far as ever from fulfillment, and his native state still struggling to reconstitute itself for a postrevolutionary world. When the British finally departed Charleston in the dying days of 1782, they took with them all but seventy-three of the once-enslaved refugees under their care. Some of these people made the voyage to new lives of freedom in Canada or England, but the vast majority were shipped to Jamaica and East Florida, where slavery continued under the flag of the British empire.[34] David Ramsay later claimed that "the prospects of gain, from the sale of plundered negroes, were too seducing to be resisted" by the Royal Navy officers.[35] Meanwhile, tensions quickly flared between Charleston's returning patriots and those who remained after the British departure. Battles raged over contracted debt and confiscated property. Safe in their independence, South Carolinians now faced the long struggle to define the postwar social, economic, and political order.

By the time the republican government returned to Charleston, elections for a new assembly had already taken place. Elected under the same exclusionary rules, Governor Mathews could expect an assembly of similar character to that of Jacksonborough. Still, Christopher Gadsden for one hoped it would provide an opportunity to look again, in a more sober light, at the legislation of the previous year, especially the Confiscation Act. He would "endeavor to have its severities at least mitigated," he wrote to an ally, General Francis Marion. Gadsden believed the act would "spread the resentment of citizens one against another," for the benefit only of rich land speculators: "artful, ambitious men" with "detestable selfish purposes."[36] He was not the only member of South Carolina's political establishment who had a bone to pick with confiscation. Many believed that the measures at Jacksonborough had gone too far in their acquiescence to the popular mood. They now sought the opportunity to reverse what had happened, and to re-establish their own gentlemanly conceptions of justice.

Chief among these enemies of confiscation was Aedanus Burke, a member of the state's circuit court. Born in Galway in 1743, Burke had arrived in Virginia at the end of the 1760s already well educated. He read the law there before moving south via the West Indies, arriving in Charleston in the mid-1770s. He served in the army for almost three years—just short of the length of service required for Cincinnati membership—before resigning early in 1778, and was immediately elected to the judicial bench.[37] It was only later that year that the war moved into the southern theater. His role as a judge placed him at the difficult interstice of republican order and the chaos of what became effectively a civil war, an awkward middle ground that came to define Burke's career as a political writer. He identified himself with what he saw as neutral principles of justice, against monarchy, aristocracy, licentiousness, and disorder. For his opposition to the Confiscation Act at Jacksonborough, the electors failed to return him to the new assembly in 1783. It was perhaps the bitter sting of this defeat that led him to take a more public approach to opposition.[38]

Before the Charleston newspapers had even resumed their runs, on January 14, 1783, Burke published an outspoken pamphlet under the pseudonym of the Roman tyrannicide, Cassius.[39] *An Address to the Freemen of the State of South Carolina* denounced the "political mischief" of the Confiscation and Amercement Acts, rebuked the legislators for undermining the proper constitutional order, and offered a catalogue of learned authorities to back up his legal case against confiscation. The acts of the Jacksonborough assembly had undermined the very rights Americans had fought for in the late war, Burke argued, not least of which was the right to a fair trial by a jury of one's peers.

By seizing property from alleged loyalists without such trials, assemblymen had abused their power. Not only that, but they had also violated the principles of international law, as laid down by "all those writers whose authority we rely on in law-matters," including Samuel von Puffendorf, and Emer de Vattel.[40] In short, "the injustice of this measure is so enormous," he wrote in frustration, "that the endeavouring to prove it is like proving that the Sun shines at noon-day."[41]

Burke argued that the assembly's acts were arbitrary invasions of natural rights. Those who had accepted the protection of the British crown during the war had not forfeited their rights when they did so. They were, after all, a conquered people. "In this situation," Burke wrote, "*necessity*, whose dominion triumphs over all human laws pointed out to our inhabitants, that as there was neither government, laws, nor army to protect them, they were at liberty to protect themselves.... This is the law of Nature and of Nations." Thomas Hobbes made the same point. "The obligation of subjects to the State is understood to last so long, and no longer than the power lasts by which it is able to protect them," Burke quoted. Yet during South Carolina's occupation, he argued, "our government was dissolved: it did not exist." Therefore, "as the Republic could not give the citizen protection, which is the equivalent he receives for allegiance, he owed none," and so had committed no offense.[42]

Moreover, the decisions made at Jacksonborough would have pernicious effects for the new republic in the future. "Unthinking are those who imagine," Burke wrote, "that one arbitrary exertion of power will not open a door for many others! ... For if the legislature can, without ceremony, or forms of law, seize the property, or banish the person of the meanest or worst member of society; what I pray can hinder their stripping or banishing men of virtue?" The "cruelty and injustice" of the Confiscation Act would be a "curse on ourselves and posterity."[43] As he had pointed out at the time to Arthur Middleton, the real problem was that once the legislature started seizing property, who could say where it would end? The democratic power of an assembly had to be carefully restricted by the dictates of natural and international law—dictates that gave property rights pride of place. Legislators had rejected one measure that would have endangered property: Laurens's "black project." Burke was asking them to reconsider confiscation in the same light.

A few months later, Burke published a second pamphlet, his *Considerations on the Society or Order of the Cincinnati*. There, he argued not only that the establishment of the Cincinnati was leading the state inexorably towards aristocracy, but that this end had been inadvertently furthered by the actions of the Jacksonborough assembly. "From their wanton, extravagant abuse of their powers as legislators," Burke wrote, the assemblymen themselves "have been the melancholy cause, that the very name of a democracy, or government of the people, now begins to be hateful and offensive." A "revolution" had been "effected *by law*, in the famous Jacksonborough assembly," and consolidated thereafter. "In short, the public opinion and power of the government is on the side of the aristocracy, at the same time that the spirit of the people is thoroughly broken." The state's military leadership, which had "opposed the [confiscation] measure with cool, gentleman-like reasoning," now threatened to swing the pendulum too far the other way.[44] Burke saw himself as a proponent of the classical balanced republic in the face of excesses on both sides. As such, he was increasingly alienated from both the elite establishment and the democratic populists. His vision of a society split between factions, however, was not wholly inaccurate.

A symptom of that division was the conflict over British merchants' role in the newly reoccupied city of Charleston. Alexander Gillon and his Marine Anti-Britannic Society, drawing on the frustrations of urban workers as well as patriot merchants, undertook a campaign of harassment and public demonstration meant to drive away the "traitors and cowards" who were also, incidentally, competing for their business.[45] At least partly in response to Gillon's violent and disordered outdoor politics, the South Carolina legislature moved to set up a city corporation, with extensive powers to preserve social and moral order, especially against mariners. Church wardens were to patrol the streets on Sundays "to observe and suppress any riotous, indecent, or disorderly conduct."[46] Gentlemen thus employed the mechanisms of law and police to restore order, and protect the normal conduct of the city's trade. Questions of loyalty could not be allowed to interfere with the revival of commercial prosperity. Contracts and property rights had to be protected.

In South Carolina, then, neither the victory at Yorktown nor the British departure from the state just over a year later led directly to a stable and peaceful settlement of the revolutionary crisis. Exacerbated by the material depredations of a highly destructive partisan war, and no doubt also by its emotional and personal toll, social conflict remained a potent factor complicating efforts to re-establish civil, republican government. How could South Carolina re-enter a wider Atlantic commercial economy still dominated by British credit and British merchants without giving up—in reality or appearance— the independence many had just fought for? How could those who had suffered in pursuit of that goal—who had lost family, friends, and property, been imprisoned, or spent years in brutal fighting—relinquish their hatred for so-called loyalists and accept them back into the community of citizens? Aedanus Burke's message of forgiveness was hard to swallow. As the new republic adjusted itself to life after war, other states faced similar problems and similar social conflicts. It was just as difficult, it seemed, to end a revolution, as it had been to begin one.

II. The Priority of Property

While Governor Mathews of South Carolina was negotiating over slaves and debts with General Leslie in Charleston in October 1782, commissioners of the United States and Great Britain were engaged in similar but much more far-reaching discussions in Paris. Informal talks had begun early in the year between America's ambassador to France, Benjamin Franklin, and the Scottish slave trader Richard Oswald, both in their seventies and both already well acquainted with each other. Oswald reported to his friend the Earl of Shelburne, Home Secretary under the new Rockingham administration which took office in March. By the middle of summer, Shelburne had become prime minister; Franklin had been joined by former president of Congress and ambassador to Spain, John Jay; and Oswald by the experienced undersecretary of state, Henry Strachey. Dogged by illness and a disagreement over the formalities of independence, it was not until autumn that the talks began to come together. The agreement that eventually emerged, however, demonstrated a surprising amount of sympathy between the rival negotiators. This was not only because Shelburne was eager to make a quick peace with the United States in order to continue fighting the European powers. It was also because, beneath their two countries' strategic differences, the gentlemen in Paris shared certain assumptions about justice.[47]

The Americans certainly sought to drive a hard bargain. Franklin's initial demands included granting all of Canada to the United States. Over issues like the extent of territory in the northwest, and rights over the fisheries off Maine and Newfoundland, they sought maximal concessions from Oswald and Strachey. Other than the fisheries, however, the final issues to be discussed were ones that had a more basic connection to the tenets of a genteel and commercial sense of justice—the security of debts owed by Americans to British creditors, the status of loyalists and the property they still held in America, and compensation for those who had their property confiscated during and after the war. From the British perspective, protecting the rights of loyalists and securing their compensation was politically important. Angry refugees from the American war could cause too much trouble for the ministry in London. But for the American commissioners, there were in fact reasons of principle to acquiesce, at least on the first two points.

It was at this point that John Adams made his signal contribution to the negotiations, if his own account is to be believed. Adams had arrived late, on October 26, after lingering in the Hague trying to get a commercial treaty finished, and then taking weeks to travel south to Paris. The first thing he did in Paris was to fit himself out with a new wig, suit of clothes, and pair of shoes. The second thing was to speak to Benjamin Franklin. "He told me," Adams recorded in his diary, "of Mr. Oswald's demand of the payment of debts and compensation to the Tories."[48] It was Franklin's position that the Americans could not accede to such a demand, because they had no power to do so. Even Congress did not. Despite the end of the fighting, the confederation's financial situation remained desperate. Robert Morris and his allies had so far failed to win a federal power of taxation from the states. In fact, Congress could hardly make the states do anything. Adams's gambit was, however, to turn Franklin's position on its head: what mattered was that the treaty, and its British signatories, *assumed* Congress had the power to do what it said.

The first step was to separate the two issues. "The question of paying debts, and that of compensating Tories were two," Adams told Franklin. Indeed, when he made "the same observation" that day to Oswald and Strachey at Jay's house, it provoked a pleasing reaction. When he put it to Strachey, Adams recalled, "I saw it instantly smiling in every line of his face." The point went over so well because by separating the two issues Adams demonstrated a willingness to back down on one of them. Franklin was right when he said the Americans had no power to compensate the loyalists. That would involve raising money, which Congress certainly could not do. But the question of debt was a different matter. "Congress should recommend it to the states," Adams suggested, "to open their courts for the just recovery of all just debts."[49] As long as it seemed plausible that states would follow this recommendation, the British could be satisfied with the concession. "The earnest recommendation of Congress is equivalent to our king's recommendation to Parliament," Strachey told his superiors. It would "have all the effect we proposed."[50]

As Adams explained to Franklin, "I had no notion of cheating anybody." The truth was, he believed in the rights of British creditors just as much as Oswald or Strachey did. A draft of the treaty written in early November made the point clear: paying debts was a matter of justice. It also included a provision on confiscated land calling on states to "correct" laws passed by their assemblies:

> Whereas it is *just* that private contracts made between individuals of the two countries before the war, should be faithfully executed, and as the confiscation of the said lands may have a latitude not justifiable by the law of nations, it is agreed that the British creditors shall notwithstanding, meet with no lawful impediment to recovering the full value, or sterling amount of such bona fide debts as were contracted before the year 1775, and also that Congress will recommend to the said states, so to correct, if necessary, their said acts respecting confiscation of lands in America belonging to real British subjects as to render their said acts consistent with perfect justice and equity.[51]

In the final treaty, signed on September 3, 1783, it was stipulated that the revisions should be "perfectly consistent not only with justice and equity, but with that spirit of conciliation which on the return of the blessings of peace should universally prevail."[52]

Like Aedanus Burke in South Carolina, Adams believed the only true basis for the success of the republican states was a spirit of forgiveness towards their former enemies, governed by a shared—property and contract-oriented—sense of justice. John Jay felt the same way. From his diplomatic post in Spain, early in 1780, he had written angrily about confiscation to George Clinton, the governor of his native state. "New York is disgraced by injustice too palpable to admit even of palliation," Jay told Clinton. "I feel for the honor of my country."[53] As a lawyer, but more importantly as a gentleman, Jay subscribed wholeheartedly to a morality centered around the sanctity of contract. "Let it never be said," he had written a year earlier as president of Congress, "that [America's] infant glories and growing fame were obscured and tarnished by broken contracts and violated faith."[54] That same morality governed contemporary ideas about the international order, and came at least in part to animate the Treaty of Paris.

On the other side of the Atlantic, however, loyalists in the one remaining zone of British occupation—New York—knew that this spirit of justice and reconciliation was not at all shared by the patriot majority. As they saw it, the treaty guaranteed them practically nothing. From November 1782, when the provisional articles were agreed, these New York loyalists petitioned and pleaded with the British government in growing desperation "not to withdraw . . . royal protection from us." To do so, they claimed, would make their position "absolutely insupportable, absolutely insufferable."[55] When a copy of the provisional treaty actually appeared in the city, on April 5, 1783, loyalists were forced to finally accept the reality of American independence on Shelburne's generous terms. They had no illusions about what would come next, or about the true capacity of Congress to enforce its recommendations with regard to debts and confiscation. From the day the terms were printed, one New Yorker wrote, a "settled gloom" hung over the city.[56]

If loyalists inside New York were gloomy, some patriots outside the city did their best to intensify the mood of anxiety. "Remorse, despair and shame will crowd upon your imagination," one patriot broadside told the city's loyalists in August 1783. "Be assured that the irresistible vengeance of a grateful people will speedily demand your blood or your banishment from this land of liberty." With such promises, the author Brutus encouraged loyalists to flee the city when the British force departed. He showed nothing but contempt for advocates of reconciliation like Adams and Jay. "Perhaps there may be some amongst us, who you may flatter or bribe, or peradventure *contract* with (for we have *contractors*) to plead in your behalf; but promise yourselves no relief from their agency." Here, *contractor* was a term of abuse, denoting precisely the kind of gentleman who would prioritize contract rights over popular rule and vengeance. "By appearing in your favour," Brutus warned loyalists, "they will as certainly render themselves odious and contemptible to their fellow citizens, as they will fail in accomplishing the ends of your preservation."[57]

George Washington rode into New York on a white horse, escorted by Governor Clinton and the local worthies, on November 25, 1783—Evacuation Day. There was feasting and drinking among the returning patriots, and a firework display on Bowling Green that "exceeded any former exhibition in the United States."[58] But tension over the treatment of loyalists was not far beneath the surface of the celebrations. Just as it had been in Charleston a year earlier, the re-establishment of republican control was a delicate political operation. It involved the careful balancing of forces within the republican camp, as genteel elites worked to restrain the popular spirit of redistributive vengeance. Thus Clinton's speech to the assembled patriots began by acknowledging the "manly fortitude" with which they had withstood "the rigors of a long and painful exile, superadded to the grievous calamities of a vengeful war." But he went on to urge a spirit of "reverence for the laws." Americans would be unworthy of the liberty they had won, Clinton said, if they should "suffer the authority of the magistrate to be violated for the sake of private vengeance."[59]

Clinton hoped to avoid the kind of scenes that Brutus had predicted that summer, extending a tentative hand of protection over those who had chosen to remain in the city following the British departure. Like John Mathews in South Carolina, however, Clinton knew that his political survival, and the legitimacy of his state government itself, depended on a degree of popularity—and that meant a certain amount of leeway for popular antiloyalist demands. Those demands expressed themselves on the streets, in the press, and in the city government elected on December 15. Earlier that spring, the state legislature meeting at Poughkeepsie had passed acts that stripped loyalists of voting and citizenship rights, and authorized the confiscation of their property. When they entered the city at the end of the year, many patriots were determined to see those acts carried into effect. Especially at first, there was only so much the political establishment could do to stop them.

This was the environment in which Alexander Hamilton arrived that November, moving with Elizabeth into a house on the less fashionable end of Wall Street. They brought with them a baby son, named Philip after his grandfather, who would be two years old in January.[60] Entertaining fantasies of a lucrative and dignified retirement from public life, Hamilton had written to Clinton from Congress asking for new delegates to be sent to replace him. "Having no future view in public life," he wrote, "I owe it to myself without delay to enter upon the care of my private concerns in earnest."[61] With his young family and no estate, Hamilton faced the plight of many other young officers re-entering civilian life after the war. But he had more than his Cincinnati connections to support him. Through his father-in-law and old friends, men like his college roommate Robert Troup, he was well placed to succeed. He intended a career in the law. What he found in New York, however, soon threw him back into the fray of public life. If he was to be a lawyer, he would also have to be an advocate for the authority of law itself, and for his own commercial view of justice.

That January, then, Hamilton published a pamphlet: *A Letter from Phocion to the Considerate Citizens of New York*. "A few heated and inconsiderate

spirits," he wrote, were attempting "to practice upon the passions of the people." Not only that, but "the public papers are made the channel of the most
inflammatory and pernicious doctrines, tending to the subversion of all private security and genuine liberty." Private security, in Hamilton's mind, was
indeed the very essence of genuine liberty. Those who argued for the expul-
sion or disenfranchisement of loyalists, and the seizure of their property, were
helping to undermine the kind of republic Hamilton and other gentlemen
believed they had fought for. Rather than listening to reason or justice, they
were endeavoring "to put in motion all the furious and dark passions of the
human mind ... revenge, cruelty, persecution, and perfidy." These "designing
men" sought to manipulate the public, but "the people, at large," Hamilton
wrote, "are sure to be the losers in the event whenever they suffer a departure
from the rules of general and equal justice, or from the true principles of universal liberty."[62]

A Letter from Phocion was timed to coincide with the beginning of the
new state legislative session, to be held in the city. This new assembly was due
to reconsider the Alienation and Confiscation Acts passed the year before in
Poughkeepsie, which had been vetoed by the Council of Revision. New York's
conservative constitution, drafted largely by John Jay in 1777, had recognized
that "laws inconsistent with the spirit of this constitution, or with the public
good, may be hastily and unadvisedly passed"—so all acts first had to face review by the Council, made up of the governor and some of the state's highest
judges.[63] An assembly could override the Council's veto at the next session,
however, and that was exactly what many New York gentlemen feared would
happen with the antiloyalist legislation in early 1784. Hamilton's pamphlet was
designed to put pressure on the assembly's conservative and moderate members to stand up against those who favored confiscation and alienation. Like
Aedanus Burke in South Carolina, he played both gadfly and voice of reason.

In his speech opening the session on January 21, Governor Clinton likewise tried to steer a path of moderation and conciliation. "While we survey
the ruins of this once flourishing city," he proclaimed, New Yorkers must also
be grateful to God for the war's victorious end. As much as they might recol-
lect the "cruelty and rapine" that had marked the war, they should also be
pleased when those returning to the city showed "obedience to the laws" and
"care to preserve peace and good order." Clinton avoided any real criticism of
the violence and intimidation that had marked the reoccupation of the city.
But his message to the legislators was clear enough. "Let us give, to all," he
urged, "protection, encouragement, and security, by providing that equal justice be administered to the stranger as well as the citizen, that the recovery of
debts be speedy and effectual, that the fulfilment of contracts be enforced.…
By these means," he concluded, "credit, the parent of commerce, will multiply
her benefits."[64]

Hamilton too held out the benefits of commerce as the result of adhering to "the rules of general and equal justice." Anyone "the least acquainted with trade" understood, he wrote, that "every merchant or trader has an interest in the aggregate mass of capital or stock in trade." The more capital in a community, the easier it would be for the merchants to get credit. The more prosperous the merchants, the better off everyone else would be. "The only object of concern with an industrious artisan, as such, ought to be, that there may be plenty of money in the community, and a brisk commerce to give it circulation and activity." Hamilton's was a free-trading vision consonant with Adam Smith's. "All attempts at profit, through the medium of monopoly or violence, will be as fallacious as they are culpable."[65] His commercial morality worked with his understanding of political economy, each supporting the other, just as he believed the merchants and mechanics did—so long as no one, including the elected assembly, interfered.

"Viewing the subject in every possible light," Hamilton wrote in the closing pages of his pamphlet, "there is not a single interest in the community but dictates moderation rather than violence." To "gratify" the "momentary passions" of the populace in a moment of "heat and violence" would always set "precedents which afterwards prove fatal to themselves." Power to disenfranchise groups of citizens created a slippery slope towards the establishment of "an aristocracy or an oligarchy" in which "no man can be safe, or know when he may be the innocent victim of a prevailing faction." Like others who theorized about republican politics, in ancient times as well as modern, Hamilton believed too much democracy would soon degenerate into a worse form. Power in the hands of the people was a dangerous thing. Thus, he cautioned New Yorkers:

> Abuse not the power you possess, and you need never apprehend its diminution or loss. But if you make a wanton use of it, if you furnish another example, that despotism may debase the government of the many as well as the few, you like all others that have acted the same part, will experience that licentiousness is the fore-runner to slavery.[66]

On February 11, 1784, the state legislature accepted the recommendation of Clinton's Council of Revision and declined to pass the alienation law.[67] A few days earlier, Hamilton's friend James Duane had been made mayor of the city. As the rule of law and its genteel advocates regained their footing in the city, courts were beginning to take over from the streets and the newspapers as its principal battleground. Unlike in South Carolina a year or two earlier, loyalists in New York still had the right to a trial to determine their liabilities. That meant there was plenty of work for lawyers. As Hamilton put it to his friend Gouverneur Morris, "legislative folly has afforded so plentiful a harvest to us lawyers that we have scarcely a moment to spare from the substantial business of reaping."[68] Part of the reason things were different in New York was that, in January 1784, Congress had ratified the Treaty of Paris. Loyalists had not got all they wanted from the peace negotiations, but the treaty at least offered them a new line of defense. From the point of view of gentlemen like Hamilton, the treaty could be used to shackle popular legislative power.

In the months that followed, New Yorkers debated the true meaning and effect of the treaty both in print and in court. They parsed the details of the treaty's text—but they always did so in relation to broader principles of justice and policy. For the physician Isaac Ledyard, who replied to the *Letter of Phocion* under the name of Mentor, the crucial thing was to protect republican liberty against the inimical "tory principle" embodied by loyalists. "Considering what it has cost us to establish this government," he wrote, "I am not willing to trifle with the acquisition." But how, asked Hamilton in his reply to Mentor that April, "shall we ascertain who are aliens or traitors?" To do it simply on the basis of where they lived during the war—one side or the other of the British lines—"would be to measure innocence and guilt, by latitude and longitude." It would deprive individuals of trial by jury and an opportunity to defend themselves. "God forbid," Hamilton went on, "that the body of the people should ever be corrupt enough to wish it, or even submit to it!"[69]

This idea that the people might be—or become—corrupt and unreliable was central to the gentlemanly conception of politics expressed in Hamilton's Phocion letters. The "rights" of "republican government" had to be "modified and regulated by the principles of such a government," he wrote: principles that included the right to trial by jury, and the sanctity of property and contract. Likewise, they had to be bound by the principles of international law. The United States, he wrote, "have taken our station among nations, have claimed the benefit of the laws that regulate them, and must in our turn be bound by the same laws." On both counts, Americans were wrong to think that government could simply enact what the people wanted. "Among the extravagancies with which these prolific times abound," Hamilton wrote, "we hear it often said that the constitution being the creature of the people, their sense with respect to any measure, if it even stand in opposition to the constitution, will sanctify it and make it right." This fallacy of popular rule threatened "to convert the government into a government of will and not of laws," no more than a popular tyranny.[70]

Hamilton's Phocion letters expressed the concerns and interests of New York's commercial gentlemen, whether they were loyalists who had stayed in the city under British occupation or patriots who had lived elsewhere during the war. Their success depended on the strength of New York as a major Atlantic port, and maintaining that status after the war would not necessarily be easy. Loyalists' capital and networks were important contributions to that project. Even more vital, though, was the state's reputation for providing a secure legal environment, and the impartial enforcement of contracts—what commercial gentlemen called justice. Ports up and down the continental seaboard were actively seeking to attract trade and capital. If British traders, or those of other nations, felt they could not rely on their property and personal rights being protected in New York, they could move their business elsewhere. So it was imperative that democratic power be confined within strict limits, and that merchants know they could trust the state and its laws to look out for their interests.

At the end of June, Hamilton had a chance to make his own commitment to loyalist rights clear in court. He was defending Joshua Waddington, a British-born merchant who had occupied and operated an abandoned brewery after the patriots left the city in 1776. Waddington also happened to be a director, along with Hamilton, of the recently founded Bank of New York. The plaintiff was Elizabeth Rutgers, the brewery's original owner. Having reoccupied the site, Rutgers and her attorney were now suing Waddington for rent to cover the period of his occupation, a sum of £8,000. In the public mind, the case was surely a foregone conclusion. Rutgers was an elderly widow, forced to leave her business behind while fleeing British forces. Waddington was an obstinate loyalist who had profited from her misfortune. Vengeful patriots the summer before had prophesied that "contractors" would earn the contempt of ordinary citizens by defending loyalists. Knowing full well what he was up to, Hamilton chose to cast himself in this very role. The judge in the case would be the city mayor, Hamilton's friend, James Duane.[71]

Rutgers's case was based on the Trespass Act passed by the New York assembly at Poughkeepsie in March 1783, which offered restitution to the patriots whose property had been used by someone else during the British occupation. Because men like Waddington had acted under the orders of British authorities, the act stipulated that the defendant "shall not be admitted to plead, in justification, any military order or command whatever, of the enemy."[72] Arguments like the one Aedanus Burke had made in South Carolina, that people could not be blamed for things they did under the threat of an invading army, were supposed to be nullified by the New York assembly's act. After all, couldn't civilians like Waddington have fled the city at the same time as patriots like Rutgers? Hamilton's defense argued that this provision was itself null and void, since it violated both the Treaty of Paris and the law of nations—the same generalized body of international law to which Burke appealed. Those principles, Hamilton argued, were superior to the law of a mere state legislature.

After two months of deliberation, Duane gave his verdict. He sided effectively with Waddington, ordering him to pay rent for the time he occupied the brewery under civilian rule, but not for the much longer period he did so under military orders. He paid £800, a tenth of what Rutgers had sought. The case was a victory for Hamilton, but it did not settle matters in New York.

Legislators quickly passed a motion censuring Duane's decision, calling it, "in its tendency, subversive of all law and good order." The idea that international law trumped the law made by the people's representatives would lead, they said, "directly to anarchy and confusion."[73] Two weeks after the verdict, a group of New Yorkers condemned it in the *New York Gazetteer* for holding "the vague and doubtful custom of nations" above "a clear and positive statute."[74] To the advocates of the assembly, it was clear that Duane, Hamilton and their allies wanted to curtail democratic power in order to protect their ideals of commercial justice.

"It is to be deplored that fœderal attachment, and a sense of national obligation, continue to give place to vain prejudices in favour of the Independance and Sovereignty of the individual States," wrote Duane to George Washington later in 1784, enclosing a copy of his decision in the Rutgers case. "I have endeavourd ... to inculcate more enlarged and liberal principles," he told the general, "but the Spirit of the times seems opposed to My feeble efforts, and I have lost credit with our Assembly, tho' I hope not with the world."[75] Duane saw himself as standing up for a truly important set of principles, a "more enlarged" view of the world that went beyond the parochialism of local assemblies. His commercial vision encompassed the networks of trade and finance that crossed the Atlantic and stretched into every corner of the globe. He also knew that those priorities ran contrary to the democratic "Spirit of the times." As Washington surely knew, reading Duane's letter in his study at Mount Vernon, the *Rutgers v. Waddington* case was a symptom of deeper social conflict that affected not only New York, but the entire country.

III. Debt and Servitude

On Evacuation Day, November 25, 1783, General Washington received the thanks of grateful New York patriots. "We hope the salutations of long suffering exiles, but now happy freemen, will not be deemed an unhappy tribute," they declared. "In this place, and at this moment of exultation and triumph, while the ensigns of slavery still linger in our sight, we look up to you, our deliverer, with unusual transports of gratitude and joy."[76] The flags of the Royal Navy, flying from the ships of the British fleet as they left New York harbor that afternoon, looked to watching patriots like "ensigns of slavery" now departing. But they had a different meaning in the eyes of the three thousand formerly enslaved people transported in the hulls of those ships to freedom in Nova Scotia and beyond. For those other "now happy freemen" it was the Stars and Stripes, flying over New York harbor as it slipped out of sight, that looked like an ensign of slavery—and it looked that way, too, to the thousands more enslaved people left behind, condemned to remain in the United States.

Slavery was not solely a southern concern. At the end of the War for Independence, enslaved people could be found in every state of the union. In Pennsylvania, the home of America's Quaker tradition, there were almost seven thousand. In New York, there were at least twice that number, and as many as eighteen-thousand. These people were servants, farmhands, craftsmen, and laborers. They lived in both the country and the city. Men and women living in the new republic, recently emancipated from the "tyranny of Great Britain," were familiar with the reality of slavery in their midst. Some were also increasingly uncomfortable with that reality. In 1780, Pennsylvania legislators passed an act of gradual emancipation that promised to free the children of enslaved mothers—but still bound them to service for their first twenty-eight years. Thanking God for their victory against the British, the assemblymen wrote, "we conceive that it is our duty, and we rejoice that it is in our power to extend a portion of that freedom to others, which hath been extended to us." Only a portion. In effect, slavery would live on for another generation.[77]

In the year that followed the British evacuation of New York, both Rhode Island and Connecticut passed similar gradual abolition laws. To their north, in Massachusetts and New Hampshire, there was no such legislation, but several enslaved men and women won acknowledgement of their freedom in court cases. Others, it seems, simply left their owners. Thus without an act or an official declaration, slavery came to a piecemeal end. New York, however, had a much larger enslaved population than its New England neighbors. Before the revolution, New York City was home to more slaves than any other town except Charleston. When the patriots returned, there were 2,000 enslaved people. In the spring of 1784, as order was restored after the riotous first months of patriot re-occupation, the city council passed new laws forcing them to carry lanterns at night, banning them from gambling or riding horses, and limiting Sunday gatherings to three people.[78] Such restrictions, enforced by the threat of public flogging, sent a message to enslaved New Yorkers that they should expect no contagion of freedom in their city. The primary concerns of the republican establishment were to maintain order and support the re-establishment of commerce.

By the time the legislature met at the beginning of 1785, however, some gentlemen in the city had grown more interested in the cause of New York's enslaved people. On January 25, they held the first meeting of a new organization, the New York Manumission Society, which would lobby for general emancipation as well as encouraging its members to free their own slaves. Mayor James Duane was a founding member, as was his friend Alexander Hamilton. John Jay, who now served as secretary of state to Congress, was elected the society's president. Indeed, this flurry of antislavery activity took place at the very moment Congress moved into the city. The New York gentlemen who joined and helped organize the Manumission Society intended to align the city with what was increasingly seen as a rational and enlightened stance on slavery. By no means did they advocate immediate abolition, but they recognized the difficulty of promoting natural rights and liberty while holding human beings in bondage. "The time may soon come," Jay wrote to Benjamin Rush in Philadelphia, "when all our inhabitants of every colour and denomination shall be free and equal partakers of our political liberty."[79]

That spring, a variety of emancipation and antislavery bills came up for debate in the state legislature. Aaron Burr's proposal for immediate abolition was soundly defeated, as he no doubt knew it would be. A program of gradual emancipation on the Pennsylvania model, however, was much more successful. The bill promised to free the children of enslaved women born after its passage, once men reached the age of twenty-five, or women twenty-two. Yet, at the behest of proslavery legislators, it also contained several provisions targeted at free black people. "No negro, mulatto or mustee whatsoever" was to hold public office, serve on a jury, or even bear witness in court "against any citizen or white person whatsoever."[80] Interracial marriages were to be outlawed, and black people were to be denied the vote. Slavery would disappear eventually, but racial division would only be further entrenched. The senate forced the assembly to abandon these provisions—all except for the restriction on the franchise. Slavery might be abolished, but those who were freed were not to be "equal partakers" of New York's "political liberty."

When the bill was sent before the Council of Revision, chaired by Governor Clinton, they vetoed it. It was illegitimate, the council argued, to create "an order of citizens, who are to have no legislative or representative share in the government." If the children of enslaved people were to be citizens, then "they are as such, entitled to all the privileges of citizens." Anything less would be "shocking" to the principles of "equal liberty." Hamilton had made similar arguments about loyalists. Either they were entitled to the rights of citizens, or none at all. Moreover, like the loyalists, "this class of disfranchised and discontented citizens ... at some future period, may be both numerous and wealthy.... Under the direction of ambitious and factious leaders," argued the Council, they might "become dangerous to the State, and effect the ruin of a constitution whose benefits they are not permitted to enjoy." By freeing enslaved people while keeping them separate from New York's civil society, the bill threatened to create a powerful internal enemy. Conversely, it would make an "aristocracy" of all "those person[s] who deduce their origin through white ancestors only."[81] In short, it would be a travesty of both political order and republican principles.

It was clear to members of the New York Manumission Society that the city's gentlemen remained divided on the question of slavery. "A great number of Persons," they reported, "are violently opposed to the Emancipation of their Slaves." The opponents of emancipation had not been able to shut out the bill completely, but by amending it to include the voting restriction, and then voting not to override the Council's veto, they managed to prevent the plan from passing. In the time between the failure of the bill and the census in 1790, the number of slaves in the state—and the city—actually increased. Yet at the same time, antislavery rhetoric multiplied. The 1785 legislature did ban the importation of enslaved people into the state, and it made it slightly easier for owners to free their slaves privately, as Virginia had done in 1782. Members of the Manumission Society hoped that "the good Example set by others, of more Enlarged and liberal Principles, and the face of true Religion, will, in time, dispel the mist which Prejudice, self Interest and long habit have raised" among the defenders of slavery.[82]

To men like Hamilton, Duane, and Jay, the promotion of "enlarged and liberal principles" with regard to property, contract, and commerce went hand in hand with the antislavery movement.[83] The reality of slavery in New York and elsewhere in the United States served to undermine arguments about "the true principles of universal liberty," and so made it all the more difficult to justify a world of inequality founded on private, individual rights. Commercial gentlemen in the 1780s, including the New York Manumission Society, tapped into an antislavery rhetoric that emphasized this "universal morality," which extended beyond the borders of New York and the United States to encompass humanity as a whole, including Africans and their descendants. As the editor of the *New York Packet* put it a few years later, "that one rational being should be claimed by another as his absolute property [is] repugnant to all the principles of humanity."[84] The rationality and consistency of these principles was integral to their vision of justice. In this way, the rights of enslaved people and of loyalists fitted a single pattern—a pattern woven together by the ties of the modern, commercial world.

In a 1783 election day sermon titled *The United States Elevated to Glory and Honour*, Ezra Stiles, president of Yale College, foretold a wonderful and harmonious future for both Americans and Europeans. The outcome of the successful revolution "may occasion and originate a commercial system among the maritime nations, on both sides of the Atlantick, founded in justice and reciprocity of interest," he declared. Such a system would "establish the *benevolence* as well as the *opulence* of nations, and advance the progress of Society to civil perfection." Now that the British had finally been brought to the negotiating table, and had recognized the new republic's independence, Americans like Stiles predicted the creation of a transatlantic and even a global order built on principles of enlightened universalism and Christian charity. "We shall have a communication with all nations, in *commerce*, *manners* and *science*, beyond any thing heretofore known in the world," he told electors assembled in Hartford that May.[85] The revolution had been an epochal event, Stiles believed. It would change the way the world worked.

Across the Atlantic, the United States' commissioners had been trying to make a reality out of such prophecies. The original treaty of peace said nothing about commercial arrangements, because the British negotiators were not empowered to alter the Navigation Acts made by Parliament. As soon as the peace terms were agreed, though, late in 1782, the diplomats began work on a separate commercial treaty. Lord Shelburne, the prime minister, was quite amenable to American ideas about opening free trade between the two nations. Shelburne had John Pownall, a civil servant with decades of experience in American affairs, draft a bill for Parliament that would "evince the disposition of *Great Britain* to be on terms of the most perfect amity" with the United States, abolishing the restrictions brought in during the war. Pownall's brother Thomas, a former governor of Massachusetts, had publicly advocated liberal commerce with the new republic. But before these plans could be brought to fruition, maneuvering in Parliament brought down Shelburne's ministry. With the help of Shelburne's rival Charles Fox, Lord North returned to power in April 1783.[86] By the time Ezra Stiles gave his optimistic oration in March, the chances of an Anglo-American free-trade deal had suffered dramatically.

Among the voices raised in opposition to Shelburne's plans, the loudest and most influential was that of John Baker Holroyd, the Earl of Sheffield. His pamphlet, *Observations on the Commerce of the United States*, urged Parliament not to abandon the Navigation Acts restricting American trade. The revolution had, he wrote, "encouraged the wildest sallies of imagination," and led to a preference for "Systems" and "Rash theory" over experience. The Navigation Acts were "the guardian of the prosperity of Britain," claimed Sheffield, and it was in the kingdom's true interest to maintain and even to strengthen them.[87] John Adams believed, or in any case hinted, that the pamphlet had actually been written by a group of loyalists now in London, including Silas Deane and Benedict Arnold.[88] Its effect was certainly damaging. Within three months of Shelburne's fall, the new ministry took Sheffield's advice and ordered harsh restrictions on American trade with the West Indies. In spite of all Adams's efforts as ambassador, this exclusionary order was to set the pattern of British policy for the next decade.

The failure of trade negotiations with the British, however, did not immediately undermine American confidence in the new world of free trade. Writing to Robert Morris, superintendent of finance, in September 1783, John Jay's greatest concern was that making too hasty and permanent commercial treaties might restrict the future growth of American trade. In his reply, Morris expressed the same kind of visionary sentiments that Hartford citizens had heard from Ezra Stiles. "If all Governments were to agree that Commerce should be as free as Air," wrote Morris, "I believe they would then place it on the most advantageous footing for every Country and for all mankind."[89] The difference was that Morris was beginning to realize how difficult that vision would be to achieve. British imports flooded the American market when peace was declared, and customers who had spent eight or more frugal years bought plentifully on credit. When the restrictions on West Indies trade hit, American merchants found their cash flow cut off, and many could not keep up payments to the British export firms. A rash of bankruptcies on both sides of the Atlantic in early 1784 heralded the end of easy terms of credit, and an economic slump that lasted through the middle of the decade.[90]

By the time the British evacuated New York, and John Jay had returned from Europe to take up the role of secretary of state, American gentlemen had adjusted their views of the situation. "The silly, malign principles of Lord Sheffield," as Richard Henry Lee described them to George Washington, had put the system of free trade out of reach for the time being.[91] Few doubted that British restrictions were capable of doing great harm to American interests. Sheffield's "ill-digested and pernicious system ... would be entirely subversive of a commercial connection" between the two nations.[92] But there was also a potential silver lining. For those who advocated a closer union among the United States, and an increased concentration of power in Congress, America's commercial and diplomatic weakness in the face of British power only made reform seem more necessary. "If European commercial restrictions produce unanimity and tend to raise a national spirit in our country, which will probably be the case, then I shall think them blessings," Jay wrote in April 1784.[93] Predicated on the notion of American weakness, Sheffield's comments stung Americans—and their allies abroad—into a sense of greater urgency about reform of the federal system.

"Without all doubt the powers of Congress must be enlarged," declared Richard Price, the radical British friend of American independence, in a 1785 pamphlet. Urging Americans to prioritize paying off the war debt and forming a government that would be respected on the international stage, Price reflected the views of gentlemen like Jay and Hamilton. "The credit of the United States, their strength, their respectableness abroad, their liberty at home, and even their existence," he wrote, "depend on the preservation of a firm political union." At the same time, though, Price equivocated over commerce. "Foreign trade has, in some respects, the most useful tendency," he wrote. But he did not subscribe to Stiles's vision of civil perfection. Instead, Price feared luxury would corrupt American virtue. It would be "better infinitely ... to consist of bodies of plain and honest farmers, rather than opulent and splendid merchants." The most corrupting commerce of all, of course, was the slave trade, "a traffick which, as it has been hitherto carried on, is shocking to humanity, cruel, wicked, and diabolical." Until Americans abolished it entirely, he wrote, "it will not appear they deserve the liberty for which they have been contending."[94]

John Adams was appointed the United States' ambassador to Great Britain the same year Price published his pamphlet. By that time, it was clear that his role would be a difficult one. The British ministry had shown little inclination to negotiate with what they perceived to be an ineffectual Congress. Several important articles of the Treaty of Paris remained unfulfilled on both sides—Britain still held posts in the northwest that should have been ceded to the United States; some of the states, meanwhile, had continued to interfere with loyalist property and debts owed to British creditors. Still, Jay was not prepared to give up the notion that straightforward commercial sense would win out in the end. "You will represent to the british Ministry," he told Adams, "the strong and necessary Tendency of their Restrictions on our Trade, to incapacitate *our* Merchants in a certain Degree to make Remittances to *theirs*."[95] Loosen the bonds on free trade, and everyone would benefit. As Benjamin Franklin's British friend David Hartley put it, "narrow Selfish projects are the Effects of Shortsightedness.... The only cure is that both sides should *feel* those consequences of passion & prejudice wch they cannot *foresee*."[96]

The problem was that Americans were feeling the effects much more painfully than the British. Things were a long way from Stiles's utopian predictions. Along with the failure of the emancipation bill in New York, the British restrictions were just another sign that universal principles of justice, humanity, and liberal trade were yet to revolutionize the Atlantic world, let alone the globe. At home, it was becoming increasingly difficult to persuade Americans that following the dictates of commercial justice, without preference or prejudice, would ultimately be for the best. As hard times bit harder, local interests grew in clarity and force. For gentlemen who saw things with a "more enlarged" view, this meant it was all the more vital to find some way to force Americans to make the temporary local sacrifices needed—or so they believed—for a broader, national prosperity. For those who were suffering, on the other hand, the mid-decade economic slump was just another reason to resist the imposition of a genteel and commercial model of justice.

Many years later, the Pennsylvania-born historian David Ramsay reflected on the economic condition of South Carolina after the British evacuation at the end of 1782. After the depredations and sacrifices of the war, the port of Charleston was once more overflowing with goods for sale, shipped in by British traders from overstocked warehouses in London, Liverpool, and Bristol. "The impoverished inhabitants of South Carolina now experienced no other want but that of money," Ramsay explained. "As a substitute for cash they stretched their credit to the utmost, and contracted debts which to several were ruinous and to all inconvenient."[97] The first flurry of postwar purchasing created new chains of debt that would quickly come back to haunt Americans, especially after the British Caribbean trade was closed several months later. What was more, the provisions of the Treaty of Paris raised the specter of old prewar debts as well. The treaty's provision that creditors should meet with "no lawful impediment" to recovering debts contracted before the war was, thought one of Henry Laurens's friends, potentially "ruinous" to the state.[98] Pinned between that threat and the requirements of justice as they understood it, the lower south's genteel establishment found itself in an increasingly tight spot.

For some, that pressure led to a political pivot. Aedanus Burke, the champion of loyalist property and creditors' rights at the Jacksonborough assembly and through the first year of Charleston's re-occupation, made the most dramatic about-face. "I am now sorry that I fell into such an error," Burke wrote in a new pamphlet in 1784. The reality, he now perceived, was that British merchants and creditors were intent on destroying the new republic. "They let loose upon us, as from a Pandora's box, a ruinous luxury, speculation, and extravagance," wrote Burke, which "vitiated our taste, corrupted our manners, plunged the whole state into a private debt, never before equalled, and thro' the means of their trade, luxury, and good things, brought the Republic into a dilemma, an example of which has not before happened in the world." Local courts and sheriffs were obliged to act on creditors' behalf, seizing and selling property when payments fell behind. When such sales were insufficient, Burke concluded, "the debt is still unpaid, and the citizen is a slave."[99]

Slavery as a metaphor applied by white slaveholders to each other no longer referred to British tyranny over colonial subjects, but to British commercial domination over notionally independent American citizens. If the war had been to free Americans from British power, it was almost as if it had been fought for nothing. "Now," Burke wrote, "in the capacity of creditors, they have us in worse servitude, if it is possible." In such circumstances, even the advocates of commercial justice had to reassess their priorities. By describing British creditors as prejudiced agents of the government in London, whose "hearts still rankle with bitterest animosity against us and our republic," South Carolinians worked to find a way out of their moral commitment to the justice of contracts. The solution they sought was a legislative intervention to protect debtors and stop the forced sales. "He who reads this proposal, must shudder at the injustice that is to flow from the measure to creditors, whether they be foreigners or citizens," acknowledged Burke. "But ours is ... one of those cases of desperate necessity."[100] The threat of "servitude" trumped claims of justice in the end.

Most of the pressure for debtor-protection laws—such as so-called stay laws regulating the frequency and amounts of demands for payment—came from South Carolina's middling sort: the artisans, merchants, and smaller planters who were most at risk from the postwar credit crunch and economic downturn, including Alexander Gillon and his Marine Anti-Britannic Society. But members of the elite planter establishment were also vulnerable. Just as they had been during the confiscation debates of a year or two earlier, the state's commercial gentlemen were wrong-footed by the strength of public resentment and the fragility of the economic situation. As committed as they were to the principles of justice, by mid-decade their position no longer seemed tenable. "Ruin," declared Governor William Moultrie at a special session of the legislature in 1785, "is now pendant over the heads of hundreds. ... It is in the power of the law if it is allowed to operate forcibly to transfer the whole property of a large part of your own citizens, into the hands of aliens." Reluctantly, he called for "an interposition of the legislature in private contracts."[101]

This policy put the state of South Carolina in contravention of the treaty with Britain, making it all the more difficult for John Adams, on the other side of the Atlantic, to press for the British to fulfill their side of the agreement and give up the forts in the northwest. As the South Carolinian Ralph Izard put it to Thomas Jefferson, it would have been far better if the treaty had stipulated that British creditors should meet with "no *greater* obstruction ... *than those of the citizens of America.*" But that was not what Adams, Jay, and Franklin had agreed.[102] Adams's instructions as ambassador told him to "represent in strong Terms the Losses which many of our, and also of their Merchants, will sustain, if the former be unseasonably and immediately pressed for the Payment of Debts contracted before the War."[103] Again, Jay hoped commercial good sense would prevail. In his view, the two nations should relate to one another like two merchants—neither would prosper if one was pushed into ruin.

There was one other consideration. Jay also instructed Adams to "remonstrate against the Infraction of the Treaty of Peace, by the exportation of Slaves and other american Property" at the end of the war.[104] Americans who had lost human property, especially in the south where the devastation had been greater, saw no good reason why they should ruin themselves meeting the treaty's stipulations before the British did their part and offered compensation. Thus the negotiations, which began with such grand hopes for justice, equity, and the spirit of conciliation, broke down to the level of quid pro quo. As decades of revolutionary rhetoric had shown, Americans were perfectly capable of complaining that they were the slaves of tyrannical creditors while simultaneously insisting on their rights of ownership over other people. Victory in the revolution by no means dissolved this paradox. Indeed, throughout the lower south, expansion of slaveholding was part of the settlement that reconciled gentlemen planters with middling white citizens. It helped build a stable, white, republican regime.

That stability, however, also depended on continuing compromise over debtor legislation. Gentlemen continued to resist calls for more extreme protective measures, aiming to limit, as much as they could, legislative interference with contract and property. Arguing against measures put forward by Alexander Gillon early in 1787, David Ramsay made the same point Alexander Hamilton had made the year before in his Phocion letters. "The power of all legislative bodies," he told fellow lawmakers, should be "limited by the eternal law of justice and reason." No assembly, and no electoral majority, had the right to "secure debtors in the quiet possession of their creditors' property," no matter the circumstances.[105] Ramsay understood the constraints placed on state leaders by the economic hardship of the postwar years—but just as he stood up for his principles by voting for John Laurens's emancipation project, he also stood up against the injustice of debtor legislation. In both cases, he was on the losing side. In the latter, at least, many voted against their own consciences in what they felt to be the short-term interests of their state.

Weeks after this defeat, Ramsay wrote to Thomas Jefferson, then touring France and Italy, to report on the act, "by which all debts contracted before Jany. 1787 (with a few exceptions) are only recoverable by three equal instalments" in the next three years. "I fear the comments that will be made on this act in Europe. I do not pretend to justify it." But it had been compelled by "political necessity," he wrote. The fact was, assemblies all over America faced popular demands for similar laws. Massachusetts and its neighbors had just faced an armed rebellion sparked by the rural debt-resistance struggle. "Our governments in the southern states are much more quiet than in the northern," Ramsay told Jefferson, "but much of our quiet arises from the temporising of the legislatures in refusing legal protection to the prosecution of the just rights of creditors." In other words, it was only because of the southern establishment's relative weakness that it had escaped rebellions of its own. Frustrated commercial gentlemen like Ramsay himself had proved unable to impose their vision of justice. "Our eyes now are all fixed," he wrote, "on the continental convention to be held in Philadelphia in May next."[106]

CHAPTER FOUR

Capital

The rich have an interest in their poor fellow-citizens, and (as some men use their wives) however tyrannical they may be themselves, they will not suffer any body else to tyrannize over them.

—PELATIAH WEBSTER, PHILADELPHIA MERCHANT, 1786

IN EUROPE, titles of nobility and distinctions of social rank were granted by hereditary monarchs and passed down through generations. The American Revolution abolished that system in the United States, and the struggle over the Cincinnati ensured that nothing similar replaced it. There was only one thing that determined the divisions of power and social status in America, and that was access to wealth—capital.[1] When American gentlemen fought to ensure that property and contract were protected from the interference of the revolutionary democratic states, they were fighting to secure an economic order that underpinned social inequality. As they worked to build a new republic that would reflect and defend their interests, they created institutions— corporations—that were neither fully public nor completely private. In this way, they solved the problem of both needing and fearing the power of their governments.[2]

Most important among these semipublic institutions were the banks. In Philadelphia, New York, and Boston, banks consolidated capital and economic power in the hands of networks of commercial gentlemen who owned and controlled them. Not only the cities but their rural hinterlands were brought under the influence of banking—and as the people of both town and country-side soon realized, the power bankers wielded was more than merely economic. As the force of capital spread westward over the land, it reshaped the lives of farmers and settlers, artisans and merchants alike.[3] But it did not do so without opposition. By the middle of the decade, movements emerged that set out to challenge the tyranny of rich over poor, and of capital over democracy.[4] In the face of this resistance, American gentlemen had to develop new accounts of the relationship between society, politics, and the economy.

I. Visions of the West

In June 1783, a few months after the crisis over pay that swept the army camp at Newburgh, George Washington wrote to his younger brother John. He was waiting "with much impatience," he wrote, for "the arrival of the Definitive Treaty" with Britain, which would "put a period not only to my Military Service, but also to my public life." But Washington had by no means lost interest in public affairs. In his brief letter to John, he set out his hopes for the new nation, hopes that reflected the political ideals he had developed as both a British subject and an American revolutionary. The states should "adopt a liberal & proper line of Conduct for the Government of this Country," the general wrote. "It should be founded in justice." Like other gentlemen, Washington believed that "liberty, when it degenerates into licentiousness, begets confusion, and frequently ends in Tyranny or some woeful catastrophe."[5] In order to prevent such a degeneration, liberty had to be constrained by justice; and at the core of that notion of justice was a commitment to the sanctity of contracts.

"We are a young Nation & have a character to establish," Washington wrote.[6] Just as a gentleman needed to prove himself to others in order to gain their trust and create credit for himself, a nation had to demonstrate that it was capable of sticking to commitments. Back in 1779 the president of the Continental Congress, John Jay, had used a similar metaphor while discussing the payment of national debts. "A bankrupt, faithless republic," Jay wrote, "would be a novelty in the political world, and would appear among reputable nations like a common prostitute among chaste and respectable matrons."[7] Jay's choice of words emphasized the moral dimension of public credit—but what mattered was not inner virtue; it was how the nation would appear to others. "If we do not fulfil our public engagements," Washington asked his brother in 1783, "if we do not religiously observe our Treaties—If we shall be faithless to, and regardless of those who have lent their money, given their personal Services, and spilt their Blood; and who are now returning home poor & penniless; in what light shall we be considered?"[8] Like a gentleman of commerce, the United States would have to exist in an interdependent world. It would need character and credit to succeed.

Two days later, Washington wrote to Elias Boudinot, the president of Congress, endorsing a petition "from a large number of officers of the army" which called for the establishment of military colonies in the "unsettled country" to the westward, land that the United States expected to control in the wake of the Treaty of Paris. How the status and boundaries of that land would be defined, and how exactly it was to be taken from its Native American inhabitants and transformed into the private property of white men, were central issues in the politics of the 1780s. There were many people in the new republic who had stakes in that land, including the soldiers who were promised farms in place of pay, and the public creditors whose own hopes of payment rested in the value of lands sold by state and federal authorities. As for Washington, he told Boudinot he was "perfectly convinced that it cannot be so advantageously settled, by any other Class of Men as by the disbanded Officers and Soldiers of the Army—to whom the faith of Government hath long since been pledged."[9]

While the peacemakers in Paris chose to simply ignore Native Americans, granting the United States notional control of all lands south of Canada and east of the Mississippi, the future of Indian relations remained unstable and uncertain through the 1780s. Here, Washington's metaphor of the United States as an individual was unsustainable. American sovereignty was in fact as fragmented as that of the Native Americans. States argued with other states over century-old boundary claims, and states also argued with Congress over who had the right to negotiate for purchases.[10] All the while, settlers were streaming westward hoping to work things out in their own way, by violence if necessary. There was no unified land or Indian policy, only a series of negotiations punctuated by frontier violence and treaties of dubious validity.[11] In short, the war with the British may have ended, but that peace was all but meaningless in the west. The concepts of justice and contract that meant so much to gentlemen in the east were difficult to apply in western circumstances, and too often those same gentlemen were happy to take advantage of the ambiguity for their own purposes.

Washington himself had been amassing western lands since long before the revolution. By 1772 he owned over 20,000 acres in the Ohio valley. The onset of war had brought chaos to much of the west, however, and severely dented landlords' profits. If the west was to become the source of great wealth Washington expected it to be, it was vital to restore and maintain order there. In September 1783, the general wrote to James Duane, who was then in charge of his correspondence with Congress, expounding on "the line of conduct proper to be observed not only towards the Indians, but for the Government of the Citizens of America, in their Settlement of the Western Country (which is intimately connected therewith)." Washington argued that both purchases and settlement should be strictly controlled. He would not suffer competing speculators to overrun the country, like a "parcel of Banditti, who will bid defiance to all Authority while they are skimming and disposing of the Cream of the Country."[12] Congress had to exert its authority to keep control of the west in the hands of those, like himself, who would use it wisely.

Meanwhile, Native American nations should be told "that their true Interest and safety must now depend upon *our* friendship." He continued:

As the Country is large enough to contain us all; and as we are disposed to be kind to them and to partake of their Trade, we will from these considerations and from motives of Comp[assio]n, draw a veil over what is past and establish a boundary line between them and us beyond which we will *endeavor* to restrain our People from Hunting or Settling, and within which they shall not come, but for the purposes of Trading, Treating, or other business unexceptionable in its nature.[13]

As Philip Schuyler, Alexander Hamilton's father-in-law and one of northern New York's largest landowners, had told an Iroquois delegation earlier that year: "We are now Masters, and can dispose of the lands as we think proper or most convenient to ourselves."[14] Americans chose to believe that their victory against Britain meant they had conquered the Indians too, and had a right of conquest over the lands of any nation who had fought the republic. If they did not choose to exercise that right, it was a sign of "compassion" for defeated enemies.

In the closing months of 1783, after overseeing the British evacuation of New York, Washington resigned his command and made the journey south back to Mount Vernon. There he found his financial affairs in a "deranged situation ... occasioned by an absence of almost nine years." Eighteen of his slaves had escaped during a British raid in 1781, and nine others had been sold to raise money for taxes during the war.[15] Even worse were the "attempts to take from me the property I have in the back-country," and the failure of his agent to collect rent from the tenants on his vast western estates.[16] In some ways, the situation of Washington's personal estate seemed to mirror that of the republic he had helped create. In both cases, the war had left financial damage that would be difficult to repair. The question was, who would take charge of the new nation to set things in order?

"The prospect before us is, as you justly observe, fair," wrote the general that winter to Benjamin Harrison, Virginia's new governor. "But what use we shall make of it, is exceedingly problematical." Washington repeated the metaphor he had used with his brother eight months earlier: the country itself was a gentleman, and it had to live by gentlemen's rules. "Like a young heir," he wrote, "come a little prematurely to a large inheritance, we shall wanton and run riot until we have brought our reputation to the brink of ruin, & then like him shall have to labor with the current of opinion when *compelled* perhaps, to do what prudence & common policy pointed out as plain as any problem in Euclid, in the first instance."[17] For half a decade or more, the childless Washington had been called Father of his Country. His attitude towards the new republic had come to fit the epithet. He hoped the nation would take on the character of a respectable gentleman, and live up to the principles that entailed. In order to do that, it would have to make the most of its greatest "inheritance," the national domain. Only through careful management of western land could it fulfill the obligations it had created in the process of revolution.

In the summer of 1784, Washington decided it was "indispensably necessary to visit my Landed property West of the Apalacheon Mountains." His principal aim was to bring order—and profitability—to his own estates. But the journey was also an opportunity to observe the behavior and attitudes of America's western settlers. The nation's future, he believed, depended on the west and the people who lived there. Now that the war with Britain had been won, the political calculus of frontier settlement, including the ongoing war against Native Americans, was foremost in Washington's mind. On the first day of March, 1784, the state of Virginia completed the transfer of its land claims north and west of the Ohio River to congressional control. That was the beginning of a new era of policy making for the national domain. Exactly six months later, Washington set out for the west. What he found there made him angry and anxious, but it also spurred new ideas and hopes for the future.

"I am well pleased with my journey," Washington wrote on the day he got home. "It has been the means of my obtaining a knowledge of facts—coming at the temper & disposition of the Western Inhabitants—and making reflections thereon, which otherwise must have been as wild, incoherent," or as inconsistent as the reports he had previously received about them.[18] Within a week, he penned a long letter to Governor Harrison, describing the situation he had encountered. "The western settlers (I speak now from my own observation) stand as it were upon a pivot," he wrote. "The touch of a feather would turn them any way." Washington was writing not only as a landowner, but as a general and a strategist. The lands east of the Mississippi may have been granted to the United States by the Treaty of Paris, but the Spanish, French, and British remained poised on the new republic's borders. "I need not remark to you, sir," Washington told Harrison, "that the flanks and rear of the United States are possessed by other powers—and formidable ones, too."[19] With no reason to stay loyal to the independent states or to Congress, there was every chance that settlers on the frontier would be lured into the arms of one of those rival powers.

How could the west and its settlers be more firmly tied to the new United States? The solution was not to invoke a common national identity: as yet, no such identity existed. Many of the settlers were recent immigrants who had never had strong ties to colonial governments before the revolution, and who received little protection or support from the new republican states. In places like western North Carolina and western Virginia, new structures of government were being organized to meet the needs of settler communities that felt ignored by eastern establishments—the states of Franklin (in modern-day Tennessee) and Kentucky both held constitutional conventions in 1784.[20] With the war over, the power and relevance of Congress was waning dramatically, in spite of its newly ceded claims on western land. If it could not protect those claims from squatters or find a way to market the land profitably and securely, it would do little to bolster congressional authority. Americans with a strategic perspective feared their enemies abroad would take advantage of these tendencies toward disintegration, undermining the viability of an independent United States, and therefore their own respectability as gentlemen revolutionaries.

Yet even before he went west, Washington had something in mind that promised both profit for himself, and an answer to the problem of the west. In March, he had received a letter from Thomas Jefferson, who was then serving in Congress at Annapolis. Jefferson was pessimistic about the "crippled state" of Congress, but his letter was full of fantastic prophecies for the glorious future of Virginia. "All the world is becoming commercial," he told Washington, and so "we must ... in our own defense endeavor to share as large a portion as we can of this modern source of wealth and power." The answer to making Virginia the commercial center of America was the Potomac River, which if it was improved and made passable with canals, could link the state to large swathes of the continental west. "Through that channel," he wrote, nature "offers to pour into our lap the whole commerce of the Western world."[21] As it happened, the idea was nothing new to Washington. He had contemplated it ten years earlier.[22] But Jefferson's letter reanimated the project in the general's mind. He was still thinking of it as he traveled west that September.[23]

Jefferson's letter had focused on the commercial benefits to be won for Virginia through a Potomac canal project. By the time he returned from the west in October, however, Washington had come to realize that it could be more than that. "There is a political consideration," he told Benjamin Harrison, "which is of still greater importance." The canal could be used to tie western settlers to the state—and the United States—by "indissoluble bonds." It could be the means of applying what Washington called "the cement of interest." With a convenient transport link from the western country to the Atlantic, settlers could bring their produce onto the international market much more easily. At present only the Mississippi and the Hudson offered suitable routes. The Potomac could potentially rival them both. Once linked into transatlantic commerce through Virginia, western farmers and settler families would come to rely not only on the canal, but on the credit system run by eastern merchants and storekeepers. Gradually, they would be fully integrated into an interdependent economy. It was that commercial integration, rather than cultural or ideological ties, that Washington trusted to hold the west within the union. Interest was the force that mattered.[24]

There was a second area where Washington's plan for the project differed from the one proposed by Jefferson in March, and that was in its answer to the question, who would pay? Jefferson had simply proposed that a new tax should be levied from Virginians to pay for the canal's construction. As with his proposal for overhauling the state's education system, Jefferson did not let the political realities of financing get in the way of his visionary schemes. Washington was more realistic. The fact was, Virginia's economy—like the economies of every other state—was overstretched and fragile. Just as stay laws were being used to protect debtors in South Carolina through the middle of the decade, so similar measures were being taken in Virginia. The state had issued paper money to help boost circulation. And it had delayed the collection of taxes. Gentlemen like George Mason, who believed in commercial justice, usually opposed all such measures. But even Mason voted for the tax postponement in the spring of 1783. "It appears," wrote Washington, that despite "all the sufferings of the public creditors, breach of public faith, and loss of public reputation, that payment of taxes which are already laid will be postponed as long as possible! How then are we to expect new ones, for purposes more remote?"[25]

The solution Washington proposed, in his letter to Governor Harrison, was to shift the burden of initial costs from the public purse to private fortunes. By setting up a chartered corporation, the state could attract investors who would pay for the project. In exchange, these "private Adventurers" would be able to profit from tolls on the new canal for a limited time.[26] As Washington told his friend James Madison, then serving in the Virginia state legislature, the aim was to reach a happy medium" that would not "vest too much power and profit in a private company," yet would nevertheless "hold out sufficient inducements to engage men to hazard their fortunes in an arduous undertaking." For Washington, there was something a little distasteful in this mixing of public good with private profit. He preferred to see himself as a gentleman of independent wealth, in the old English style, rather than as a commercial gentleman who relied on networks of exchange. But he knew that the project would rely on the latter. "Resort ... must be had to mercantile funds," he told Madison, "from whence nothing can be extracted if there is not a prospect of great gain, present or future."[27] Washington held himself aloof, yet pushed the project forward.[28]

If it was successful, the Potomac canal promised to create a new stream of commerce, flowing through Virginia between the west and the Atlantic. At the same time, it would bring the western settlers into closer contact with the east and, Washington hoped, make them more loyal to eastern state governments and Congress itself. These visions relied on the idea that "the motives which predominate most in human affairs is [sic] self-love and self-interest."[29] Merchants and men of finance in the east would fund the canal project because they expected to make profits from it. Likewise, western farmers would eagerly produce crops for the international market as soon as they had easy access to it. Washington may not have thought his own motives could be described that way, but as a politician and a strategist, he was willing to bet it was how most people behaved. It was that same basic principle of mutual self-interest that allowed commercial gentlemen to deal with one another as equals—it implied a kind of predictability that was vital to long-distance trade and long-term investment. Without this assumption of predictability, the rules of commercial justice and the system they supported would collapse.

While Washington was touring his property in the Ohio valley in September 1784, congressional negotiators were meetings with Iroquois representatives at Fort Stanwix in western New York to make a treaty of peace. The negotiations were complicated by New York's attempts to claim the Iroquois territory as its own. But federal commissioners, including the French *chargé d'affairs*, the Marquis de Barbé-Marbois, shrugged off the New Yorkers' claims and asserted the exclusive power of Congress to treat with Native Americans.[30] From the perspective of Congress and its supporters, peace with the Indians and a clear supremacy over the states in matters of western land both served the same purpose: to create a national domain under federal ownership that could become a stock for sale to defray the war debt. By the time a second treaty was signed early the next year at Fort MacIntosh in Pennsylvania, with several nations of what Washington called "Western Indians," the beginnings of peace on the frontier seemed to be at hand.[31] The next step was to consider exactly how Congress should go about selling off its "inheritance."

From his home at Mount Vernon, Washington watched the process closely. He was in touch with three of the members of the Congressional committee appointed to review the question of western land: William Grayson and Richard Henry Lee of Virginia, and Hugh Williamson of North Carolina. In letters to all three of them, the general set out his own vision of a western policy for the republic, expanding on the ideas he had shared with James Duane while still commander-in-chief. Like many eastern gentlemen, Washington was made uneasy by the potential for disorder and conflict the west represented. His idea of American empire involved a continuation of white settlement all the way to the banks of the Mississippi, and eventually, perhaps, across the continent. But he distrusted the men and women who made up the leading edge of that settlement, frontier squatters who had no respect for the rights of landowners like himself. He had no love for Native Americans, but he hoped to avoid the provocation and bloodshed that always ensued when white settlement was left unrestrained. Finally, he supported the rights of absentee owners—after all, he was one himself—but he feared the effects of rampant speculation. In short, the west was not only a great resource for the new nation, it was also a cauldron of potential trouble.

Writing to Williamson in March, Washington set out the two principles that guided his thinking on western land. First, the sale of the federal territory "ought not to be delayed," and second the settlement of the land itself "ought not to be too diffusive." Settlers usually preferred to take up as much land as they could, and they also sought to locate their farms on the best, most fertile tracts. Both of those considerations led to neighbors living far apart from each other. The problem was, such a dispersed pattern of settlement not only took up more land than seemed strictly necessary, it also made it more difficult to supply public goods like roads and defense. "Compact and progressive Seating," Washington wrote, "will give strength to the Union; admit law & good government; & fœderal aids at an early period." Moreover, if purchasers were allowed to make extensive claims wherever they liked, the way would be open for "land jobbers and speculators, who are prouling about like Wolves in every shape."[32] Instead, Washington argued, people should only be able to buy limited tracts next door to already existing farms. The rest of the land should be left open and untouched.

Washington also believed that the sales of public land should be made either as close as possible to the land itself—which would be an advantage to actual settlers—or, failing that, at the seat of Congress, then in New York. What he opposed, on the other hand, was that the sales should be conducted separately in each state. Yet the latter is exactly what the committee decided. It also ended up ignoring most of Washington's advice about "compact and progressive Seating." Clearly, his influence had limits when it came to the complexities of congressional politics. Writing to Washington in early May, just before the Land Ordinance was passed, William Grayson reported that the whole process had been gripped by "interfering interests" and "ill founded jealousies." If it had not been for the pressing need to pay the public creditors, nothing might have been agreed at all, Grayson concluded. "I verily believe it is the best that under present circumstances can be procured."[33] From Washington's perspective, it was an example of just how dysfunctional Congress could be. The Ordinance, as he saw it, was a victory for unscrupulous speculators.

It was well known that some of those speculators were congressmen themselves. As a representative of Pennsylvania at the Congress of 1785, the lawyer and honorary Cincinnatus James Wilson made good use of his time in New York. On the fourth of May, just weeks before the Land Ordinance passed, Wilson went into partnership with the New York surveyor-general Simeon De Witt and a third gentleman to buy lands on the edge of Indian territory in both New York and Pennsylvania. They called themselves the Canaan Company, and they expected to find the land flowing with milk and honey, at least for themselves. The trio called on William Bingham, one of Robert Morris's most successful Philadelphia partners, to supply funds for the scheme. By the following year, they were possessed of tracts valued at over thirty times what they had paid for them.[34] Wilson's networks as both a congressman and a Philadelphia lawyer were what allowed him to pursue such lucrative opportunities. Far from an old-style independent landowner, he thrived in the world of commercial interconnections.

Activity like Wilson's inevitably created tensions with the families seeking to settle on the land they bought and sold—or in some cases those who already lived there. If Washington's absentee landowning was one thing, and

settlers resented and sometimes refused the rent he charged them, speculators were worse because they had bought the land purely in order to sell it
again at an increased price. Speculators forced settlers to pay more for their
land, and used local sheriffs and soldiers to force them off if they would not
pay up. In April 1785, federal troops from Fort MacIntosh, where the new Indian treaty had just been made, raided land on the north bank of the Ohio.
After confronting a group of seventy settlers refusing to leave, the commander
gave them a two-week deadline to quit the area.[35] Local communities in the
west organized to resist speculators' claims and the government that tried to
enforce them. They also sent their protests back east. Speculators "treat us
with more cruelty than the Indians were capable of," one petition to the Pennsylvania assembly put it, "and have the affrontery to Stamp on their Proceedings the Sanction of the Law."[36]

Such conflicts helped drive a wedge between the commercial vision of
justice, and the interests and ideas of people in the rural west. Even those
who were not forced to move on experienced higher prices as a result of speculation. Legislators and congressmen in the east seemed to live in a different
world from that of settlers and farmers out west. In terms of sheer numbers,
westerners were under-represented because they lived in districts that were
often scarcely populated when seats were apportioned in the legislatures.
They were also further from state capitals, and so less able to monitor and
influence politics there. Before the revolution, a series of insurrections called
Regulations had broken out in the Carolina backcountry, spreading into Virginia and Pennsylvania as well—conflicts over colonial governments' failure
to look after the west. Regulators took it upon themselves to enforce order
in their own communities, drawing the suspicion of colonial officials. During
the war, many former Regulators fought as patriots. Yet when peace came in
the 1780s, they found that the new state governments were often little improvement over what came before. The old Regulator spirit re-emerged to
animate backcountry politics in the first decades of the new republic.

Gentlemen like Washington hoped schemes such as the Potomac canal
could help bring western settler communities into closer relations with the
east, extending the benefits of international commerce further into the countryside and connecting rural people to larger networks of credit and market
exchange. They feared that imperial rivals—especially the Spanish, who controlled the Mississippi—would encourage westerners to split from the United
States and cut off the route of expansion for the fledgling republic. Extending
the commercial economy into the backcountry was never a straightforward
proposition, however. In fact, it was a double-edged sword. Where land was
surveyed and sold, especially if it boasted good water-transport links, it attracted speculators as well as settlers. Rising prices meant settlers who paid
to secure their claims were more likely to be in debt. Commercial farming encouraged the extension of credit arrangements too. When hard times hit, these

debts became fetters that left westerners at the mercy of creditors in the east. In the county of Westmoreland, for example, two families in every five faced foreclosures in the decade from 1782 to 1792.[37] That was the price settlers paid for joining the commercial world.[38] Before long, it also became the source of powerful resistance movements that redoubled the anxieties of gentlemen back east.

II. Bankers versus the People

The institution that most came to symbolize the expanding, credit-based commercial economy in the 1780s was the Bank of North America, in Philadelphia. The bank had first been conceived at one of the darkest moments of the revolutionary war, early in 1781, when the Continental Congress was near bankruptcy, its money practically worthless, and army commanders left unable to provision their troops. In that time of desperation, Congress turned to one of the country's wealthiest merchants, Robert Morris, to serve as its first superintendent of finance. Taking the advice of Washington's young aide, Alexander Hamilton, Morris set about establishing a national bank that could offer a new mechanism of public credit. A bank on the model of the Bank of England, Hamilton wrote in April, would "offer adventurers immediate advantages analogous to those they receive by employing their money in trade." Moreover, it would "not only advance their own interest and secure the independence of their country, but in its progress have the most beneficial influence upon its future commerce and be a source of national strength."[39] Over the year that followed, Morris set about turning this visionary proposal into a reality.[40]

By pooling the resources of Congress along with those of the country's richest businessmen, the idea of the bank was to create a large enough stock of capital that it could give security to a much larger "mass of credit." Bank notes would be exchangeable for specie—that is, coins of precious metal—but the bank would be able to print more notes than the specie it actually had on deposit. As long as the public had faith that the bank would honor its notes, they could circulate at more or less the same value as actual metal coin. The whole scheme would thus increase significantly the amount of circulating value, which could then be loaned to the government to continue the war. Where would the initial stock of specie come from? Morris's first move was to borrow from the Spanish, who had $400,000 worth of gold in Cuba which they could not ship across the Atlantic for fear of capture by the British. This plan was scotched, however, when Morris's ship was itself captured en route to the island. The second, and successful, plan was a diplomatic mission to France, carried out that summer by the unlikely duo of Thomas Paine and John Laurens: $200,000 of the loans and gifts they came back with would be the starting capital of the Bank of North America.[41]

Continental currency before 1781 was backed by a simple promise on behalf of the United States to pay for the note at a future date. Faith in the notes depended on the expectation that Congress would be able to raise revenues, either through taxes or, more likely, through sales of federal land. The notes from Morris's bank differed substantially from that, because they could be readily exchanged, at least in theory, for real gold or silver, a universally accepted store of value. As Morris pointed out, his bank notes might "even be preferable to those precious metals" since they were safer and easier to transport.[42] Individuals and even governments could deposit specie with the bank, which would then add to its stock and support public faith in the notes. Banking thus facilitated the flow of value through the economy. The more readily exchangeable the notes, the smoother the flow: a characteristic referred to as liquidity. This was part of the reason men like Hamilton and Morris preferred specie as the bank's capital basis, in spite of the difficulty of rounding it up. Land, which Congress had in abundance, was distant and variable in quality, so much harder to exchange.

In 1784, the Bank of North America was flourishing. Its investors, who included foreigners as well as some of the richest merchants in the new republic, granted themselves massive dividends to reap the rewards of controlling such a useful institution. Other states sought to replicate this success by incorporating banks of their own. But there was a problem. To set up a money bank like the Bank of North America, you needed plenty of specie. The only place to get that specie, unless you were Congress and could borrow it from France or Spain, was rich merchants who had capital to spare. Chartering a money bank to be owned by merchants meant giving more power to the already powerful, and that was difficult in the political circumstances of the 1780s. State legislatures were not keen to give their sanction to such institutions. Land banks, on the other hand, were potentially much more democratic, since they could be based on land the state already owned, and controlled by directors appointed by the legislature, rather than stockholders. It was this kind of bank that Chancellor Robert Livingston tried to set up in New York soon after the British evacuation.

Hamilton, who was already in discussions with certain merchant friends about setting up a money bank for New York, strongly opposed Livingston's project. He called it absurd and inconvenient, deleterious to "the commercial interests of the state." The supporters of the land bank, Hamilton told his brother-in-law John Church, were "country members" of the legislature, ignorant rural representatives who had been "persuaded that the land bank was the true Philosophers stone that was to turn all their rocks and trees into gold."[43] Land banks operated for the benefit of farmers and other landholders by offering mortgages, but they were of little use to merchants like Church. Moreover, Hamilton, like everyone else, believed that banks worked best when they did not face competition within their own region. If it went ahead, the land bank would funnel capital away from a potential money bank. In order to stop that from happening, Hamilton worked with other New York merchants to set up their own bank before Livingston could get a charter from the legislature. In the end neither project was granted a charter, but it was the money bank that went ahead regardless. New York's merchants had effectively organized to shut out the "country" influence and keep the advantages of banking in their own hands.[44]

With a third bank established the same year by a group of Boston merchants, financial activity in the three leading port cities of the republic was now, by the summer of 1784, organized in the hands of its leading mercantile gentlemen.[45] Just because these were money banks did not mean that farming and the countryside was left out of the picture. Indeed, Hamilton argued that "by promoting industry and commerce" a bank also "necessarily promotes agriculture and renders landed property more valuable."[46] Banks helped integrate local and regional economies by pooling investment capital and providing loans to entrepreneurs. Often, however, those loans simply went to bank directors themselves, or their friends and relatives. Bankers had to judge the credit of applicants, and the best way to do that was through personal connections. Gentlemen who were well known to each other, and who had the chance to build up a reputation for keeping their word, had better access to credit than unknown outsiders—and of course, those with better access to credit were more likely to succeed in business and prove that trust in them was well-founded. The entire mechanism was self-reinforcing.[47]

If anyone was at the center of the network that made up the new republic's financial elite, it was Robert Morris. His influence and connections had been the very reason he was appointed to be superintendent of finance in the first place. Leaving that office at the end of 1784, Morris returned to private business but remained at the head of the Philadelphia commercial community. When George Washington wanted to interest America's monied gentlemen in his Potomac canal company, he naturally turned to Morris, the man who helped fund the march to Yorktown. As soon as the process of acquiring charters from the Virginia and Maryland legislatures was complete, Washington wrote to Morris outlining the scheme. "Were I disposed to encounter present inconvenience for a future income," wrote the general, "I would hazard all the money I could raise upon the navigation of the river. Or had I inclination and talents to enter into the commercial line, I have no idea of a better opening than the one I have descanted upon to make a fortune."[48] As a result, Morris bought shares for his children, and told Washington he would encourage his "Friends to become adventurers" in the scheme.[49]

Philadelphia society revolved around the circle of wealthy financiers associated with Morris and his bank. Thomas Willing, the bank president, had been Morris's partner in business since before the revolution. William Bingham had been Congress's agent in the West Indies during the war, where he had performed profitable service to Morris and Willing as an agent for their private trading as well as government business. In 1780, Bingham married Willing's daughter Anne, who quickly became one of the most glamorous women in the country. It was on the Binghams' porch in 1782 that Benjamin Rush had first conceived of Dickinson College, and Bingham's money that helped pay for it. As Rush had put it in the summer of 1784, he intended the college to "soften the tempers of our turbulent brethren" in the west, and to "inspire them with liberal sentiments in government and religion."[50] Just as Washington believed that his canal would turn westerners into loyal and productive constituents of the Atlantic economy, Rush hoped to make them obedient citizens of the commercial state. Both ultimately served the ends of Philadelphia's commercial elite.

While gentlemen in the east worked to extend their influence into the back-country and across the Appalachian mountains, communities in the west were also organizing to protect their own interests and autonomy. With the chains of credit tightening in the years after the Peace of Paris, and foreclo-sures becoming a common occurrence throughout the west, farmers and set-tlers developed tactics to defend their homes and livelihoods. Local tax and court officials could interfere with the process and delay collections to protect their neighbors—and when they were prosecuted for failing to do their duty, local juries voted to acquit them. Juries could also let off neighbors accused of not paying their debts or taxes. As an institution, juries gave power to local people to enforce their own vision of justice, quite different from the one held by commercial gentlemen. At the same time, rural communities organized themselves to resist speculators and debt collectors by gathering at auctions where seized property was being sold, preventing bids from being made. These intimidation tactics undermined the legal process of foreclosure with-out overtly defying it. As one Pennsylvania county treasurer put it in July 1784, "the laws are eluded without being openly opposed."[51]

Farmers and settlers in rural Pennsylvania—and across the new republic—also worked for changes in the law itself. Such people were rarely elected to state legislatures themselves. Those positions were still mostly taken by gen-teel landowners who could afford to treat voters to whisky and beer at the polls, and who could take time out to attend the sessions in distant state cap-itals. One group of Pennsylvanians did try to campaign against their local assemblyman in 1783. They published an open letter criticizing "lawyers" and "anti-constitutionalists"—opponents of the relatively democratic 1776 state constitution—who only made laws "to suit themselves. . . . Let us have a set of Farmers to serve us this year," the authors of the letter wrote, "and no doubt but we shall be honestly represented." But the target of their criticism, George Woods, successfully sued the authors for libel. The case seemed to prove that the law was a friend to established politicians, not rural people.[52] What they could do, though, was get together at local meetings to debate issues and sign petitions putting forward their views. Through the 1780s, petitions flooded state legislatures calling for tax and debtor relief, paper money, and easier access to credit.

Petitioners framed their proposals as simple common sense, but to elites in the cities their ideas represented a dangerously radical alternative. During the war, mercantile leaders like Robert Morris had argued that stringent fiscal measures had to be taken to show public creditors that the state government was responsible and reliable. New paper money emissions and land banking were supposed to undermine the state's credibility, and the value of its currency, in a time of crisis when Continental currency was experiencing massive inflation. At the end of the war, though, gentlemen had shown no sign of rolling back those measures, or of trying to make things easier on farmers in the west. "The State of Pennsylvania is now in a Situation entirely Different from any they have been in Since the beginning of the late National Contest," rural petitioners reminded the assembly in Philadelphia. "We now stand upon entire new ground, so firm, that nothing but an unwarrantable timidity can occasion distrust." The time was ripe for a new set of policies, including a return to "the Ancient, Safe and Successful plan" of land banking, that would relieve country communities from the burdens of debt, taxation, and the scarcity of money.[53]

It was not that farmers wanted to remain isolated from the commercial economy in which Washington and Morris aimed to enmesh them. Access to trade would benefit rural communities by giving them more access to manufactured goods and other exotics from the east and abroad. Selling their wheat on the international market offered the opportunity to improve the quality of rural life. Petitioners emphasized, then, that they had no wish to "obstruct the Extension of trade." What they wanted was to "enable the citizens of this state to discharge their debts" over time, without fear that their land would be taken from them. They also sought to rebalance the scales between farmers and the speculators who competed for control of the land. The law should "give the Preference To those whose Lives have been Spent in Endeavouring To Procure an honest Livelihood on Lands," read one petition. Surely, farmers argued, the most valid rights belonged to "those only who have been Tillers of the ground & Livers on the Land."[54] Settlers were strong believers in property. To them, ownership of land had a moral quality. When speculators traded land like so much paper, left it undeveloped, and even forced off cultivators, that was when the two visions of justice diverged.

Many farmers saw themselves as part of a struggle for power that was both economic and political—and they identified their enemy in that struggle as Robert Morris's bank. The republican rhetoric that became ubiquitous during the revolution had emphasized the importance of equality among citizens. Inequality, by contrast, was understood to be a cause of aristocracy, dependence, and corruption. Yet, as petitioners from Pennsylvania's rural communities pointed out, the bank served to concentrate power and wealth in the hands of a few. Morris and his associates were using the bank "to acquire influence in our public councils, and an ascendancy in the government, subversive of the dearest rights of the people," read a petition printed in the *Pennsylvania Evening Herald.*[55] Merchants, too, complained about the bank's power. "The directors of the bank," wrote a group from Chester County, "are able to give such preferences in trade by advance of money to their particular favourites when it is most needed, as to destroy the equality that ought to take place in a commercial community."[56] For all those who experienced the hard times that followed the peace, the bank seemed to be a source of oppression, not prosperity.

By the 1784 elections to the Pennsylvania assembly, some politicians were beginning to pay attention to this movement for an alternative economic policy. In rural counties across the state, not just in the west, new representatives emerged at state level who were prepared to argue for the reforms already outlined in community petitions. The most prominent leader of this group was William Findley, an Irish-born settler from Westmoreland County. Findley had been active in the local committee of safety since the beginning of the revolution. In 1784, he came to Philadelphia for the first time and became an outspoken advocate of the rural reform agenda.[57] Established politicians who identified with the Constitutionalist Party, the supporters of the 1776 constitution, also took up the country petitions' call. Their opponents, the Republican Party—which included Robert Morris, James Wilson, and Benjamin Rush—had dominated the state government since the end of the war. At the election in October 1784, though, opposition to Morris and the commercial elite coalesced around the demands of farming and settler communities, sweeping a wave of reform-minded legislators into office. The balance of the new assembly was overwhelming: fifty-seven Constitutionalists to nineteen Republicans.[58]

When they got to Philadelphia that winter, the members of the new assembly began to take action on their plan of reform. As promised, they passed a new emission of paper money, mandating that interest to the public creditors be paid in paper, not specie. They also established a new land bank, which would offer mortgages to farmers and settlers, giving them access to credit that had hitherto been locked up in the Bank of North America. The land bank would have offices in each county, instead of forcing farmers to trek all the way to Philadelphia to get a loan. Two-thirds of those who received loans from the land bank were farmers. Only one-sixth were gentlemen and merchants. But there were limits to the new assembly's program. The land bank had a smaller fund than the one that had existed in colonial times, and was "too small ... to give adequate relief to the several counties," as one petition charged in February 1785. Its terms were also worse: it charged higher interest and gave loans for shorter periods than the colonial version. For many farmers, the new assembly was a disappointment. Politicians, they said, were merely trying "to keep us quiet."[59]

One thing they did do, however, was to follow up on popular outrage against the Bank of North America. A committee was established to consider whether Morris's bank was "compatible with the public safety, and that equality which ought ever to prevail between the individuals of a republic." Among the committee members was Robert Whitehill, a Cumberland County representative who had helped draft the original 1776 constitution and had been a consistent advocate of farmers' policies. He could be trusted to pursue the reforming agenda.[60] When the committee made its report, on March 25, 1785, it came down clearly on the side of those who wished to see the bank abolished. Not only did the bank make it more difficult for farmers to access money and credit, the committee concluded, but it endangered the political basis of the state. "The accumulation of enormous wealth" in the hands of a perpetual corporation "will necessarily produce a degree of influence and power, which cannot be entrusted in the hands of any set of men whatsoever," they wrote. "We fear the time is not very distant, when the bank will be able to dictate to the legislature, what laws to pass and what to forbear."[61] In calling for the end of the bank, Whitehill and his colleagues must have known that they were embarking on a bitter struggle.

The bill to repeal the Bank of North America's state charter passed the assembly on April 4, 1785. That did not, however, mean the charter was immediately revoked. Pennsylvania's constitution of 1776 included a provision that any bills passed would not become law until the following session. What followed, then, was six months of vigorous campaigning on behalf of the bank. Shocked out of their complacency, commercial gentlemen attached to Morris's network began to mobilize their rhetorical and political abilities. By no means were they prepared to concede defeat at the hands of a mob of farmers and mechanics. Rather, their struggle with the assembly helped such gentlemen further develop and articulate their shared vision of justice. Revoking the charter, wrote a correspondent to the *Pennsylvania Gazette* on April 6, was "a direct violation of the social compact, on which all government is founded." Charters, he argued, should be held "as sacred as private property," and for the government to break such a contract was "to introduce the manners and vices of barbarians and savages."[62] These were the outraged sentiments that would appear again and again as the battle over the bank continued.[63]

Meetings of the bank's directors became strategy sessions for the campaign of defense. One advantage they still had was that the bank had actually been chartered twice: once by Pennsylvania, but also by Congress itself. In May, the board decided to appeal to Congress to intervene on the bank's behalf. If state laws could be nullified by international norms, as Alexander Hamilton and James Duane had shown in *Rutgers v. Waddington*, the year before, then could not the same set of priorities apply in the bank's case? James Wilson, already a distinguished lawyer, had been a director of the bank until 1784. Now in its hour of need, Thomas Willing asked Wilson to act in its defense by putting the case directly to Congress. "When this political child of theirs has once breathed its last," Willing wrote, "they have no Promethean power to call another such into existence. Confidence, once lost, is not often, if ever, to be regained." The assembly of Pennsylvania had "violated" the confederation of the states. "A stab, a mortal stab, is given to the honor of Congress,—& the credit of all America."[64]

Willing urged Wilson to put these arguments into the legal language that would force Congress to intervene. To him, it was a matter of personal honor as well as public policy. "I have devoted a large portion of my time ... to the service of my Country in the establishment of the Bank," wrote its president. "It is my pride, it is my greatest glory that it has thus far succeeded ... I conjure you," he told Wilson, "by every tie you have to the institution of which you was [sic] an early protector, by every tie you have to the country you live in, to exert every nerve in its defense."[65] But that summer, Congress could hardly raise a quorum to pass the Land Ordinance. Its power over the states was questionable at best. What Wilson wrote in answer to Willing's plea was not a petition to them alone. He decided instead to publish a pamphlet laying out in detail all the arguments against the revocation of the charter. It was not designed primarily to persuade ordinary Pennsylvanians—"other fugitive and weekly pieces will directly follow," Willing told his son-in-law William Bingham, "to suit the people at large."[66] Rather, Wilson's "very ingenious pamphlet" was more like a statement of principles that would guide the campaign to defend the bank.[67]

Wilson divided his *Considerations on the Bank of North America* into two main parts. In the first, he offered a legal argument to prove that, regardless of the actions of the Pennsylvania legislature, the charter granted by Congress would remain both valid and sufficient to protect the bank as a corporation. "The United States," he argued, "have *general* rights, *general* powers, and *general* obligations, not derived from *any* particular states, nor from *all* the particular states, taken *separately*; but resulting from the union of the whole." Congress had powers that had not been specifically granted to it by the states, but had been created by the act of union itself. The two examples Wilson gave were Congress's power over "the purchase, the sale, and the government" of western lands, and its power over "an institution for circulating paper, and establishing its credit over the whole United States," that is, the bank. "Any argument ... against the power of Congress to grant a charter to the Bank of North America" could be applied "with equal strength and fitness" against its power to create new states in the west.[68] Anyone who sought to undermine the bank's Congressional charter would also be attacking the national domain.

The shadow of western land also fell over the second major part of Wilson's pamphlet. Quoting at length from the contemporary Scottish economists Adam Smith and James Steuart, Wilson noted that "the improvement of that country," Wilson's own native country, was "entirely owing" to its banks. "The judicious operations of banking," Adam Smith had written, enable a country not only to augment its capital but to render "a greater part of that capital active and productive," and "increase the industry of the country." If "gold and silver money," specie, was a metaphorical highway by which goods were circulated, banking created "a sort of wagon-way through the air," freeing specie from circulation so that it could be used in investment.[69] The difference between Smith's wagon way in the air and the reformers' paper money policies was that bank notes could still be exchanged for hard money. The role of the state, according to this commercial vision of justice, was not to try to set values directly through paper money and legal tender laws. It was simply to protect the operation of a free market. That meant making sure that people could put trust in things like contracts and charters.

Business and commerce required the security of government protection through incorporation, but also freedom from government interference. Revoking the bank's charter, Wilson argued, would undermine the foundations of credit and confidence on which future prosperity would rest. "Those acts of state, which have hitherto been considered as the sure anchors of privilege and property, will become the sport of every varying gust of politics, and will float wildly backwards and forwards on the irregular and impetuous tides of party and faction."[70] If democratic assemblies had the power to break contracts and alter economic relationships, institutions and entrepreneurs alike would be "at the mercy of the community." According to Wilson, such interventions would violate the "rules of justice, of faith, and of honor."[71] Having established the Bank of North America as a corporation "for ever hereafter," the Pennsylvania legislature had bound itself to "the rules and maxims by which compacts are governed."[72] In the eyes of Philadelphia's commercial gentlemen, it was those rules and maxims that were at the root of all justice. To violate them would not only damage the "credit of the United States," it would also be a moral failing on the part of the new republic—signaling a defect of character.[73]

Wilson's pamphlet offered Pennsylvanians a choice between progress and backwardness, prosperity and poverty. But his model of progress and prosperity was eighteenth-century Scotland, where he was born and lived until the age of twenty-four. There, new models of justice, order, and commercial life had been imposed on the countryside by aggressive and often violent English policies, designed as much to break the power of Jacobite rebellion as to create a flourishing economy. For men like James Wilson and Adam Smith, who had been his tutor at Glasgow University, this was a success story to be emulated. That meant imposing new ideals and patterns of life on recalcitrant rural citizens. In order to belong to the enlightened commercial economy, all men had to adopt and internalize the "rules of justice, of faith, and of honor" that characterized ideal relations between merchants. Older conceptions of the right to land had to be left behind. If Pennsylvanians were to enter the modern world, they would have to reject the reform program of men like Findley and Whitehill, and put their faith in Wilson, Morris, and their bank. Accepting the new rules of justice would eventually help all alike.

These arguments did not sway the bank's opponents in the legislature over the course of their summer recess. When they reconvened in September, the assembly did accede to Thomas Willing's request for a hearing to be held before the final vote on the charter's revocation. Wilson, on behalf of the bank, spoke at length, going through each charge in turn laid at the bank's door in the original committee report. "The truth is," he declared, "that banks are calculated to be the servants of the people. Their aim is profit not ambition."[74] But when the assemblymen voted a few days later, they did not change their minds. The Bank of North America no longer operated under charter from the state of Pennsylvania. That did not mean, of course, that the bank closed its doors. It still had its congressional charter, as Wilson's pamphlet emphasized. The Bank of New York had been operating for a year without a charter, and while it had made smaller profits than its Philadelphia cousin, it showed no signs of disbanding. If the opponents of Morris's bank thought they had the institution beaten, they were premature. Its backers would not give up so easily.

III. Resurrecting the Bank

In New York, news of the charter repeal frightened gentlemen who had investments in the Bank of North America. Two of the largest stockholders were the Connecticut merchant Jeremiah Wadsworth and his erstwhile business partner John Church. Living in England, Church entrusted his American business affairs to his brother-in-law, Alexander Hamilton. Thus in January 1786, Hamilton met with a group of New York–based investors to assess the situation. "The step lately taken by the legislature of Pennsylvania," they agreed, "has given rise to questions of a delicate and important nature." The investors decided to send Wadsworth as their agent to the next meeting of bank shareholders. Wadsworth's mission was to determine whether the bank could be "continued with safety and advantage," a prospect which the New Yorkers deemed "inseparable from its existence as a corporation.... If this cannot be maintained all hopes of security or utility in our apprehension fail." He was to examine the bank's legal status, and its financial activities. "We cannot help feeling great anxiety to know what our true situation is; and to extricate ourselves from one (if such it is) in which we might hazard much more than we intended."[75]

Of all the bank's activities, what made investors most anxious was speculation in western land. And of all the speculators supported by the bank, the
most worrying was James Wilson himself. When he arrived in Philadelphia,
Wadsworth discovered that without complying with the "usual forms," Wilson
had drawn $100,000 from the bank for use in speculative purchasing. A num-
ber of men acted as guarantors for Wilson's debt, including Robert Morris for
$10,000. John Nixon, a bank director, held mortgages on the land "for the
security of these individuals." The value of Wilson's land was, in the nature of
speculation, far from certain, and this left his guarantors and the bank with
considerable exposure. It was clear to Wadsworth that the directors had indeed been guilty of "partiality" in making loans.[76] That raised the question of
whether the directors were properly representing the interests of the shareholders at large. Church, for one, was unconvinced. "After the unwarrantable
lengths they have gone in assisting Wilson," he told Hamilton, "I do not think
the property can with propriety be confided to their management."[77] Fortu-
nately for the bank, however, Church was too far away to exert an immediate
influence on events.

Rather than seeking to dissolve the bank, Wadsworth forced a motion past
the board that was designed to protect the group's investment. The bank could
continue to operate profitably, the directors agreed, as long as it remained
protected as a corporation under Pennsylvania law. So an "experiment should
be made without delay" to judge the security of the original congressional
charter, and to ascertain "in what light it may be perceived by those laws."[78]
Wadsworth's motion, seconded by Gouverneur Morris, instructed the bank's
directors "to obtain as speedily as may be a legal decision" on whether the
bank was still to be treated as a corporation. If it was not, all present agreed,
then the contract between the shareholders and the bank itself would have
been broken, and as Robert Morris put it, "every stock holder might withdraw
by right."[79] Until some sort of decision was obtained, the bank's future continued to hang in the balance.

In the year that followed the charter revocation, the bank's proprietors or-
chestrated a political campaign to save the institution. Petitions arrived at the
legislature, letters appeared in the newspapers, and Philadelphia society—the
networks surrounding Morris, Willing, and other wealthy gentlemen—began
to exert pressure on legislators to reverse their decision. Philadelphia, as one
westerner later observed, was a "nursery of corruption." When legislators
arrived, they found themselves the object of friendly attention from gentlemen, plied with dinners, wine, and introductions into exclusive circles. These
"Enchanting allurements," wrote the disappointed reformer, were "honors
too powerful for human nature to resist." Soon, legislators found themselves
adopting the perspective of their new hosts, and changing their minds about
the promises they had made to constituents.[80] It was these people for whom
pamphlets like Wilson's were most effective, for they provided arguments to

match and bolster their new point of view. What was more, by January 1786 the campaign for the bank had gained an advocate well-placed to sway the opinion of Constitutionalists in the city. The next major pamphlet to support the charter was by none other than Common Sense himself—Thomas Paine.

To judge from the abuse he received at the hands of the bank's opponents, many interpreted Paine's work on its behalf as a betrayal of the revolutionary cause. Assemblyman John Smilie said he was an "unprincipled" author who "hires out his pen for pay." One poet wrote of Paine, "*Janus* is our own who props a bank, altho' he scorn's a throne; / And, should his breast with just resentment burn, / Would scorn a bank and prop a throne in turn."[81] Yet Paine's career in the 1780s had been remarkably consistent. Soon after returning from France in 1781, where he had helped negotiate the loans of silver that had established the bank in the first place, Paine entered the service of Congress as a paid propagandist for Robert Morris's fiscal program. His job was to "write and publish such pieces respecting the propriety, necessity and utility of taxation as might be likely to promote the public service of America."[82] That contract ended when Morris stepped down as superintendent of finance in 1784, but by 1786 Paine had "between eight and nine hundred pounds" on deposit at the Bank of North America.[83] It was only natural for him to defend it.[84]

Titled *Dissertations on Government, the Affairs of the Bank, and Paper Money*, Paine's pamphlet was a substantial rendition of his ideas about political economy. The longest, central section was dedicated to a painstaking dissection of the assembly's position on the bank, even more forensic than James Wilson's speech at the hearing of September 1785. "I have now gone through, line by line," Paine wrote, "every objection against the bank" put forward by the legislative committee in March, "and a more irrational, inconsistent, contradictory report will scarcely be found on the journals of any legislature in America."[85] But this direct attack was buttressed, at its beginning and end, by more philosophical discussions of the nature of republican government and finance. As Paine recognized, the question of the bank was deeply linked to a much larger debate that had been emerging through the middle of the decade. What kind of power did citizens and their elected representatives really have? What was it that made those citizens equal? And what were the limits of that democratic power, that equality? Paine's pamphlet, unlike Wilson's, addressed these questions head on.

As if to underscore the gravity of its subject, the pamphlet began with a definition of sovereignty, "a power over which there is no control, and which controls all others." Its first fifteen pages described a theory of sovereignty and government based on Paine's distinction between "despotic" states and republics. In a republic like America, he wrote, sovereignty was "where nature placed it, in the people." This difference was crucial. "A despotic government knows no principle but will," wrote Paine. By contrast, the citizens of a republic "renounce not only the despotic form, but the despotic principle, as well of governing as of being governed by mere will and power, and substitute in its place a government of justice." If ever "the administration of a republic" were to deviate from "certain fundamental principles of right and justice ... there is a kind of stepping out of the republican principle, and an approach towards the despotic one."[86] Republican government was defined, according to Paine, by its adherence to certain rules of justice.

These rules did not simply emerge from the will of the majority, even the majority of enfranchised citizens. Rather, republican citizens renounced the power to do anything "not right in itself, [merely] because a majority of them may have strength or numbers sufficient to accomplish it." This social "compact" was the "foundation of the republic." It meant there was no legitimate power to redistribute property or control from the wealthy to the many, as reformers wanted. "The security to the rich and the consolation to the poor is, that what each man has is his own," safe from "the despotism of numbers." Likewise, "the people in their original compact of equal justice or first principles of a republic, renounced, as despotic, detestable and unjust, the assuming a right of breaking and violating their engagements, contracts and compacts." Whereas despots could declare right wrong and wrong right, "the sovereignty in a republic is exercised to keep right and wrong in their proper and distinct places, and never to suffer the one to usurp the place of the other." In this way it would remain "a sovereignty of justice in contradistinction to a sovereignty of will."[87]

By constructing this dichotomy between despotic and republican sovereignty, Paine argued implicitly that there was only one viable option: the kind of government he advocated. By drawing this point out over the course of eight pages at the beginning of his pamphlet, Paine sought a quite different and much broader audience than James Wilson had done. Whereas Wilson addressed a political and financial elite that took the need to secure property against majoritarian tyranny for granted, Paine's step-by-step explanation was addressed to the ordinary constituents of the Pennsylvania legislature, those who had voted for reforming representatives in the last two elections. Nonetheless, Paine was making precisely the same point as Wilson. Legitimate power in a republic was limited by "rules of justice, of faith, and of honour." Revolutionary committees had given themselves powers "suited to the spur and exigency of the moment," Paine reminded his readers. But now it was time to stop thinking like "committee-men" and start thinking like "legislators," to govern not only "by the rule of the constitution" but also by "the principles of the republic."[88]

Paine, like Wilson, held up the prospect of future prosperity put in jeopardy by the unjust actions of the assembly. Even such "great improvements" as "inland navigation, building bridges, [and] opening roads of communication through the state" relied on the government's ability to secure credit through public confidence. Yet "the faith of the government, under the present mode of conducting it, cannot be relied upon," he concluded.[89] Westward economic development, predicated on extending inland communications, was tied up with what Wilson had called "the rules and maxims by which compacts are governed." Paine repeated Wilson's argument that different kinds of legislative acts had to be treated differently. The charter of incorporation "is of the nature of a deed or contract" between the republic and the bank, "signed, sealed, and delivered; and subject to the same general laws and principles as all other deeds and contracts are." It could not be retroactively undone. "That this is justice," Paine declared, "that it is the true principle of republican government, no man will be so hardy as to deny."[90]

At the same time as Paine's, another substantial essay appeared, defending the cause of the bank. The author was the elderly Philadelphia merchant, Pelatiah Webster, a cousin of Noah's and a fellow Yale graduate once ordained to the ministry in Massachusetts. The elder Webster had published a series of articles since the beginning of the revolutionary war in which he discussed financial and commercial matters. A supporter of Robert Morris and an advocate of centralizing the fiscal powers of the confederation, Webster had published his most famous work, *A Dissertation on the Political Union and Constitution of the Thirteen United States*, in 1783. James Madison would later cite this essay as providing the outlines of the federal constitution.[91] In his 1786 *Essay on Credit*, Webster followed James Wilson in asserting the authority of Congress and its charter of incorporation. More important, though, the repeal itself was a blow to "mutual confidence ... that band of union, which holds the states together." By withdrawing its "public and vigorous support" from the bank, Pennsylvania's assembly would "weaken the union" and "lessen its power of operation."[92]

Where Paine began with the question of sovereignty, Webster opened on another general principle. "Credit," he wrote, "is the confidence which mankind place in the virtue and good character of its object ... in a commercial sense, [it] is the confidence which people place in a man's integrity and punctuality in fulfilling his contracts and performing his engagements."[93] Speaking from the perspective of Philadelphia's merchant community, Webster set out to explain the role of credit in society, and of banking in particular. He gave a brief account of the history of banking in Europe before going on to detail the operations of the Bank of North America, and its advantages to the people at large. This explanation was designed both to dispel public misconceptions about the bank and to impress readers with its importance. "The force and energy of credit," Webster asserted, "perfectly well established and permanent, is vast beyond conception." Harnessed by an institution that was at once private and "in some sense" public, such force and energy had "extensive utility and public importance."[94]

If a bank was so useful to society, why not operate one directly through the government, under public ownership? Webster answered this question in two ways. First, because merchants were the best people to direct the operations of a bank, being the most "acquainted with its nature and principles." Second, to prevent it from becoming an instrument of "tyranny in the government." A privately owned bank, by contrast, would be "a check and restraint on government, when it becomes oppressive." The bank's proprietors, "the rich men of the state," would oppose "needless popular clamors," for Webster declared, "the rich have an interest in their poor fellow-citizens, and (as some men use their wives) however tyrannical they may be *themselves*, they will not suffer *any body else* to tyrannize over them."[95] Just as husbands ruled over their wives, according to Webster's clerical training, so the rich through the agency of the bank would protect Pennsylvania from the tyranny of the legislative majority. "The influence of merchants is the safest of any that can affect a government," he noted.[96]

Such sentiments can have had little influence on the farmers and artisans addressed by Paine. As in his earlier writings on political economy, Webster made his appeal upwards, to an imagined set of detached and relatively uninformed statesmen. In other words, his rhetorical strategy did not register the revolutionary change in the location of sovereignty that Paine's did. The older man's writing reflected the pattern of colonial politics under which he had spent most of his career. He showed an awareness of the conditions of contemporary debate only while ironically signaling his disapproval. "*Public faith*," he wrote, "is an old threadbare topic of argument, and is as much *out of fashion* as going to *church* or reading the *bible*, and has been dinned in the ears of some folks, till, like the doctrine of repentance to sinners, it rather nauseates than convicts."[97] Like the New England ministers Enos Hitchcock and Zabdiel Adams, Webster mistrusted revolutionary upheaval. Like them, he associated the practices and values of Christianity with those of the liberal social order characterized by his broad notion of credit.

Webster's social and political vision was founded on "the sacred force of contracts." In this, if not in his explicit invocation of religion, he aligned perfectly with Wilson and Paine. Sensing his own distance from the popular mood, Webster feared his arguments would do more to "disgust" than to "persuade" the postrevolutionary public.[98] It was clear to him that not all Pennsylvanians, not all Americans, shared his commitment to the concept of public faith or to the primacy of contractual justice. Not broad consensus but precisely the opposite was what led these doctrines to be "dinned into the ears of some folks," by his own essays and, in a different form, by the likes of Thomas Paine. Webster no doubt had a confused and anachronistic sense of his own audience, but he also shrewdly identified the limits of his rhetoric. He bluntly and tactlessly aligned himself with "the rich men of the state," with the mercantile influence, and therefore with the Bank of North America. The public good would be best served, he concluded, by committing the government's support to their interests.

However different were their relationships to the bank, the foundations of their arguments, and the social outcomes they envisioned, Wilson, Paine, and

Webster's thought overlapped in one crucial respect. They each saw the conflict over the bank charter as a battle between legislative, majoritarian sovereignty and what they believed to be a deeper republican principle, the rule of
law and the "sacred force of contracts." Especially in Pennsylvania, where the
constitution of 1776 had deliberately vested so much power in the unicameral
assembly, this was a battle over the meaning and outcome of the revolution
itself. Addressing it required defining fundamental concepts like sovereignty
and credit. It required each author not merely to assert the contest between
majoritarian and contractarian justice, but to argue the merits of the latter. In
doing so they helped to formulate more explicitly than ever before the linea-
ments of a general political vision. This was a vision with diverse appeal, but
one which unmistakably favored the private power of property and contract
over the public power of popular legislatures.

In the months after Paine and Webster's pamphlets came out, petitions organized by friends of the bank began to reach the assembly in Philadelphia,
"praying that the charter of the bank of North America may be revived, in
such manner that in future its existence be determined by the laws of the
land, administered in the courts of justice, and not otherwise."[99] The courts,
not the legislature, and therefore legal principles rather than popular politics,
should govern the bank's fate in future. Thomas Willing published a note of
thanks "for the honorable and voluntary aid thus publicly given by my fellow-
citizens."[100] All this led up to an assembly debate held over several days towards the end of March, published the same year by the young Irish-born
journalist Mathew Carey. "No subject of debate that has been agitated before
the legislature of Pennsylvania ever drew such crowded audiences as attended
the house during the four days the debate lasted," reported Thomas Paine.[101]
This time Robert Morris spoke on behalf of the bank, and William Findley
against it. In many ways, it was the culmination of two years of struggle.

Yet that meant the arguments put forward had all been rehearsed many
times before, first in the antibank petitions and in the report of the original
legislative committee, then in Wilson's counterblast, in the debate surrounding the final passage of the repeal act, and in the letters, pamphlets, and petitions on both sides that had continued to flow since that decision was made
in September 1785. Findley pointed once again to the bank's tendency to concentrate power and wealth, and to the way that concentration undermined
republican equality. He also argued that repealing the charter did not interfere with property rights. The proprietors could simply carry on their business
without the protection of incorporation. Morris responded with a point-by-
point response to the specific charges against his bank, much like James Wilson's speech a year before. Denying that the bank had undue influence over
the politics of the state, Morris pointed to the irony of the charge, given that
the bank was under a political attack. "There are certain gentlemen from the
country, who possess a kind of magic," he said, that seemed to be far more

influential than his own "reasoning."[102] It was this democratic magic that had led to the charter's repeal in the first place.

When the debate was over and a vote called, the bank was defeated once again, by a vote of forty-one to twenty-eight. The same reforming politicians who had been elected in 1784 still controlled the majority in the assembly. The publicity campaign mounted since the previous September had not changed that. But, on the other hand, it was yet to have its effect at the polls. The new elections in the fall of 1786 presented the opportunity for a change of legislators and a corresponding change of fortunes for the bank. As the newspaper war grew more and more heated through the summer, with publicists on each side accusing the other of corruption and ulterior motives, Willing took pains to reassure his investors that the bank was "going on with our business, having experienced no diminution of confidence among the trading or country interest."[103] Amidst charges of corruption and betrayal, the reform movement had failed to turn around the hard times faced by western farmers. They had little faith in the political system. That gave the supporters of the bank an opportunity to take back the assembly.

The election of 1786 was a victory for Morris and his party. Seven of their number did not return to their seats, while fully twenty-four of the forty-two reformers had been defeated. Not counting the new members, the probank party now had a majority of six. Artisans in the city broke with the reform slate, reflecting Paine's split with his fellow Constitutionalists. His pamphlet had done its work. Benjamin Franklin, a figure of enormous influence who was not only a Constitutionalist but also, like Paine, a friend of Robert Morris and the bank, had returned to the state and taken the post of president of the Executive Council. And even in the countryside, where voter turnout was especially low, many of the reforming delegates had failed to win re-election. Those who arrived in Philadelphia that winter to replace them had ambivalent views on the bank. Among them was a lawyer, Hugh Henry Brackenridge, elected for Westmoreland County alongside William Findley himself. During the campaign, Brackenridge told his constituents that Findley and his allies were ignoring the true interests of the west in order to pursue their vendetta. "All last year was taken up about the bank," he wrote. "The devil take them and the bank both."[104]

"There are local interests of this western country to which it is necessary that particular attention be paid," Brackenridge had written in the new *Pittsburgh Gazette*. The real problem for western and rural people, he claimed, was not the bank but speculators and "land jobbers" who were "running away with our property." [105] Brackenridge promised Westmoreland voters that he would work to give them the same advantages as speculators when it came to buying up land with state debt certificates. The problem was, when he got to Philadelphia, he quickly began to change his mind. "A representative is not supposed to be a mere machine," Brackenridge wrote, "a clock wound up, to run for many hours in the same way."[106] Rather, legislators should be open to persuasive arguments and new ways of thinking. Once in Philadelphia, the young lawyer soon found himself taken under the wing of the city's commercial gentlemen. Never strongly committed to Findley's reforming ideas in the first place, Brackenridge soon came to see things from Robert Morris's perspective. Claiming to have been *"struck by the power of reason,"* he led the campaign *against* the land payment bill he had pledged to support.[107]

Of course, this excuse did not convince Brackenridge's constituents, nor even his friends. "History, in my opinion, can scarcely produce a man so eminent for his vanity, so prone to corruption and servility, as well as every other baneful quality proper to dignify a contemptible tool," said one westerner later. "On his appearance in this country I considered him as a man of virtue and was his friend ... I am not now his enemy, but I despise him, as I have and ever will engines of oppression."[108] Even before the report of his speech was published in Pittsburgh, word had traveled westward. Brackenridge, wrote one correspondent to the *Gazette*, had "sold the good will of his country for a dinner of some stockholder's fat beef."[109] He was just another example of the corrupting influence of wealth and society in the state capital. "He may expect the people to look upon him with indignation and treat him with contempt," wrote Findley. When confronted with his broken promise, Findley claimed that Brackenridge had replied, "the people were all fools."[110]

"If they would let Mr Morris alone, he would make Pennsylvania a great people," Brackenridge was said to have remarked, "but they will not suffer him to do it."[111] In fact, it was no longer the voters of Pennsylvania who stood in the way of Morris's ambitions, at least when it came to his central concern, the bank. He already controled enough of the new assembly. As Brackenridge reminded the inhabitants of Westmoreland county in a lengthy defense of his legislative conduct, he had never promised to vote one way or the other on the bank. "This case of the certificates is the only one with respect to which I changed my mind." With the help of his new allies, he had succeeded in having five thousand acres assigned to endow an academy for Pittsburgh, and in establishing a new county with the city as its seat.[112] A vote for the bank was an easy gift for him to give in exchange. All that remained for Findley and his allies were legislative delaying tactics. "The opposers of the bank, finding their cause as unpopular as it is unjust, are endeavouring to confound what they cannot confute," wrote Paine in early March, 1787.[113] A week later, the bill for rechartering the bank was passed.

Had Brackenridge and others betrayed their own voters? Or were they simply taking a more enlarged and liberal view? In November 1786, just as the new legislators were arriving in Philadelphia, George Washington wrote to his brother Bushrod on the subject of representation. "That representatives ought to be the mouth of their constituents, I do not deny," he wrote. But when it came to "national matters," it would only cause "embarrasment" if they held themselves strictly to voters' instructions. In such matters "there must be a yielding of the parts to coalesce the whole." Whereas "a county, a district, or even a state might decide on a measure" thought to be beneficial "in its separate and unconnected state," that measure "may be repugnant to the interest of the nation, and eventually to the state itself" as part of the union. Surely, then, it was better if the legislators were left "to judge from the nature of the case and the evidence before them."[114] As he had put it more bluntly the month before: "I am no friend to instructions."[115] Representative legislatures could be tools for Washington's idea of good government, but only if representatives themselves were free from popular control—free to follow the dictates of their own reason, and the "rules of justice, of faith, and of honor."

Battles like the one over the Bank of North America were part of a larger struggle to define what those ideas meant, and entrench them in the political culture of the new republic. Gentlemen at the seats of American commerce in Philadelphia and New York worked to extend their intellectual influence into the hinterlands of the west at the same time as they solidified their economic control over the same regions. In the novel he wrote some years later, Hugh Henry Brackenridge declared that "genius and virtue are independent of rank and fortune."[116] In practice, though, those things were difficult to distinguish. Mostly, those who had the rank and fortune to travel widely and have diverse business interests, hold positions of command, and influence public affairs, were those who seemed the most possessed of "genius and virtue." They were the ones most likely to present "enlarged" and "federal" opinions, and to help define what those words meant. This process of definition was an ongoing one, tangled up with the day-to-day action of politics. It was, in fact, just like the way the bank itself slowly and imperceptibly augmented its own capital and influence. Over time, gentlemen carved out the exclusive power to define justice itself.

CHAPTER FIVE

Rebellion

*Unless power is lodged somewhere to control the vice and folly of the people
we shall soon be involved in all the horrors of anarchy and confusion.*

—WILLIAM ELLERY, NEWPORT LAWYER, 1786

EVERYWHERE IN THE United States during the 1780s, commercial gentlemen struggled against popular movements and representative assemblies
over the nature of society and the balance of power in the new republic. These
struggles were far from uniform. They differed from state to state and region
to region, determined by circumstances and forces that could be traced far
back into the colonial past. In the southern states, as David Ramsay pointed
out to Thomas Jefferson, the weakness of gentlemen's control resulted in the
"temporising" measures that protected debtors and, in Ramsay's view, undermined the pursuit of justice.[1] There society was relatively tranquil. But the
case was different in the north. It was there that the social conflict simmering
since the war's end finally broke out into armed insurrection. It was there that
the new republic's future seemed to be once more at stake. And it was in this
moment, finally, that gentlemen could begin to acknowledge just what kind
of struggle they were waging.[2]

I. Countryside Rising

Of all the revolutionary constitutions adopted by the newly independent
American states, the one designed for Massachusetts by John Adams was
among the most conservative. Adams's vision of politics demanded that only
those whose personal wealth made them truly independent of all other men
could properly participate in matters of state. His classical notion of a balanced
constitution demanded representation for property as well as people, the aristocratic as well as the popular element in society.[3] Thus, the politics of Massachusetts in the mid-1780s differed substantially from those of Pennsylvania.

Subject to minimum property requirements, the bicameral General Court sitting in Boston was consistently dominated by commercial and mercantile interests centered in the east. The reform movement that determined the shape of Pennsylvania politics was stymied in Massachusetts. Not that such a movement did not exist. But unable to find expression in legislative politics, unhappy rural and western communities looked to other measures, other strategies with which to make their voices heard and to defend their interests. It began as it had in Pennsylvania, with conventions and a flood of petitions to the government. But by the summer of 1786, unrest in the countryside would begin to overflow into rebellion.

Where governments in South Carolina and Virginia, for example, passed stay laws and delayed tax collection in the face of economic hardship, Massachusetts led the way in taxing its people and paying its war debts. At the end of 1776, after the fight against Britain moved southwards, taxation began to increase. It continued to do so after 1781 as both Congress and the state faced the burden of public debt. Petitions for relief, and public conventions airing grievances against the state government, were commonplace from the beginning of the decade. An excise levied in November 1781 on wines and spirits, coaches and carriages, and on tea, generated particular anger. "We esteem it as a matter of great grievance that excise should be paid on any articles of consumption in a free republic," complained the townsmen of Hadley, in Hampshire, one of the westernmost counties.[4] Massachusetts had not fought a revolution to pay taxes on tea. Nor did western farmers think it fair that such taxes should go into the pockets of eastern merchants who held public securities, or even worse, to pay the salaries of public officials like Governor John Hancock.

Heavy taxes, scarce money, and high burdens of debt naturally went along with each other. Conventions like the one in Hadley sought remedies across the board. As rural people were doing all over the United States, they called for the state government to halt tax and debt collection until the economic situation improved. Sometimes they went further than that. In February 1782, for example, three hundred people gathered in Pittsfield, Berkshire County, to prevent the court of common pleas from sitting. Samuel Ely, a Yale graduate and former Connecticut preacher, led demonstrations against the courts in Northampton, Hampshire's county seat, where the state Supreme Court held its circuit session. Ely was sent to jail in Springfield, but in June supporters came to set him free, resulting in a major confrontation between protesters and government troops. Nor was it only men who escaped the custody of the courts with the help of angry western citizens. In September, a crowd rescued two oxen from the sheriff of Berkshire County. Such disturbances continued throughout the west in 1782 and 1783, with Continental officers' pay joining the list of grievances after the Newburgh conspiracy.[5] From the countryside's perspective, the revolution had not turned out as expected.

Petitioners and would-be reformers, let alone rioters and disturbers of the peace, received little sympathy from gentlemen in Boston. "Some men among us ... under the guise of watchful patriots, are finding fault with every public measure, with a design to destroy ... just confidence in government," wrote Samuel Adams to his cousin John in 1783.[6] The following year, he wrote to Noah Webster about the state of public affairs, outlining his concerns about "county conventions." These conventions, he told Webster, were stirred up by "designing men" in order to gain personal influence. Demagogues prayed "upon credulous though well meaning persons," intending "to keep this country, who may be happy if they will, long in a state of discord and animosity." It was right that the people should be vigilant towards their government, Adams wrote. "Such attention is the people's great security. But," he went on, "there is decency and respect due to constitutional authority." Those who opposed "the weight of government lawfully exercised, must be enemies to our happy revolution and the common liberty." Elections, not conventions, were the proper means of making the legislature accountable to public grievances, "without the aid of any self-created conventions or societies of men whatever."[7]

Adams's attitude was representative of mercantile interests in Boston and other seaport towns. A Boston town meeting in March 1784 "unanimously determined to express the sorrow of the town" at the behavior of the western counties. The General Court made only small gestures towards the accommodation of western demands, especially with regard to credit arrangements. While South Carolina was passing installment acts to regulate collection of debts, the furthest Massachusetts went was to make them payable in property as well as in specie, and to make sure that the value of property would be assessed by a neutral third party, not creditors themselves. The creditors could, however, simply wait for the law to expire before demanding payment.[8] In 1784, the state did finally reduce the tax burden. Consequently, there were no county conventions or demonstrations that year. At the same time, however, this concession put pressure on the public accounts and threatened the holders of public debt. Commerce in Massachusetts was depressed as a result of the British Navigation Acts. As in Charleston, local merchants in the port towns faced competition from their British counterparts, who were busy flooding the market with cheap goods. From their perspective, commotions in the west only made economic recovery more difficult.

Many blamed Massachusetts' economic hardships on the moral failings of its citizens. They had, some said, developed an addiction to luxury which led them to buy beyond their means and build up debts they could not pay. Americans were betraying the revolutionary cause by "imitating the Britons in every idle amusement and expensive foppery [and] every unmeaning and fantastic extravagance." As Samuel Adams put it to his cousin, "You would be surprised to see the ... expensive living of too many, the pride and vanity of dress which pervades through every class, confounding every distinction between the poor and the rich and evincing the want both of example and economy."[9] For Adams, social order and public virtue relied on clear distinctions between classes, while economic hardship went hand in hand with excessive consumption. "We are exchanging prudence, virtue, and economy," the *Massachusetts Centinel* lamented, "for those glaring spectres of luxury, prodigality, and profligacy."[10] Yet these vices could hardly be pinned on western farmers. Rather it was the behavior of rival urban elites that shocked Adams's sensibilities. City luxury and country revolt were two sides of the same coin, in his view: they were aspects of a general breakdown of the proper social order.

The reality was that an older generation of political leaders had begun to fear that they were losing their grip on Massachusetts politics and society.[11] Clubs like Boston's Sans Souci seemed to represent the rise of new men, upstart merchants who had profited in the war and were now seeking to displace the old establishment. As one writer complained to the *Boston Gazette* in 1785, such men had little respect for the sacrifices and achievements of their elders. "How are our worthy patriots treated? Men who risked their lives and property in the cause of freedom—lent their hard money to assist in the contest, and took securities or paper money for it, which now lie dormant in their desks." These *"once valuable men,"* the *Gazette*'s correspondent concluded, are now "held up in polite assemblies as rigid republicans, men of contracted minds, only because they will not conform to gaming, sabbath breaking, drinking and every other vice."[12] This kind of profligate behaviour, charged Adams and his allies, set a bad example to the countryside. Luxury was corruption. Republican virtue required discipline. How could Boston expect to enforce justice among rural debtors if gentlemen there were not frugal and virtuous themselves?

John Hancock had been governor ever since the new state constitution had come into operation in October, 1780. It was he who, in the eyes of the old guard, most represented the degeneration of leadership and republican values in postrevolutionary Massachusetts.[13] His style of life resembled that of Robert Morris or William Bingham, Philadelphia's merchant princes, more than the self-denying Christian ideal promoted by the likes of Adams. His public salary was a matter of disgust in rural petitions. By the end of January 1785, under mounting pressure from his enemies in Boston, Hancock finally resigned his office. In the contest that followed, Samuel Adams put his support behind James Bowdoin, a merchant, scientist, and the first president of the Bank of Massachusetts. Bowdoin was also an investor in state securities. He vowed to defend the public credit and meet rural agitators with a firm hand. In the voting, he won in commercial districts and lost heavily in rural ones. With the decision thrown into the senate, the representatives of property and aristocracy did what was expected—they chose Bowdoin. "I confess," wrote Adams, "it is what I have long wished for."[14] The days of the old republicans were not over yet.

For farmers and rural communities, Bowdoin's victory signaled a new phase of austerity and merchant rule. One of the new governor's first acts was to issue a "Proclamation for the Encouragement of Piety, Virtue, Education and Manners, and for the Suppression of Vice," drafted by Samuel Adams himself, which declared the government's commitment to strict public order.[15] Without outright support in the General Court, Bowdoin's tax proposals—which involved raising massive new sums and beginning to pay off the principal as well as interest on the public debt—failed to pass in his first year in office. Yet the pressure of both tax and debt continued to weigh on western communities, and a renewed flow of petitions began to arrive in Boston, calling for paper money and tender laws. Rather than give way, the General Court hardened, and with it the commercial interests in the east fell into step behind Bowdoin. In the spring of 1786, he easily won re-election. The assembly wholeheartedly rejected the paper money proposal, and they levied heavier taxes that year than any since the end of the war.[16] While all this was taking place in Massachusetts, however, its southern neighbor Rhode Island was taking a quite different path.

Through the middle of the decade, agitation for relief measures had taken much the same form in Rhode Island as it had in other states. By the spring of 1786, however, it had reached a dangerous pitch. "The people are almost drove to desperation," one Rhode Islander wrote. Pressed by heavy taxation designed primarily to meet payments on the public war debt, people assembled in town meetings to demand a package of measures similar to those sought by the townsmen of western Pennsylvania and western Massachusetts. Paper money, a land bank, and the postponement of tax and debt payments were the Rhode Islanders' key demands. In February, Gloucester County's meeting called for "a more easy and equitable way of paying taxes," and Coventry's for "a paper currency . . . to relieve the present distresses of the inhabitants of this state."[17] The state assembly was reluctant to accede to such demands. In the run-up to elections that spring, it granted bounty payments to sheep and hemp farmers, a four-month postponement of tax collection, and some protections to the property of debtors. But it rejected the land bank and paper money. The latter, claimed one newspaper correspondent, would be "a perversion of law, of justice, and of humanity."[18]

Meanwhile, towns continued to pass resolutions and write petitions calling for reform and relief measures. Their leaders met two weeks before the election to agree upon a pro-reform slate, naming John Collins as their candidate for governor. At the head of their ticket was the slogan, "To Relieve the Distressed." When it came, on April 19, the election was a landslide. The governor, his deputy, and most of the mercantile party were thrown out of office, and a radical, reforming legislature was installed. All this was in spite of the over-representation of Providence and Newport, the bulwarks of merchant power, mandated in the 1663 Charter. The state's small size, in contrast to

Massachusetts, might have made it easier for the reformers to organize. More important, though, was the absence of property requirements for voting and officeholding. "We are now experiencing one of the greatest revolutions ever known in this state which has long been noted for one of the most fluctuating governments in the union," wrote one astonished supporter of the old regime. "A paper currency is thought to be inevitable, which if made will be fraught with a thousand evils." For poor and rural Rhode Islanders, the triumph over "numerous gentlemen" was celebrated like another Lexington and Concord.[19]

Among the first acts of the new government was to introduce emissions of paper money. As the law's preamble put it, its aim was "to quiet the minds and to alleviate the distressed situation and circumstances of the good citizens of this state."[20] At the same time, the new government made these new paper bills legal tender in all contracts and debts. That meant that if a creditor refused to accept the money, the debtor could lodge it with the local court and consider the debt paid. If the creditor did not relent and accept the money within three months, it was forfeited to the state.[21] From the perspective of commercial justice, this measure was tantamount to robbery. But even more offensive to the merchant community and its representatives were the penalties the legislature imposed in June for actions that would contribute to the new currency's depreciation, actions that included refusing it, accepting it at depreciated rates, and even criticising it in conversation. Such "subversive" behaviour was to be punishable by a heavy fine, and ultimately disenfranchisement.[22] Radical legislators knew that if their policies were to succeed, they would need to force merchants into line—or else, exclude them from the community altogether.

Not everyone, however, was willing to take such a hard line. June's draconian measures passed with a reduced majority of only six votes, over the strong objections of the opposition members. Moreover, even these measures did not succeed in breaking the merchants' resistance. Paper money continued to circulate at depreciating rates, and the depreciation was getting worse. So in August, Governor Collins called a special session of the assembly. There had been, he wrote, a "combination of influential men against the good and wholesome laws of the state." Henceforth, according to an act passed by the special session, any case arising from the paper money laws would be heard by a court immediately. Fearing that juries might be subjected to intimidation tactics by the merchants and their allies, the assemblymen also stipulated that such trials would be held before judges alone. Opponents, of course, immediately sprung on this provision, claiming that it violated "the natural and constitutional rights of the citizen."[23] Once again, the debate took on the contours of the battles in South Carolina and New York over loyalist property and confiscation. On one side was the will of the democratically elected legislature. On the other, natural right, the common law tradition, and a notion of justice founded on property and contract.

Fierce opposition to the new government's measures met with equal anger on the side of the reformers. Violence lay just under the surface. Some radicals talked of carrying the heads of their enemies on poles through the streets. "How unhappy the people," lamented one merchant, "where the laws are so unstable as ours, or rather where there is none at all."[24] Nonetheless, a core of Rhode Island merchants and their allies refused to be cowed, either by the measures of the radical assembly or by the intimidation tactics of paper money advocates. In Newport and Providence, at least, there were sufficiently strong mercantile communities to establish a resistance. They could draw strength and courage from their out-of-state connections, from the firm stand of the Massachusetts government, and from the scorn that was beginning to be heaped on the Rhode Island radicals from many of the presses across the new nation. "The merchants have shut up their stores," recorded one Congressman, "notwithstanding the severe penalties of the law. How the matter will terminate remains uncertain, some are apprehensive of a dissolution of government in that state."[25] As long as both sides refused to back down, it seemed as though the outcome might be anarchy.

Within Rhode Island, the merchant faction drew strength and support from other elements of the state's social and political establishment—from the clergy, and from organisations like the Society of the Cincinnati. Although openly disparaging paper money was now, of course, illegal, its opponents found ways of sharing their views and encouraging one another in their resistance. Exclusive bodies like the Cincinnati provided ideal venues for organizing local elites against the government—and nothing could have better fulfilled the officers' fantasy of reliving the glory of the revolution. At that year's Fourth of July Dinner, the oration was given by none other than Enos Hitchcock, the old army chaplain who had been friends with Joel Barlow, whose *Discourse on Education* had been published the year before, and who now served at Providence's First Congregational Church. Ostensibly, Hitchcock simply recounted the tale of the revolution itself. But his listeners would have been able to see through his words to their parallels with the contemporary situation.

"By their increasing wealth and power," Hitchcock told his audience that Fourth of July, the prerevolutionary colonists of British America "became the object of avarice, envy and jealousy. Measures were formed to drain them of all the fruit of their labor and industry, upon principles totally subversive to the rights of men." Clearly, the same jealousy that had once motivated the British ministry now motivated Collins and his party of reformers. "But," Hitchcock went on, "the evil was too alarming and detestable to pass unnoticed. The genius of America, roused by reiterated and atrocious acts of tyranny and oppression, called forth the generous efforts of her sons, to oppose the destructive system; yea, to resist unto blood, rather than part with their freedom."[26] Was Hitchcock inciting the former officers to violent resistance against the new government of Rhode Island? No one would have been able to prove it in court. Yet for the commercial gentlemen of Providence and Newport, and their allies in the state establishment, the situation had become something akin to revolutionary. Once more, as they saw it, they were being forced to defend their property—and what they understood to be their fundamental rights—against a government that did not share their vision of justice.

While the stand-off in Rhode Island between merchants and reformers had "convulsed the state nearly to a civil war," things were also coming to a head in Massachusetts.[27] According to Samuel Adams, the countryside was beset with "internal enemies . . . influencing many weak men to withhold the necessary aid of taxes, to destroy the public faith."[28] Some in the east believed those agitating for reform were in fact agents of the British, "whose every wish is for our overthrow and ruin"—a charge that was not totally outside the realm of possibility, given how recently the leaders of Vermont's republic had been open to negotiation with Britain.[29] As in the years before 1784, farmers went beyond simply holding conventions and writing petitions to the legislature. Courts were the closest and most direct embodiments of eastern authority and financial oppression, so they became protesters' primary targets. If the judges could not sit, they could not perform the legal rituals necessary to deprive men of their livelihoods, to have their land and cattle seized and sold, or to censure and punish the protesters themselves. The strategy of western resistance that emerged in the summer of 1786, then, was once more to shut down the courts.[30]

By September 2, Governor Bowdoin was forced to respond to the insurgents. He issued a proclamation against their "high handed offence . . . fraught with the most fatal and pernicious consequences." Preventing the operation of the courts, Bowdoin declared, "must tend to subvert all law and government; to dissolve our excellent constitution, and introduce universal riot, anarchy, and confusion, which would probably terminate in absolute despotism." He called on the officers of government, "civil and military . . . to prevent and suppress all such violent and riotous proceedings," and on "the good people of this commonwealth" to help them. Finally, he authorized the state's attorney general to prosecute the "ringleaders and abettors" of the court-closure in Northampton, and "of any similar violation in future, whensoever and wheresoever it shall be perpetrated in this commonwealth."[31] In short, Bowdoin sought to mobilize all the apparatus at his disposal, including not only the formal instruments of the state, but sympathetic elements of the social order as well. As in Rhode Island, the stage was set for a struggle between gentlemen and their inferiors, except this time the state itself was on the gentlemen's side.

Or rather, the core leadership of the state was for the gentlemen. But not all its representatives were. In the first weeks of September, 1786, the chief justice of the Court of Common Pleas of Berkshire county, Dr. William Whit-

ing, wrote an essay that declared him to be on the side of the insurgency. Calling himself Gracchus, after the Roman tribune who had favored redistribut-
ing land to citizen farmers, Whiting invoked an egalitarian concept of justice
to condemn the policies of the Boston administration. "Whenever some citizens have it in their power by compulsion to enrich themselves by the same
means that impoverishes and depresses some other orders of people," wrote
the judge, "that government is either defective in its original constitution, or
else the laws are unjustly and unequally administered." Listing the people's old
grievances, including taxation, debt, seizures, and the scarcity of money, he
declared that "it is the indispensable duty of the people to exert themselves"
to remove such injustices. "Whoever brands them with the odious names of
mobbers, rioters, and disturbers of the peace, ought to be considered as being
of the number of those who wish to enrich themselves by the plunder of their
fellow citizens." It was, in essence, a call for renewed revolution.[32]

Men in Berkshire took him at his word. On September 12, they shut down
the county courts. With the hay harvested, this was the time of year when
there was little work to be done in the fields. Farmers could instead take
up the work of insurgency. Across Massachusetts and New Hampshire, then,
early autumn saw an upswelling of organized dissidence, with courts stopped
in Northampton, Worcester, Concord, Taunton, Exeter, Great Barrington,
and Springfield. Yeomen in Connecticut declared themselves "in readiness at
a moment's warning, to embody" as a mass and stop the debtor's court at New
Haven.[33] From New York, where Congress was, General Henry Lee wrote to
George Washington with the alarming news. "The period seems to be fast approaching," he reported, "when these United States must determine to establish a permanent capable government or submit to the horrors of anarchy and
licentiousness.... Weak and feeble government are not adequate to resist such
high handed offences."[34] By October, things were looking even worse. "The
insurgents," Lee wrote, "have in very formidable shape taken possession of the
town of Springfield, at which place the supreme court was sitting."[35] By shutting down Massachusetts' courts, protesters struck a powerful blow against
gentlemen's justice.

Meanwhile in Rhode Island, it was in a courtroom that the next battle was
being fought between the state's merchant community and its reforming government. In the case of *Trevett v. Weeden*, the defendant was being sued for
refusing to accept paper money. Held before a regular session of the state's
highest court, without a jury, it was to be the test case for the whole system of
paper money and tender laws established by the assembly. On the side of Mr.
Weeden, the defendant, two attorneys had agreed to appear without charging
a fee. One was the established Newport lawyer Henry Marchant, and the other
was the president of Rhode Island's Society of the Cincinnati and a delegate
to Congress, Major General James Varnum. These formidable gentlemen represented the full weight of the state's legal and political establishment—but

rather than a rich merchant, their client Mr. Weeden was a simple butcher. The case gave every appearance of having been carefully chosen by the merchant side. It was to be as much an exercise in public relations as a legal battle, with the aim of influencing public sympathy against the government and its measures.

The trial began on September 25 in a courtroom packed with spectators. It was Varnum who handled most of the argument—at least according to the pamphlet he published the following year, which told the tale with himself in the role of hero. Varnum summed up his position in the preface to this work. "The late political measures," he wrote, had produced "a system of revenue and finance, subversive of private contracts, and public faith!"[36] What Varnum had to accomplish in *Trevett v. Weeden* was similar to Alexander Hamilton's task in *Rutgers v. Waddington.* He needed to show not that his client had not broken the law, but that the law itself was null and void. To do that, Varnum needed to establish the principles that would restrict and counteract the power of the assembly. He also needed to convince the judges, who were appointed on one-year terms by the legislature itself, that they had the power to annul its laws. It was a daunting task. But if successful, Varnum would add another plank to the bulwark that was gradually being constructed by American gentlemen in defense of property and contract, against the political power of legislative majorities.

At the center of Varnum's argument was the assembly's attack on trial by jury, which was, he said, protected by both Magna Carta and the English Bill of Rights. The legislature, Varnum argued, had "aimed ... at a summary process, flattering themselves that the judges, being elected by the legislators, would blindly submit to their sovereign will and pleasure. But, happy for the state, our courts in general are not intimidated by the dread, nor influenced by the debauch of power!"[37] Indeed, "the attempts of the British Parliament to deprive us of this mode of trial were among the principle causes" of the revolution; and that revolution had not been made in order to institute legislative tyranny. "Were there no bounds to limit and circumscribe the legislature," Varnum told the court, "were they to be actuated by their own will, independent of the fundamental rules of the community, the government would be a government of men, and not of laws."[38] And just as Hamilton had done, he cited Vattel on the "general principles that are equally binding on all governments ... the laws of nature and of nations." The judges, argued Varnum, were "bound by the laws of nature in preference to any human laws."[39]

Closing with emotive invocations of liberty and the "fathers of our country," Varnum demanded that Rhode Island's judges nullify the assembly's law—and to the cheers of genteel onlookers, they did.[40] While the chief justice recused himself, his four colleagues rendered a verdict for the defense, declaring the law inconsistent with the constitution and therefore impossible for them to enforce. It was a dramatic victory for the side of commercial justice. But of course, it was far from the end of the matter. To the majority in Rhode Island, the decision was an outrage. The townsmen of Coventry declared that the judges had acted beyond their mandate, and the state assembly called them to a special hearing. Here again, Varnum succeeded "by masterly display of legal talents" in preventing the judges from being replaced. Appointed on good behaviour, they could not, he argued, be dismissed "for a mere matter of opinion, without a charge of criminality."[41] Yet the victory did not have the lasting effect Varnum and his allies might have hoped for. Rather, it opened a new phase of hostilities between the majority and its opponents. Just when disturbances in Massachusetts reached the level of open rebellion, the very constitution of Rhode Island had begun to tear itself apart.

II. The Gentlemen Respond

"For Gods sake tell me," demanded George Washington in October 1786, "what is the cause of all these commotions?"[42] He had just been informed that "every thing is in a state of confusion in the Massachusetts" and "Rhode Island continues in a state of phrenzy and division on account of their paper currency."[43] In an effort to understand what was going on, Washington asked his correspondent which of three possible causes lay behind the upheavals. "Do they proceed from licentiousness," he asked, "British influence disseminated by the Tories, or real grievances which admit of redress?" The problem was, that last question was a political one—it depended on one's understanding of justice. From the perspective of commercial gentlemen, there could be no legitimate grievance against the system of property and contract that lay behind the insurgents' distress. There was no question of abandoning commitments to the public creditors that had to be met by taxation, nor of undermining public credit itself by adopting paper money and other debtor-relief measures, for any such measures would mean doing injustice to the creditors themselves. The insurgents would get no sympathy from gentlemen like Washington.

Instead, just as Samuel Adams had done the year before, Washington and his correspondents returned to "licentiousness" as the explanation for popular resistance. This was the idiom of the New England educationalists who argued that schooling must teach citizens obedience, or the republic would descend into anarchy. Freedom deserved the name of liberty as long as it was carried out within the rules of gentlemanly conduct—namely, of law, property, and contract. But if it followed other rules, such as the notion that settlers and not speculators owned their land regardless what the deed said, then it became licentiousness. In the minds of gentlemen, that kind of freedom bore a close resemblance to the anarchy predicted by ancient republican theory whenever the people had too much power. Whether it took the form of elected governments like Rhode Island's or popular insurrection like Massachusetts', the improper use of freedom was a threat. This notion allowed gentlemen to consider democratic assemblies and rural insurgencies as two sides of the same coin, and to pit themselves against both in the name of liberty and the republic.

Of all those who kept Washington informed during the crisis, none was more regular than his old army friend, General Henry Knox of Boston, who had served since the peace as secretary of war. Moving between Boston, Springfield, and New York, Knox was a vital conduit for information. He also had strong opinions about the insurgency, which he did not hesitate to include in his dispatches to Mount Vernon. As both a soldier and a Massachusetts native, he took to heart the fact that citizens of his own country were now in arms against the government he had fought to establish. He felt a duty to restore order and dignity to the state. As a good federal man, Knox saw events on a national scale too. What was happening in Massachusetts was only part of a larger problem among all the United States. "The machine works inversely to the public good in all its parts," he wrote to Washington. "Not only is state against state, and all against the federal head, but the states within themselves possess the name only without having the essential concomitant of government, the power of preserving the peace."[44]

Knox understood the insurrection in Massachusetts, first and foremost, as a struggle between rich and poor. It was the weakness of government that had allowed the situation to get out of hand, but it was inequality that actually lay at its root. "The insurgents," Knox told Washington, "feel at once their own poverty, compared with the opulent, and their own force, and they are determined to make use of the latter, in order to remedy the former."[45] Their "creed," he wrote, declared that since all had participated in protecting American property from the British during the war, it "therefore ought to be the common property of all." Any opponent of this plan must be "an enemy to equity and justice, and ought to be swept from the face of the earth. In a word," Knox concluded, "they are determined to annihilate all debts public and private and have agrarian laws which are easily effected by the means of unfunded paper money which shall be a tender in all cases whatever."[46] It was clear to Knox that such people had a very different sense of justice from him and his fellow gentlemen—a difference that sprang ultimately from the inequality of power and wealth.

What was stirring in Massachusetts was "a formidable rebellion against reason, the principles of all government, and the very name of liberty," Knox declared. "This dreadful situation has alarmed every man of principle and property in New England." Such men had formerly been overly sanguine. They had believed that the virtue of the people would support a mild government. But now, "they start as from a dream," to "find that we are men, actual men, possessing all the turbulent passions belonging to that animal." "What is to afford us security," they ask, "against the violence of lawless men?" Thus, the "men of reflection, & principle, are determined ... to establish a government which shall have the power to protect them in their lawful pursuits." Americans could no longer consider themselves different from "other nations" in this respect. They must, Knox wrote, revert to "brutal force to support the laws," and to a government capable of exerting such force. "Unless this is done we shall be liable to be ruled by an Arbitrary and Capricious armed tyranny, whose word and will must be law."[47]

Even those who had not previously supported strengthening the federal government began to change their mind when confronted with the news from Massachusetts. "I myself have been an advocate for government free as air," wrote Rufus King to Berkshire county judge, Theodore Sedgwick. "My opinions have been established on the belief that my countrymen were virtuous, enlightened, and governed by a sense of right and wrong." Recent events, however, threatened to disabuse him. If indeed "the great body of the people are without virtue, and not governed by any internal restraints of conscience, there is but too much reason to fear," King wrote, "that the framers of our constitutions and laws have proceeded on principles that do not exist."[48] King had more sympathy than Knox for the rebels. "While I reverence the principles of rigorous justice, and earnestly desire that the constitution and laws may be superior to all opposition," he told his colleague Elbridge Gerry, "I feel compassion for those unfortunate men, who have thoughtlessly united in measures unauthorised by their sober reflections."[49] It was error, not wickedness, that inspired events in Massachusetts. But that did not mean the solution was any different. Government had to be strengthened in the face of the insurgents' leveling program.

Knox, as secretary of war to the Congress, took responsibility for planning a response to the insurrection. At Springfield was a federal armory containing 7,000 muskets along with powder and shot—when that town was occupied by the insurgents, defending the armory from seizure became Knox's top priority. From Springfield in October, Knox reported to Bowdoin that the insurgents were under the command of a revolutionary war veteran, Captain Daniel Shays. Shays had about 1,200 men, "embodied in a military manner," and 900 of them armed with muskets. Against them stood 900 men of the Massachusetts state militia mustered on Bowdoin's orders, "men of respectable character," Knox told John Jay, "and great property compared with their opponents."[50] At a meeting in Boston with Bowdoin and Rufus King, Knox developed a plan to put congressional forces at the disposal of the Massachusetts government. A federal force would be raised on the pretext of confronting Indians on the frontier, and it would be stationed at Springfield.[51] Knox told Washington that such an army would "tend to strengthening the principle of government as well as to defend the frontiers." Its real purpose was to support Bowdoin's rule in Massachusetts, to crush the rebellion and restore justice.

Yet when he returned to New York with King to put this plan into action, Knox found his efforts were of no avail. His resolution for raising new forces was passed "unanimously," as he reported to Washington. Carrying it out was a different matter. The $530,000 price tag proved to be too much for the meager resources commanded by Congress in 1786. When Congress put the requisition to the states, only Virginia answered the call.[52] Those assigned the task of recruiting the new troops found they had no money with which to do so. The federal force remained augmented on paper only, and meanwhile, Shays and his men continued to occupy the town of Springfield. To Knox, Washington, and many other gentlemen, the failure seemed to prove everything that had been said about the weakness and inadequacy of the federal government under the Articles of Confederation. There was now what amounted to open rebellion in Massachusetts, with armed men organized behind experienced leaders and threatening to take over the country's foremost military depot— and there seemed to be nothing that Congress could do about it.

"Government is prostrated in the dust," lamented Colonel David Humphreys, one of the former aides in Washington's military family. "The leaders of the mob, whose fortune and measures are desperate, are strengthening themselves daily, and it is expected that they will soon take possession of the continental magazine at Springfield." Humphreys had a clear interpretation of what was going on, and it aligned closely with Knox's view. The poor and indebted were taking advantage of the weakness of republican governments, and especially of Congress itself, to improve their situation. "The wheels of the great political Machine can scarcely continue to move much longer, under their present embarrassment." Things were rapidly advancing to a final crisis, Humphreys believed—and "in the event of civil discord," he told Washington, "you could not remain neuter."[53] There may be, he admitted, "a few real grievances ... but it rather appears to me, that there is a licentious spirit prevailing among many of the people; a levelling principle; a desire of change; and a wish to annihilate all debts public and private."[54] In such a situation, Washington himself would surely have to intervene on the side of property, distinction, and contract.

Humphreys had earlier that year returned from Paris, where he had served as secretary to the American delegation since the end of the war, under John Adams and Benjamin Franklin.[55] At home in Hartford, he returned to the company of his fellow Yale graduates, but as his letters to Washington show, he also remained connected to an incipient national political network. The core of that network, for Humphreys, was the Society of the Cincinnati. It was, he believed, no coincidence that the two New England states where rural insurrection had not become widespread were New Hampshire and his own Connecticut. In the former, John Sullivan, the president of the state Cincinnati branch, had become governor in June. "Genl Sullivan has behaved nobly," Humphreys reported to Washington in October, "& put a period to a very considerable insurrection, without the effusion of blood." Sullivan's success contrasted sharply, for Humphreys, with the prevarications of the civilian

Bowdoin. And in Connecticut, what gave Humphreys most cause for optimism was that at the recent legislative elections, "more gentlemen lately belonging to the Army, have been elected than on any former occasion." Even in Massachusetts, it was military men who put up the sternest resistance on behalf of government. Confronted by the rebels, Major David Cobb had declared, "I shall sit as a judge, or die as a general."[56]

It was clear to Humphreys that the former officers of the revolution would have an important part to play in protecting the new republic from encroaching anarchy and popular licentiousness. To preserve order and government had been one of the Cincinnati's founding purposes, after all. Yet in the summer and autumn of 1786, the organization itself was in crisis. Two years earlier, Washington had forced the national meeting of the society to accept amendments to its constitution that aimed to make the society more acceptable to its critics. But many state branches, including Connecticut's, had refused to ratify those amendments. John Sullivan's New Hampshire branch had led the movement against abandoning hereditary membership, and even Alexander Hamilton's New York branch had quibbled with Washington's proposals. With this situation unresolved, the national society was fractured and leaderless. A second national meeting was scheduled for the spring of 1787, but just what would take place, no one knew. The backlash against Washington's reforms had been strong. As Humphreys advised the general, "it would not be of any good consequence, or even advisable for you to attend the next general meeting."[57] The condition of the Cincinnati, in short, seemed to reflect the weakness of the Confederation itself.

The events in Massachusetts and Rhode Island took on a symbolic and emotional power for many gentlemen, especially those of New England. They seemed to represent the collapse and disappointment of all their bright hopes for the new republic, the opposite of Joel Barlow's optimistic predictions in the still-unfinished *Vision of Columbus*. Among the many written expressions of the shock and anxiety experienced by American gentlemen in this moment, perhaps the strangest was the mock epic poem written by Humphreys, Barlow, and several other friends, called *The Anarchiad*. The poem, published in twelve parts over the course of a year from October 1786 through the following summer, was a way of turning these poetic gentlemen's anxiety into something else, perhaps even endowing it with political power. By satirizing the insurgents and reformers, *The Anarchiad* became a weapon against change. Yet especially in its earliest numbers, it primarily served as a harbinger of chaos. A prose section published in November, for example, offered the following prediction:

> That a majority should be persuaded, by the power of intrigues and sophistry, to refuse a compliance with the requisitions of Congress— that a determination should be formed, and announced to the world, that we will not pay the interest on our foreign or domestic debts—that

we should furnish nothing for the support of the federal government—
that we should withdraw ourselves from the Union—that all government should be prostrated in the dust—that *mobs, conventions*, and
anarchy, should prevail for a limited time, and then—.... But I draw
the curtain; the picture is too melancholy to be viewed by a patriot
eye without prompting the tear of sensibility, and forcing the sigh of
sorrow.[58]

Such predictions spurred the gentlemen of the Cincinnati into action. After
the failure of Congressional requisitions, Henry Knox looked to the society he
had founded as the potential savior of the union. "I shall depend on the noble
and independent spirit of the late continental officers to step forward," he told
Jeremiah Wadsworth, vice president of the Connecticut society. The Massachusetts branch produced a series of resolutions, which expressed some sympathy with soldiers of the "*yet* unpaid army" who were tempted to join Shays
and his protestors, but warning that to do so would make them rebels. The
Cincinnati would not rest, the resolutions declared, until "public faith and
private credit are made the sacred objects of government."[59] In November,
delegates from all the New England branches, including Enos Hitchcock from
Rhode Island, met in Boston "upon confidential business," to plan their collective response to the insurrection. The network of officers maintained by the
Cincinnati since the end of the war now became the best hope of raising an
army in defense of government. As Mercy Otis Warren ironically observed in
December, "The Cincinnati who have been waiting a favourable tide to waft
them on to the strong fortress of nobility, are manifestly elated by the present
prospect."[60]

Still, there was no real progress until the early months of 1787. In December, Benjamin Lincoln wrote that "the time when and the manner how these
commotions are to end [is] concealed from me in the unturned pages of futu-
rity."[61] But when the new session of the Massachusetts legislature convened,
Bowdoin was finally able to declare a state of emergency, and set himself fully
against the insurrection. No longer would insurgent groups be given the right
to disperse within an hour of the Riot Act being read; now they were to be
treated as an enemy army. As for the matter of creating and supplying a government force, it was Lincoln, the president of the state Cincinnati, who found
the answer. "I went immediately to a club of the first characters in Boston," he
told Washington later, "and layed before them a full state of matters, and suggested to them the importance of their becoming loaners of part of their property if they wished to secure the remainder. A Subscription was set on foot in
the morning, headed by the Governour." Within twenty-four hours, the commercial gentlemen of Boston came up with the money.[62] As Lincoln had deftly
reminded them, it would serve primarily to protect their own property.

On January 25, with Benjamin Lincoln and his new army marching out
from Boston, Daniel Shays' men launched an attack against the magazine at

Springfield. They were repelled by canon fire that killed and wounded several men. Hearing of the engagement, Lincoln sped up his march, arriving in the area two days later. He was in such a rush, he reported, that "many of our supplies fell into their hands." But with the new army on the scene, any hope of the rebels taking the armoury had ended. For a few days, there was a negotiation between Shays and Lincoln, the former asking for a ceasefire while new petitions from the people were presented to the General Court. Lincoln refused. Then, on February 3, Shays attempted to escape by marching to the nearby town of Pelham. Lincoln, rapidly following, surprised the insurgent force: 150 were arrested, and the rest fled. "Thus," Lincoln told Washington, "that body of men who were a few days before offering the grossest insults to the best Citizens of this Commonwealth and were menacing even Government itself, were now nearly dispersed, without the shedding of blood but in an instance or two where the Insurgents rushed on their own destruction."[63] Shay's Rebellion was over.

For Henry Knox, the proceedings of the Massachusetts campaign had utterly vindicated the Society of the Cincinnati. He wrote to Washington in March, a few weeks after Lincoln sent his report, rejoicing in the society's success. "In the only instance in which it has had the least political operation," Knox wrote, "the effects have been truly noble." Despite the officers remaining unpaid, and "extremely depressed in their private circumstances," nonetheless "the moment the government was in danger, they unanimously pledged themselves for its support."[64] There was some irony in Knox's use of the word "noble," the same word David Humphreys had used to describe John Sullivan's actions against insurgents in New Hampshire. It was precisely the idea of a new order of nobility that frightened the Cincinnati's early critics, and led Washington to almost abandon the organization. By the early months of 1787, however, those fears had begun to feel much less acute for most of America's genteel elite. It was not the pretensions of would-be aristocrats that most seemed to threaten the republic now, but the egalitarian demands of the people. In the face of rural insurgency and radical democratic reform, the differences between gentlemen themselves faded almost into the background.

In Massachusetts, the government's political response to the rebellion—once it had been dispersed by Lincoln and his Cincinnati forces—was harsh. At Bowdoin's urging, the General Court passed a Disqualifying Act that stripped the right to vote from anyone deemed to have been involved in the disturbances. The act covered "so great a description of persons," wrote Lincoln, "that in its operation many towns will be disenfranchised." He thought it might provoke renewed unrest. But from the perspective of Bowdoin and the rest of the political establishment in Boston, the act ensured that the state government would remain in the hands of gentlemen. As the Cincinnati's memorandum had put it during the crisis, "public faith and private credit"—the fundamental tenets of commercial justice—were to be "the sacred objects of government."

Both sides of the struggle understood exactly what it had been about. On one side were the poor, the rural, and the indebted, who had been further impoverished by taxes to pay public creditors and ruthless seizures for unpaid debts to their private creditors. On the other were those being paid, and those who profited in wealth and power from the workings of the commercial economy. Those profits had to be defended with what Knox called "brutal force."

When the June elections brought John Hancock and a new slate of legislators back to power, it by no means meant a change of policy. On the contrary, Hancock took repression of the countryside still further. With Samuel Adams taking the role of president of the Senate, the two former rivals worked together to solidify establishment control and support. They passed a requisition to raise more state troops, and the legislature voted to reimburse shopkeepers who had lost property during the rebellion. These measures would not lessen the burden of taxation in the countryside. To make sure no new insurgency emerged, as Lincoln had worried it would, Hancock sent his new army to "kill, slay, and destroy if necessary, and conquer by all fitting ways, enterprises, and means whatsoever, all and every one of the rebels."[65] These orders symbolized the new regime's complete commitment to commercial justice in the face of agitation from the countryside. They did not result in actual mass killings. In the end, almost all participants in the rebellion were pardoned in a general amnesty. Even Daniel Shays escaped with his life, and was eventually pardoned. Only two men were hanged. But the lesson for the gentlemen's opponents was clear enough.

In Rhode Island, on the other hand, things remained more complicated. The balance of power had not swung decisively since the beginning of the reform government in 1785. With James Varnum's victory in *Trevett v. Weeden*, the prospect of stabilizing the paper currency and forcing merchants to accept it had been dealt a blow. A proposal to force every freeman to swear an oath that he would accept the paper money, on pain of disenfranchisement, was defeated in a referendum that October. So in December, the assembly passed a law forcing the immediate redemption of all promissory notes and short-term credit arrangements, on which most mercantile activity depended. Twice, the majority tried to amend the state constitution to remove the extra representation of Newport and Providence, and twice they failed. Yet, come April and the new election, the supporters of paper money and egalitarian reform were voted back into office overwhelmingly.[66] Paper continued to circulate at ever depreciating rates, and the government used it—or attempted to use it—to pay its public creditors.[67] Merchants, who held over half the public debt, refused to surrender their certificates for anything other than hard specie. In this impasse, both sides were gambling on their own power in the long run.

Varnum himself held a relatively sanguine view of the whole affair. Writing in early April, 1787, he did not expect a mercantile victory at the forthcoming polls. He held out little hope for gentlemen to regain power in Rhode Island politics in the short term. Nevertheless, he wrote, "I do not feel any great degree of anxiety about the impolicy of this legislature. They represent only the present humors of the state; and even the state itself is but of very little consequence in the great scale of the union."[68] With the rebellion in Massachusetts over and the power of the commercial elite restored there, Varnum was confident that Rhode Island could only hold out so long. Indeed, his optimism reflected a crucial strategic distinction between the side of rural and prodebtor reform and the side of commercial justice. Merchants, lawyers, and other gentlemen were embedded in national networks—networks of communication, trade, credit, and politics, including organisations like the Cincinnati. Even if they did not always manage to do so, they were capable of wielding their influence on a national scale. Farmers and their representatives were not. For all the similarities of interests and tactics in debtor movements up and down the country, there was no national network to stand up against the merchants' cause. As long as that remained the case, the great scale of the union would always fall in favour of gentlemen.

Perhaps the most important effect of the crisis of 1786 among American gentlemen was to underline that reality. In order to make use of their inherent advantage, in defense of their shared interests and their vision of justice, gentlemen needed to consolidate their power on a national level. "What madness has seized the people of the New England states!," wrote the Rhode Islander William Ellery that October. "I begin to think that we do not deserve the privileges which we are possessed of, and that unless power is lodged somewhere to control the vice and folly of the people we shall soon be involved in all the horrors of anarchy and confusion."[69] Most felt that Congress was the logical place to lodge such a power. But it was the states that held the power to augment Congress, and so far they had failed to do so. In November 1786, New York's assembly scuppered plans to introduce a federal customs tax, plans that had first been proposed back when Robert Morris was superintendent of finance. As the dramatic events of that autumn unfolded, more and more gentlemen became convinced of the need for action to somehow transform Congress. How that would take place, however, no one could say.

By the spring of 1787, plans for a convention at Philadelphia were underway, but gentlemen remained divided on the issue. "It cannot be expected that the Convention at Philadelphia will frame and recommend a system that will ever be federally adopted," wrote James Varnum. The states would no doubt fail to agree on a solution to "the defects of our present national government." More likely, he wrote,

> Their increasing animosities will precipitate the period of anarchy and confusion. From these exuberant sources will arise a government that may be assisted in its formation and principles by the wisdom of the

convention. For it is very possible that the majority of wealth, influence and numbers will meet their sentiments; and if so, the residue will be compelled to come in.[70]

Strong and just government would not be imposed, in other words, until an even deeper crisis forced the hands of the wealthy and influential. Henry Knox had similar ideas. "So impressed is my mind with the evils about to happen," he told Washington, "that I have no hope of a free government but from the convention—If that fails us we shall find ourselves afloat on an ocean of uncertainty, uncertain as to the shore on which we shall land but most certain as to the storms we shall have to encounter."[71]

III. Madison's Gambit

Like Alexander Hamilton and Noah Webster, James Madison came of age as a revolutionary. Unlike them, his status as a gentleman was already secure. His father, a respected planter in Orange County, Virginia, was chairman of the local Committee of Safety when James Jr. was elected to it, age twenty-three, at the close of 1774. He spent the revolution not seeking fame in the field, or a living in schools and court-houses, but as a committeeman and politician. When he arrived in Congress as its youngest delegate in 1780, it was at a moment of near bankruptcy and failure for the United States. The British had forced the republican regime out of Georgia and were now besieging Charleston. Shortages of food and supplies, not to mention pay, had sparked a string of mutinies that winter which Washington was barely able to control. It was, he told Thomas Jefferson, then governor of Virginia, the most "truly critical" moment that the revolution had yet faced. At the heart of Congress's distress lay its systems of finance and public credit—the treasury was "empty," Madison wrote, public creditors "exhausted." Each "temporizing expedient" only generated "new difficulties." Congress, he believed, lacked "adequate Statesmen" who could bring about the "mature & systematic" reforms that were urgently needed.[72]

Madison had not come to Congress as an advocate for increased federal power. He had come as a representative of Virginia and its interests. But his response to the circumstances he discovered there led him into a close alliance with those who sought to augment congressional power. When in 1781, Robert Morris was appointed superintendent of finance—a "pecuniary dictator," as the Pennsylvanian Joseph Reed put it—the foundations for a new financial system began to be put in place.[73] The Bank of North America began to issue notes that were more credible than the now-worthless continental currency. But the bank alone was not sufficient. At the center of Morris's plans was the absolute necessity of giving Congress its own source of tax revenue, independent of the states, which could serve to pay interest on its loans and thereby re-establish public credit. Morris's plan was to grant Congress the right to charge customs duties over and above what states themselves charged—an "impost" that would create a revenue without imposing direct taxes on the population. For the next six years, Congress fought to have this impost system adopted by the states. Their efforts, and their failure, shaped the attitudes of men like Madison and Hamilton toward Congress and federal power.

When Madison's term in Congress came to an end in 1783, just as the peace with Britain was ratified, he returned to Virginia and the House of Burgesses. With the war over, he looked to the commercial prospects of his state, and to its political future as a republic. Over the previous decade, Madison had developed into a canny and effective political operator. He was still reserved and soft-spoken, but his skill as a legislator had come to be widely respected. In Virginia, he made himself into the protégé of two of the state's most powerful gentlemen—Thomas Jefferson, the former governor, now ambassador to France, and George Washington, the former commander-in-chief, now retired to his estate at Mount Vernon. Madison acted as each man's particular friend in the legislature of their state. With Jefferson, he pursued an ambitious and radical program of overhauling the state's legal code, including its system of education. He also succeeded in passing Virginia's Statute of Religious Freedom, drafted years earlier by Jefferson, which stripped the Episcopal establishment of its support from public taxation. As the chairman of the assembly's committee on commerce, he led the adoption of Washington's proposals for a canal on the Potomac River—proposals that Jefferson, too, had endorsed.[74]

It was Madison and Washington's work on the canal project that led, as things turned out, to events that would transform the structure of the federal government itself. The process began with a straightforward dilemma: Virginia did not control the Potomac, and so could not grant exclusive rights to charge tolls to the new canal company. Without the prospect of profiting from tolls on river traffic, no investors would come forward with the money to build the canal. Virginia and Maryland would have to find a way to cooperate. At Christmas 1784, Washington himself met with Maryland delegates to coordinate legislation for the canal company in both states. Then in March, he hosted a meeting at Mount Vernon that went far beyond just the Potomac. Gentlemen from both states were deeply concerned with the future of American commerce, including the problem of competition from ports to the north. It was vital, they agreed, for the Chesapeake to take a more substantial role. To that end, the neighboring states should work together on coordinated measures, including a uniform currency. Moreover, the delegates at Mount Vernon also recommended annual meetings, starting the following year, that would bring together *all* the states to discuss commercial cooperation. If they were to compete with European powers, gentlemen believed, the United States would have to start acting together.

That first general meeting was due to be held in September 1786, at Annapolis. Like the Potomac canal itself, it was conceived in an optimistic spirit that looked towards future American prosperity. If sensible men could overcome the petty differences between states, there was nothing to prevent the union of new republics from becoming what nature had destined it to be: a mighty empire. But by that summer, events had shaken that optimistic vision to its core. The forces of justice—as gentlemen understood it—seemed to be on the defensive everywhere. It was not just the rural insurrection in Massachusetts and the bordering states, or the popular reforming government in Rhode Island. Nor was it just the revocation of the charter of Robert Morris's bank in Pennsylvania, or the ongoing political fight over debt and taxes in South Carolina, where even sympathetic governors seemed to be incapable of standing up for creditors' rights. In Virginia, too, the burdens of postwar debt and economic downturn had stretched genteel power to the breaking point. Taxes had been delayed, even effectively forgiven. Paper money and prodebtor laws did not seem far away. Congress, without the impost, remained too weak to resist either democrats or insurgents.[75]

Writing to Thomas Jefferson from Philadelphia in August, Madison mentioned that on his way north he had seen progress being made on the Potomac Canal. "These fruits of the Revolution," he wrote, "do great honour to it." But this optimistic gesture was no more than a foil for the darker thoughts that filled the rest of Madison's letter. There were too many other fruits of the Revolution, he told Jefferson, that should be considered sources of dishonor. "At the head of these is to be put the general rage for paper money." Even in conservative Maryland, "the clamour for it is universal," and it would require "all their firmness" from the old establishment to "withstand the popular torrent." Like the merchants who resisted it in Rhode Island, like Pelatiah Webster and Thomas Paine in Pennsylvania, and indeed like almost every gentleman whose sense of justice was conditioned by the practices of modern commerce, Madison considered paper money "an epidemic malady." Not only did it undermine justice, it also produced "warfare and retaliation" wherever relationships of credit crossed state borders.[76] That was where the meeting he was due to attend at Annapolis came in. Might some new plan, concocted far away from state assemblies, turn the tide?

"Gentlemen both within and without Congress wish to make this meeting subservient to a plenipotentiary convention for amending the Confederation," Madison told Jefferson. Such a move would be much more significant than just commercial regulation. "Tho' my wishes are in favor of such an event," he went on, "yet I despair so much of its accomplishment at the present crisis that I do not extend my views beyond a Commercial Reform. To speak the truth," wrote Madison, switching to code at this point in his letter, "*I almost despair even of this*."[77] Congress was at that moment convulsed with recriminations about a treaty negotiated between John Jay and the Spanish ambassador, Diego de Gardoqui, which seemed to harm the interests of the southern states in favor of the north. Spain, with its control over New Orleans, had closed the Mississippi River to American traffic, cutting off western settlers from oceanic trade. Rather than forcing the Spanish to reopen the river, Jay had gained concessions for the lumber and fishing industries of New England. Of course, Washington and Madison believed that the Potomac Canal would make the Mississippi irrelevant eventually. The fight over the treaty, though, made cooperation in Congress look all but impossible.[78]

By the time a rather forlorn group of officials from five states met that September in Annapolis, then, the state of the union seemed increasingly hopeless. Some states had appointed representatives who failed to turn up on time for the meeting. Others, including Maryland itself, had simply ignored the invitation to convene. The result was that those who did show up were those who shared Madison's own vision most strongly, foremost among them his old friend from Congress, Alexander Hamilton. There was no real hope, with so few present, that the convention could achieve much in the way of commercial reform. Yet what they could do was make a statement of principle, a rallying cry for those who sensed the fruits of revolution were not ripening as they would like them to. "Deeply impressed ... with the magnitude and importance of the object confided to them on this occasion," the convention asked that "speedy measures be taken to effect a general meeting of the states in a future convention." This new meeting would conduct a "deliberate and candid discussion" of the "important defects in the system of Fœderal Government." It was to meet at Philadelphia, "on the second Monday in May next."[79]

Within weeks of Madison's return to Virginia after the Annapolis convention, he found himself engaged in a battle over paper money. The "epidemic malady" that had afflicted other states was finally, it seemed, poised to engulf his own. For those suffering most from the economic slowdown of mid-decade, and burdened by taxation and debt, an injection of cash into the economy was meant to make exchange and commerce flow more easily. Just as in other states, the advocates of paper argued that without it, economic power was unfairly concentrated in the hands of those few gentlemen with access to hard money. Madison, of course, thought otherwise. If it was made legal tender, as in Rhode Island, then paper money would become the means for debtors to pay off their creditors without redeeming the true value of their debts. In that way, Madison argued, it "affects Rights of property as much as taking away equal value in land," and without the right to a trial by jury. Paper money destroyed "confidence between individuals" and created "dissentions between the states." It discouraged commerce, fostered luxury, and by helping debtors at their creditors' expense, it reversed the true aim of government, "which is to reward the best and punish the worst." It was, Madison concluded, pernicious, unconstitutional, and unjust.[80]

A large majority of the Virginia Burgesses, it turned out, agreed with him. "On the question for a paper emission," he gleefully reported back to Washington, "the measure was this day rejected in emphatical terms by a majority of 84 vs 17."[81] The assembly's resolution echoed the language not only of Madison's speech, but of a hundred other pronouncements against paper money made by gentlemen across the previous five years. They declared it "unjust, impolitic, destructive of public & private confidence, and of that virtue which is the basis of Republican Governments."[82] The experience of Rhode Island had strengthened the resolve of those, like Madison, who felt that such measures posed a threat to the very order of things. In their view, that property-based order had a strongly moral dimension—it was a matter of "virtue," and of dividing the "best" men from the "worst." That the legislators in his own state had stood so firmly on the side of his idea of justice gave Madison hope. "In general appearances are favorable," he told Washington, for the remainder of the legislative session. What he hoped was that the Burgesses would give their strong support to the proposal he and Hamilton had made at Annapolis.

Responding to Madison's news, Washington shared his pleasure with the decisive vote. While that success was important, though, larger clouds still hung over the republican experiment. If only, Washington lamented to Madison, "that most important of all objects—the foederal government—may be considered with that calm & deliberate attention which the magnitude of it so loudly calls for at this critical moment." Indulging himself in a sweeping vision of storms gathering on the American horizon, Washington shared with his young protégé the full weight of his anxieties for the future. News from Massachusetts, which the general had just received from Henry Knox, was troubling indeed. "No morn ever dawned more favourable than ours did," he wrote, "and no day was ever more clouded than the present! ... We are fast verging to anarchy & confusion!" How were American gentlemen to "rescue the political machine from the impending storm," Washington wondered? Hope lay, he now believed, in recasting the central authority of the union. "A liberal, and energetic Constitution ... might restore us to that degree of respectability & consequence, to which we had a fair claim, & the brightest prospect of attaining." If the new nation was to regain its character, in short, it needed the strong hand of wise rulers, not the chaos of democracy.[83]

These were the sentiments that guided Madison in the months that led up to the Philadelphia Convention. His cause was enormously strengthened by reactions to the events in New England that autumn and winter. Speaking of Knox's report on the insurrection in Massachusetts, Madison told Washington that "if the lessons which it inculcates should not work the proper impressions on the American Public, it will be a proof that our case is desperate." In Virginia, at least, though, things looked better. "Judging from the present temper and apparent views of our Assembly," wrote Madison, "I have some ground for leaning to the side of Hope." Not only had the Burgesses rejected paper money, they had also voted "*unanimously*" in agreement with the recommendation from Annapolis, that a convention should be held at Philadelphia to consider "a general revision of the federal System."[84] As he put it to fellow Virginian Edmund Pendleton in February, "the late turbulent scenes in Massachusetts and the infamous ones in Rhode Island have done inexpressible injury to the republican character in that part of the United States."[85] Yet they might also have made all the difference in creating a united front for constitutional revision.

Congress endorsed the idea of the Philadelphia Convention on February 18, 1787. By then, half the states had already elected delegates. Robert Morris and James Wilson were both among those chosen by the new assembly to represent Pennsylvania. Virginia's delegation included Madison, of course, and also George Washington. The selection of the general was, however, to become a slightly delicate issue. Washington had already informed the Society of the Cincinnati that, having retired from public life, he did not intend to come to the city for their own convention a month earlier. How would it look if he missed that meeting, but showed up to the one that followed? It took months of persuasion not only from Madison—who had perhaps overstepped his bounds by putting Washington's name forward for the delegation in the first place—but also from Henry Knox, one of the Cincinnati's principal founders. "It is the general wish that you should attend," Knox wrote in April. Indeed, he implied that should the convention fail, and civil war be the result, then Washington might be blamed for its failure. "Slander and malice," wrote Knox, "might suggest that force would be the most agreable mode of reform to you."[86] Both personal reputation and the fate of the nation itself seemed to be at stake.

Not all American gentlemen were convinced that the convention was worthwhile, however. David Humphreys believed the probability was "that nothing general or effectual would be done by the Convention." A crucial problem was that delegates were to be selected by the state assemblies—the very bodies, men like Humphreys thought, whose untrustworthiness had brought about the need for a convention in the first place. Rhode Island, still governed by its popular reforming party, refused to participate in the convention. "Connecticut," wrote Humphreys, "is under the influence of a few such miserable, narrow-minded & I may say wicked Politicians," that even if they did send delegates, "my apprehension is still greater that they will be sent on purpose to impede any salutary measures that might be proposed." New York had chosen, except for Alexander Hamilton, men who were "directly antifœderal." The prospects for a successful conclusion seemed slim. Many believed, including all those Humphreys had spoken to, that the situation would get worse before it could get better.[87] The rebellion in Massachusetts may have been crushed, but the spirit of dissension and popular resistance remained prevalent in the early months of 1787. Surely the crisis was too great to be resolved by any meeting.

After all, the most widespread and fundamental cause of anxiety among elites up and down the country was not to do with the details of political institutions, the balance of power between state and federal government, or even with the efficacy of Congress. It was, rather, the social transformation threatened by an upsurge of popular resistance that had taken place since the revolution. That was the message at the heart of the *Anarchiad*. The poem offered no political program, but it did successfully evoke the kind of world that most frightened its authors. Theirs was a vision of a broken and unpredictable social order, in which they and their friends were no longer guaranteed the power and status they expected from their birth or education, while men on whom they looked down could achieve the trappings of rank. The most compelling image in the poem depicts an invasion of "imps ... veiled in human guise," who "mix, undistinguished, with the common race" until they "fill every *rank*, in each *profession* blend." This was the horror at the heart of republican egalitarianism. Without clear and visible distinctions, who could tell or decide who was superior, and who inferior—or to use Madison's language, the best and the worst?

State legislatures, in their folly, were only the clearest symptom of what was going on. "See, from the shades, on tiny pinions swell," continued the poem, "And rise, the young DEMOCRACY of *hell*! ...

> O, glorious throng ! beyond all wisdom wise!
> Expert to act, eccentric to devise!
> In retrogressive march, what schemes advance!
> What vast resources, and what strange finance![88]

Newly empowered elected assemblies brought new ideas of justice and political economy: the authors scorned both alike. "Democracy" of this sort was a far more insidious threat than the open rebellion that had been crushed in Massachusetts, for it was much harder to simply stamp out. As the convention at Philadelphia approached, more and more gentlemen began to put their hope in Madison's gambit, in the creation of a powerful new government that could restore the kind of justice and the kind of social order they believed in. On May 24, the eve of the convention, the poem's tenth installment came out. In it the hero, "Hesper," the foe of anarchy, "with a solicitude and energy becoming his high station and the importance of the subject, makes his last solemn address to his principal counselors and sages, whom he had convened at Philadelphia." In the hyperbolic, apocalyptic world of the *Anarchiad*, this was the gentlemen's last stand.

One way to look at Madison's gambit—the Constitutional Convention as he envisaged and tried to implement it—is as a culmination of the struggle against state government power that had taken place during the 1780s. What commercial gentlemen had already achieved was to entrench their control of property in a variety of institutions, neither public nor private: institutions like banks and other corporations. This in turn had required a series of struggles, replaying themselves in state after state, over the extent of public, political power—in other words, popular power—over property relations, including contract, credit, and finance. Here then, the focus of elite ideas had been on *restricting* the power of government. Through their many individual battles, in courts and assemblies, and in the field of political debate, gentlemen had worked to carve out a separate sphere of power that could be safely wielded without the threat of popular interference. An ubiquitous element in this strategy had been the appeal to fundamental principles of justice, enshrined in various ways through the common law, the law of nature, or the law of nations. Republican governments, gentlemen argued, became tyrannical as soon as they overstepped these limits.

Yet these fundamental principles were not the only forms useful to gentlemen in their battle to restrict popular power. They could also draw crucial support from positive institutions, namely the Congress and its international treaties. In the case of *Rutgers v. Waddington*, for example, it was the superior or anterior quality of the Treaty of Paris that acted to curb the legislative freedom of the state assembly. Congress was also a useful tool through which to control America's most valuable potential resource, the western lands. Wresting this control from the states had been the most important congressional victory of the 1780s. The crucial point was that Congress was largely unresponsive to popular majorities in the states. While delegates did advocate on behalf of sectional interests, as gentlemen they shared certain assumptions about justice. In September 1786, for example, the Rhode Island delegation had gone so far as to write to their state's new governor, John Collins, condemning his paper money policy. Such measures, they wrote, "will infallibly terminate in the ruin of the state."[89] From a perspective like Madison's, then, national power could be trusted in ways that state power could not.

Madison's plan for reconstructing the federal government was a continuation of the strategy of strengthening Congress at the expense of the states, a strategy that Alexander Hamilton and Robert Morris had pursued avidly at the beginning of the decade, but which had begun to fall apart as soon as the Peace of Paris was signed. Where Madison broke from what had come before, and where his gambit became frighteningly radical, was in its attempt to redefine the very basis of legitimacy and authority. By writing and ratifying a national fundamental law, Madison threatened to strip away the existing foundation of the discourse of justice, the *unwritten* constitution of principle that gentlemen had worked hard to build up and cast in American terms since the revolution. This unwritten constitution could be accessed only through reason and forms of knowledge—legal, historical, and philosophical—to which gentlemen claimed privileged access. It consisted in discourse: that is, the ability to win an argument, or a court case. The institutional structures that measured and ratified such discursive claims—the legal and judicial profession, the colleges, the major press networks—were themselves constituents of elite power. Madison proposed to replace this complex assemblage with a written document legitimated through a vastly risky political process.

There were mitigating factors to that risk, and there were also reasons why it was worth taking. The existence of a written document would not preclude the need for interpretation, and would not in reality bypass the apparatus of legal and political judgment, even if it might helpfully give the impression of doing so. The same political networks and dispersed structures of power could be mobilized in the campaign for ratification. Moreover, and perhaps most important, if the whole project failed, then the unwritten constitution of principle would not have been destroyed in the process. The attempt was necessary because elite discursive and governmental strategies were *already* failing. This was the crisis of the political machine to which Washington referred in November 1786. By the following May, it had only grown deeper. James Varnum may have won in court, but Rhode Island still had paper money. James Bowdoin may have defeated the rebels in Massachusetts, but he still lost his governors' seat. Congress could not raise a quorum, let alone make its power felt in the states. To change the course of the new nation, American gentlemen would once again have to become revolutionaries.

"The nearer the crisis approaches," Madison told Edmund Pendleton that spring, "the more I tremble for the issue." He was well aware of the difficulties his plan entailed. "The necessity of gaining the concurrence of the Convention in some system that will answer the purpose, the subsequent approbation of Congress, and the final sanction of the states," he wrote, "presents a series of chances, which would inspire despair in any case where the alternative was less formidable."[90] That unthinkable alternative, whatever political ramifications Madison saw in it, stemmed from the success of majoritarian populism like Rhode Island's. "Nothing can exceed the wickedness and folly which continue to reign there," he had remarked to Edmund Randolph. "All sense of character as well as of right is obliterated."[91] Even in Massachusetts, the threat of violent unrest had given way to the much more worrying prospect of "wicked measures ... sheltered under the forms of the constitution."[92] In short, the true danger in Madison's view was not institutional breakdown but the overturning of social and economic hierarchy through state governments themselves.

America's gentlemen would tear down the union rather than submit to popular rule. Numerous observers predicted that if something was not done soon to reverse the direction of events, a civil war would be the result. So Madison thought of his own plan as a desperate attempt to save the fruits of revolution and national independence. Yet he could not imagine the possibility of accomplishing this goal from the other direction, by protecting popular legislatures and existing state constitutions. At root, he believed the vices of

American politics grew from the "injustice of the laws of the states." This more than anything, he wrote, "brings ... into question the fundamental principle of republican government, that the majority who rule such governments, are the safest guardians both of public and of private rights."[93] That was the republican principle exactly as Jefferson had expressed it in his Virginia education plan. Both men, in their respective plans, expressed this principle and renounced it in the same breath. It was not an axiom but a dilemma. The people were not safe after all. They had to be *made* so, by the imposition of elite power through institutions of elite design.

It would be absolutely vital, Madison told Jefferson as the convention approached, "to arm the federal head with a negative *in all cases whatsoever* on the local legislatures." The whole purpose of reforming the confederation was to introduce a power, at the national level, that could check and overturn the popular legislatures of the states. "Without this defensive power," he went on, "experience and reflection have satisfied me that however ample the federal powers may be made, or however Clearly their boundaries may be delineated, on paper, they will be easily and continually baffled by the Legislative sovereignties of the States."[94] Up until now, gentlemen had attempted to resist state legislatures in piecemeal and partial ways, through court cases and legal technicalities, through winning over individual politicians, and through outright civil disobedience, as in the case of the Rhode Island merchants who rejected paper money. Most important, those efforts had been entirely local. Gentlemen had not been able to make proper use of their greatest advantage —their connectedness. They might be overwhelmed by the numbers of the majority, but gentlemen were a much more coherent group. Concentrating power in the center was intended to place it in their hands.

As gentlemen from up and down the nation—though not from Rhode Island—began to convene in Philadelphia, they did so in the hope of turning a tide that seemed to be almost overwhelming. That April in Caroline County, Virginia, the home of Madison's friend Edmund Pendleton, the people had formed an association to resist auctions of debtor property. In neighboring King William County a crowd had burned down the courthouse.[95] No state was exempt from tumult. The constitutional convention was a response to the ordinary people who sought to remake society through both insurrection and election in the 1780s. It was meant to insure that they could never again turn the power of the state against what Madison and his allies saw as a just social order. Most of the attendant "demi-gods," as Jefferson dubbed them, came to Philadelphia with subdued hopes.[96] But they also came with feelings of purpose, duty, and honor. Their mission was to make sure that their own vision of justice held sway over the anarchic potential of popular politics. One of the first things they did was agree that their deliberations must be secret.[97]

Conclusion

JAMES MADISON PUT his pen to the convention's proposed constitution on September 17, 1787, knowing it was not all he had hoped for. In order to completely break the power of popular legislatures, Madison had sought "a Constitutional negative on the laws of the States." Only an absolute federal veto could "secure individuals against encroachments on their rights." Indeed, he thought it was "the evils issuing from these sources," the unchecked power of state governments, that most "contributed ... to that uneasiness which produced the Convention, and prepared the public mind for a general reform."[1] Yet the measure had not been adopted by his fellow framers. Even if they agreed with Madison's aims, they did not agree with his assessment of the public mind. They knew how much of a struggle it would be to get the document accepted in their states as it was. "It was apprehended, I believe, by some," James Wilson told the delegates to Pennsylvania's ratifying convention some months later, "that a people so highly spirited, would ill brook the restraints of an efficient government."[2] The proposal that emerged from the closed doors and shuttered windows of the Philadelphia State House was constrained by the political mood of the nation at large. In truth, gentlemen were in no position to dictate terms.

While Madison made his disappointment with the outcome clear to Thomas Jefferson in Paris, George Washington offered only the most lukewarm assessment. The framers' document, he told the Marquis de Lafayette the day after he signed it, "is now a Child of fortune, to be fostered by some and buffited by others." Washington remained concerned primarily with his own reputation. He could not say what kind of reception the proposal would meet, but "if it be good I suppose it will work its way good—if bad it will recoil on the Framers."[3] To Benjamin Harrison, the general was only slightly more forthcoming. "I wish the Constitution which is offered had been made more perfect," he wrote, "but I sincerely believe it is the best that could be obtained at this time—and as a constitutional door is opened for amendment hereafter—

the adoption of it under present circumstances of the Union is in my opinion desirable."[4] It had taken Madison months to persuade Washington to even show up at the convention. Now, returning home to Mount Vernon, the older man remained as reticent as ever. Both knew that the constitution they had helped to write that summer, even if it were adopted, would not signal the end of the political struggle.

Some of their fellow gentlemen, though, were considerably more enthusiastic. The Cincinnatus and *Anarchiad* poet David Humphreys had been deeply ambivalent in the lead-up to the convention. But now that he had seen its proposals, he told Washington, "I must acknowledge myself to have been favorably disappointed [that is, pleasantly surprised] & highly pleased with the general tenor of them." Humphreys was also straightforward about the way social networks and status would mark the political dividing lines over ratification. "All the different Classes in the liberal professions will be in favor of the proposed Constitution," he wrote. "The Clergy, Lawyers, Physicians & Merchants will have considerable influence on Society. Nor will the Officers of the late Army be backward in expressing their approbation."[5] While land-owning gentlemen might side against the framers' vision, those who were most deeply enmeshed in urban and commercial society could be trusted to stick together. Henry Knox, the Cincinnati founder, likewise expressed his support. He would have to leave the details of the document to speak for themselves, he wrote, but "sufficient it is that it contains the great principles, by which liberty and property are to be secured."[6] Predictably, it was this promise of security for property that animated many of the proposals' strongest backers.

What every gentleman hoped for was an end to the paper money policies that threatened the wealth of public and private creditors. Madison's friend Edmund Pendleton put it in the simplest terms. "The restrictions of Paper emissions & unjust tender Laws," to be found in Article 1 Section 10 of the proposed new constitution, "are alone of value sufficient to outweigh all Objections to the System," he wrote.[7] In Pennsylvania, James Wilson made the same point. "If only the following lines were inserted in this Constitution, I think it would be worth adoption: 'No state shall hereafter emit bills of credit; make any thing, but gold and silver coin, a tender in payment of debts; pass any bills of attainder; ex post facto law; or law impairing the obligation of contracts.' Fatal experience has taught us, dearly taught us, the value of these restraints." It was true that Pennsylvania itself had never passed a legal tender act. But, Wilson declared, whenever someone like him went to a state that had such a law, "you find it haunts your journey and follows close upon your heels." When debts could be paid off at two-thirds of their expected value, or even less, "how insecure is property!"[8]

In fact, some friends of the proposals believed that Article 1 Section 10 would be the greatest sticking point in the battle for ratification. David Ramsay of South Carolina wrote that it "will doubtless bear hard on debtors who wish to defraud their creditors," and would be the "real ground of the opposition" to the constitution among some people, however much they "may artfully cover it with a splendid profession of zeal for some state privileges or general liberty."[9] Henry Knox believed that as the proposed constitution "affects deeply the projects of the paper money," it would "set in motion" among popular politicians "every subtelty and art they possess to retard its progress and frustrate its adoption."[10] It was, in fact, that very subtlety and art that led James Madison to think that "the restraints against paper emissions, and violations of contracts are not sufficient." Legislatures would surely find some way to get what they wanted. "Injustice may be effected by such an infinitude of legislative expedients, that where the disposition exists it can only be controuled by some provision which reaches all cases whatsoever," he told Jefferson.[11] Only a veto could prevent the states' egalitarian—in Madison's view, wicked and unjust—designs.

And yet behind the gentlemen's concern for property itself, there lay a deeper set of interests and anxieties. This was the question of social order. What they feared most, and what they believed lay at the root of such unjust measures as the paper money laws, was the people's licentiousness. As Wilson explained, the true enemy of the republic came from within. "While she kept her eye steadily fixed on the efforts of oppression, licentiousness was secretly undermining the rock on which she stood. Those, whom foreign strength could not overpower, have well-nigh become the victims of internal anarchy."[12] His fellow Pennsylvanian, the honorary Cincinnatus John Dickinson, wrote that "the uniform tenor of history . . . holds up the *licentiousness* of the people, and the *turbulent temper* of some of the states, as *the only causes* to be dreaded."[13] Connecticut's Oliver Ellsworth reminded his readers, "it is not strange that the licentious should tell us a government of energy is inconsistent with liberty, for being inconsistent with their wishes and their vices, they would have us think it contrary to human happiness."[14] It was licentiousness, above all, that the new constitution was designed to crush.

For gentlemen, it was the fate of the republic—and the outcome of the revolution—that hung in the balance. "If the people of our nation, instead of consenting to be governed by laws of their own making, and rulers of their own choosing, should let licentiousness, disorder, and confusion reign over them," John Jay wrote in his address to the people of New York, "the minds of men every where, will insensibly become alienated from republican forms, and prepared to prefer and acquiesce in Governments, which, though less friendly to liberty, afford more peace and security." If social order and commercial justice could not be secured through the republican means offered in the constitutional proposals, Jay was saying, then it would soon be imposed by harsher means. So soon after the uprisings in New England, many Americans still feared the possibility of civil war. Opponents of the proposed constitution must "consider whether we ought to give further opportunities to discord to alienate the hearts of our citizens from one another, and thereby encourage new Cromwells to bold exploits.... In the mean time our affairs are daily going from bad to worse." The metaphor Jay chose to drive his argument home was one taken from the world of commerce. "Our distresses," he wrote, "are accumulating like compound interest."[15]

Not every gentleman in the United States supported the adoption of the Philadelphia proposals. The Virginians George Mason and Edmund Randolph, and the Adams cousins' Massachusetts ally Elbridge Gerry, all refused to sign the document at the convention's end. As the campaign for ratification swept across the states in the year that followed, there were many who took up the opposition, "antifederalist" stance. This opposition was founded primarily on fears that the new national government would wield too much power. Without a Bill of Rights like the one Mason had written for Virginia in 1776, delimiting the power of the government, the proposal of the Philadelphia convention could not win the backing of the most conservative republicans.[16] What none of these gentlemen opposed, however, was the clause so many deemed the most important—Article 1 Section 10. Over the question of revoking the state governments' ability to interfere with private contracts and the value of money, gentlemen on both sides were agreed. Even Patrick Henry, one of Virginia's most ardent antifederalists, whose supporters included middling and poor folk from the western countryside, told Madison and his allies that "we are at peace on this issue."[17]

This genteel wing of the antifederalist coalition did not represent the deeper strain of opposition to be found among the radicals and democrats. Those who had already stood up against commercial gentlemen and their idea of justice since the war now formed an important part of the movement against the constitution. In Pennsylvania, rural democrats who had fought Robert Morris and his friends throughout the last three years now made up a minority in the assembly. When they tried to block the vote for a ratifying convention by denying the assembly a quorum, some of them were "forcibly dragged through the streets of Philadelphia to the State house, and there detained by force" until the vote had been taken.[18] At the convention that followed, the same men—among them William Findley, John Smilie, and Robert Whitehill, all leaders of the campaign against the bank—found themselves once more in a minority opposition. In their memorial of dissent, they spoke of the gilded chains that had been forged in secret behind the closed doors of their own State House.[19] Like popular antifederalists throughout the states, they warned that the constitution was a machine of elite rule threatening to undermine, if not destroy completely, the state governments that offered the potential for egalitarian reform.[20]

Among the many gentlemen to publish their responses to the Pennsylvania dissent was the young educationalist, Noah Webster. Now a resident of

New York, and the publisher of the new *American Magazine*, Webster was an ardent supporter of the proposed constitution. His response to Findley and his allies accused them of fanning "the flame of opposition among the weak, the wicked, the designing, and the factious." Most importantly, though, it identified the fault lines in the larger political contest. Ratification of the constitution was not a question to be taken on its own, for its key supporters and opponents had already faced each other in years of ongoing struggle. "You are the men, Gentlemen," wrote Webster, "who wrested the Charter from the Bank, with the least justifiable pretence; sporting with a grant which you had made, and which had never been forfeited." It was all too easy to connect these causes, and to pinpoint the centers of opposition to the constitution. "There is not a spot in the United States," he went on, "where the solemnity of contracts and grants, has been so sacriligeously violated—and the rights of men so wantonly and perseveringly abused, as by you and your junto in Pennsylvania—except only, in the little detestable corner of the Continent, called *Rhode-Island*."[21]

For Webster, as for many others, it was the sacred quality of property and contract, the fundamental tenets of commercial justice, that defined the contours of political morality and wickedness. In his *Examination into the Leading Principles of the Federal Constitution*, published a few months earlier in Philadelphia and dedicated to Benjamin Franklin, Webster gave his own reading of the questions of justice and power at stake in the new republic. "Wherever we cast our eyes," Webster confidently declared, "we see this truth, that *property* is the basis of *power*." Indeed, it was a sentiment the Cincinnatus Stephen Moylan had expressed four years before in his defense of that organization. "*Property alone constitutes power*." The notion was an axiom of the republican tradition, which "being established as a cardinal point," Webster wrote, "directs us to the means of preserving our freedom." All that was needed was to get rid of entailments and "leave real estates to revolve from hand to hand, as time and accident may direct." Without a nobility accumulating real estate, "the laborious and saving, who are generally the best citizens, will possess each his share of property and power, and thus the balance of wealth and power will continue where it is, *in the body of the people*."[22]

Webster saw that the essential feature of republican society was a general equality of property. What he could never countenance was the active use of state power for egalitarian, redistributive purposes. Such a use of power, he believed, would undermine the very property that was still the basis of freedom. Rather, he proposed that simply by sweeping away the artificial constraints imposed by feudal and aristocratic societies, republics would create the conditions for a natural equality to come about. The real threat, he implied, came from the great estates of the nobility. By contrast, "the inequalities introduced by commerce, are too fluctuating to endanger government."

True, some men would become rich, but they could never accumulate enough to secure permanent advantages. There would always be the opportunity for poor men to become rich in their turn. "An equality of property," he wrote, "with a necessity of alienation, constantly operating to destroy combinations of powerful families, is the very *soul of a republic.*" True commercial justice was, for Webster, a force for the good of every "laborious and saving" citizen. Unburdened by the fetters of feudal society, the rules of property would generate a sort of constant natural leveling. Commerce itself would be America's permanent revolution.[23]

Democratic opponents of the Constitution agreed with Webster, of course, that abolishing entail and nobility, and breaking up the large estates that characterized European patterns of property holding, were important elements in creating the new republic. Like him, they believed that broad equality among white men was crucial—even while they put aside the questions of women, enslaved people, Native Americans, and free people of color. They would also have agreed with him, in concert with their republican intellectual heritage, that property was the true basis of power. All these things constituted a consensus among revolutionary Americans. Yet the two sides were intractably opposed. What set them apart was perhaps less a question of reasoned principle than one of experience—of different points of view on the world as it was. For Webster seemed to believe that economic power could be freed from its entanglement with politics, and if that could be done, that the mere working of the system would produce equality. Men like Findley, Smilie, and Whitehill saw things quite differently. From where they stood, commerce was the very force that concentrated power, corrupted political institutions, and gave some men the strength to dominate their fellow citizens. It was the effect of that force that they had been fighting since the war's end. And it was that force the constitution sought to enshrine, permanently.

When these popular antifederalists looked at the Philadelphia convention, in its "secret conclave," they saw amongst the "men of excellent characters ... others who were more remarkable for their ambition and cunning."[24] They saw men who had opposed American independence, and who even now opposed the democratic constitution of the state of Pennsylvania. They saw bankers and speculators, lawyers who cared more for property than loyalty, and politicians who fought tooth and nail to keep assemblies from making paper money or protecting farmers from their debts. They saw the networks and interests that had fought them for five years and more, men who had gained wealth and power while the people suffered, who had raised a private army to crush Shays and his insurgents, and who now sought to subvert the Confederation and impose a new system of government. For years, the gentlemen had preached obedience. They had drummed home the lesson that justice meant paying one's debts. They had railed against the wickedness of democratic states, the ignorance of voters, and the tyranny of the majority. Findley and those like him had seen all this happen. To them, the plans from Philadelphia looked very much like just another move in the long, bitter struggle. They looked like a set of gilded chains.

In the conflict over the new constitution, it was gentlemen like Webster who emerged victorious. In the process, many of them jettisoned the notions of obedience and deference that had characterized their politics at the beginning of the decade. Instead, they adopted for themselves the language of equality and popular sovereignty. James Wilson, the lawyer and speculator who had worked so hard to save the Bank of North America, went further than anyone in linking the constitutional proposals with the idea of popular rule. At the Pennsylvania ratifying convention, Wilson contrasted himself directly to William Findley. "His position is, that the supreme power resides in the States, as governments; and mine is, that it *resides* in the PEOPLE, as the fountain of government."[25] Thus the gentlemen who had for so long pushed back against democracy in the states now painted themselves as defenders of popular power. They put on the mantle of the revolution, and took up the image Thomas Paine had painted, of a crown broken in pieces and distributed among the people. But they used that rhetoric for their own purposes— purposes we can only discern if we appreciate the struggle that came before.

This reshaping of revolutionary rhetoric has had a powerful effect on how we look back on the history of the United States. Over time, the movement for the constitution came to be seen just as Wilson and his allies framed it—as a culmination of the revolutionary call for political equality and popular sovereignty. The republic that emerged over the following century was, indeed, very much like the one Noah Webster imagined in his defense of the constitution. Americans were proud of the absence of feudal constructions like entail and primogeniture. Because it lacked the overt hierarchy of nobility that continued to mark the Old World long into the nineteenth century, the United States could seem like a remarkably egalitarian place. To observers like Alexis de Tocqueville, it had produced a culture of democracy that was completely at odds with deferential societies elsewhere. Crucially, moreover, this new type of society in the United States was host to a market-based commercial economy backed by the strong legal defense of property and contract. As it seemed to many at the time, and as many historians since have depicted it, democracy and capitalism went hand in hand. That would be to ignore the huge problem of slavery—but then, the shadow of that profound evil helped make everything else look positively utopian.

It has been all too easy to forget that at the center of Webster's vision was the idea that free-flowing commerce would maintain equality, and that "equality of property" was, in his words, "the very *soul of a republic*." That desire for equality united Webster and his popular opponents. Where they differed was over the validity of his prediction. Democrats could not agree that the system of capital, contracts, and corporations that they had witnessed being built in America would act to preserve general equality in the long run. It looked, in fact, very much like the opposite. Capital, once organized in something like a corporation, tended to accumulate, and to enrich those who controlled its flows while turning others into its servants. Its rule was increasing inequality. Today's historical economists have shown that these early opponents of the constitution were correct. We need only look around and see the world as it has come to be since the end of the eighteenth century to know that Webster was much mistaken.[26] His marriage of commerce and equality had always been remarkably convenient, deployed to promote the projects of those seeking to defend their property and power. At its core, Webster's vision of justice —like that of America's other commercial gentlemen—always served the few at the expense of the many.

There are many stories to be told about the constitution. This is only one of them. What this book has been about is less the constitution per se, than the role and evolution of a particular kind of identity in the aftermath of the revolution. I began by saying that what it means to be a gentleman changed over time, in different places, and with different kinds of people.[27] The emergence of a dynamic commercial economy, alongside the banking and financial systems built by European empires, transformed the Atlantic world over the course of the seventeenth and eighteenth centuries. Power and wealth changed in ways that nobody at the time fully grasped. For one thing, the ideal of independence that was so important to the old style of gentleman began to give way to the necessity of *interdependence*. Gentility no longer offered an escape from networks of cooperation and competition. Instead, it provided a set of rules that allowed gentlemen to operate and succeed in their new environment. To those who identified with this system, the rules of gentility were tantamount to the dictates of justice and morality. Such were the men whose story I have tried to tell in this book. That story is one we should consider when we turn to face our own time.

When we examine our assumptions about justice and how to organize society, we should remember that they have complex historical roots. It is vital to acknowledge that these ideas and assumptions are not just the products of careful thinking and the gradual accumulation of wisdom by great minds. They are the results of struggles that took place across all sorts of realms, from newspapers to courtrooms, from polling places to parlors, and from the halls of America's legislatures to the battlefields of its rebellions. The American Revolution shifted the ground on which such struggles played out. It created new cultural, economic, social, and political contexts that transformed the way American people thought and argued about justice and power. Looking back, the revolution can seem like a radical moment, a watershed between an old world of aristocratic hierarchy and unenlightened deference on the one hand, and a new world of unfettered progress on the other. But to see it that way would be to mistake the kind of change that really took place. Rather than defeating inequality and hierarchy, the revolution forced it to take on new forms. It was that pressure for change, for new justifications and new modes of exercising power, that gave rise to the extraordinary creativity and innovation of the founding generation's political strategists, men like Hamilton, Madison, and Wilson.

Caught between the failure of old ideas and their contempt for the licentiousness of popular democracy, such men met the challenge by remaking their identity, and crafting a new vision of justice and power. In their wish to continue being gentlemen, they took upon themselves the task of revolutionaries. If we can see them in both of these roles, we will better understand the birth of the United States—what was at stake, what was transformed, and what, through everything, remained.

NOTES

Introduction

1. For explorations of gentility in Revolutionary America, see Rhys Isaac, *The Transformation of Virginia, 1740–1790* (Chapel Hill: University of North Carolina Press, 1982); Richard Bushman, *The Refinement of America: Persons, Houses, Cities* (New York: Knopf, 1992); Joanne Freeman, *Affairs of Honor: National Politics in the New Republic* (New Haven: Yale University Press, 2001); and Carroll Smith-Rosenberg, *This Violent Empire: The Birth of an American National Identity* (Chapel Hill: University of North Carolina Press, 2010).

2. "The defining characteristics of gentility are elusive. At first glance being a gentleman resided in the fact itself—a claim made upon the world and accepted by the world. A complex of attributes and ways of conducting oneself were required to support the claim—deficiency in some would need to be balanced by a fuller measure in others." Isaac, *Transformation of Virginia*, 131.

3. On planter indebtedness, see Timothy Breen, *Tobacco Culture: the mentality of the great Tidewater planters on the eve of Revolution* (Princeton: Princeton University Press, 1985).

4. "Gentlemen restrained their passions and controlled their words. Their manners were refined, their carriage easy. They were men of integrity and honesty whose promises could be trusted; their word was their bond." Freeman, *Affairs of Honor*, xv, and see xxi–xxii, 247. Freeman argues that "the tradition-bound culture of honor" was particularly important in the early national period when it 'provided solid ground' for an elite leadership under threat from "democratic politicking" (*Affairs of Honor*, xv). Her view is compatible with Gordon Wood's claim that "there was ... something old-fashioned, even feudal, about this gentlemanly concern with reputation and honor," which was challenged after the revolution by "the new democratic world of the nineteenth-century"; Wood, *The Radicalism of the American Revolution* (New York: Alfred A. Knopf, 1992), 40, and see 26–33, 343–347. More recently, Carroll Smith-Rosenberg has emphasized the "shifting and contested" nature of gentility, especially during the revolution; Smith-Rosenberg, *This Violent Empire*, 339, and see 32, 309–362. As this book hopes to show, gentility was more than capable of adapting itself to republican society, even while it continued to embody the influence of European aristocratic culture.

5. "Capitalism and gentility were allies in forming the modern economy." Bushman, *Refinement of America*, xvii. My contention is that this argument applies not only to the rise of consumerism, but also to the developing nature of relationships between individuals, or as economists might say, market actors.

6. The notion of landed independence, as a prerequisite for virtue, played a central role in the "country-party" or "radical Whig" politics of the eighteenth-century North Atlantic world, which Bernard Bailyn and others argued provided the ideological origins of the American Revolution; Bailyn, *The Ideological Origins of the American Revolution* (Cambridge: Harvard University Press, 1967); and see Robert Shalhope, "Republicanism and Early American Historiography," *William and Mary Quarterly* 39 (April 1982): 334–356. Historians now agree that this republican tradition co-existed with other lines of thought emphasizing mutual connection and the positive effects of commerce; Cathy Matson and Peter Onuf, *A Union of Interests: Political and Economic Thought in Revolutionary America*

(Lawrence: University of Kansas Press, 1990); Joyce Appleby, *Liberalism and Republicanism in the Historical Imagination* (Cambridge: Harvard University Press, 1992); Milton Klein et al., eds., *The Republican Synthesis Revisited: Essays in Honor of George Athan Billias* (Worcester, MA: American Antiquarian Society, 1992).

7. This international turn in the historiography of the American founding was especially influenced by David Hendrickson, *Peace Pact: The Lost World of the American Founding* (Lawrence: University Press of Kansas, 2003). Its most powerful statement is Eliga Gould, *Among the Powers of the Earth: The American Revolution and the Making of a New World Empire* (Cambridge: Harvard University Press, 2012). See also Frederick Marks, *Independence on Trial: Foreign Affairs and the Making of the Constitution* (Baton Rouge: Louisiana State University Press, 1973); Nicholas Onuf and Peter Onuf, *Federal Union, Modern World: The Law of Nations in an Age of Revolutions, 1776–1814* (Madison, WI: Madison House, 1993); and David Golove and Daniel Hulsebosch, "A Civilized Nation: The Early American Constitution, the Law of Nations, and the Pursuit of International Recognition," *New York University Law Review* 85 (Oct. 2010): 932–1066. For an overview, see Tom Cutterham, "The International Dimension of the Federal Constitution," *Journal of American Studies* 48 (May 2014): 501–515. On the importance of a strong central government to match the fiscal-military powers of European empires, see Max Edling, *A Revolution in Favor of Government: Origins on the U.S. Constitution and the Making of the American State* (New York: Oxford University Press, 2003).

8. On Smith's impact in America, see Samuel Fleischacker, "The Impact on America: Scottish Philosophy and the American Founding," in Alexander Broadie, ed., *The Cambridge Companion to the Scottish Enlightenment* (Cambridge: Cambridge University Press, 2003); and on free trade ideas, see James Fichter, *So Great a Proffit: How the East Indies Trade Transformed Anglo-American Capitalism* (Cambridge: Harvard University Press, 2010). For strongly procapitalist accounts of these issues, influenced by the field of institutional economics, see Douglas Irwin and Richard Sylla, eds., *Founding Choices: American Economic Policy in the 1790s* (Chicago: University of Chicago Press, 2011); and Robert Wright, *The First Wall Street: Chestnut Street, Philadelphia, and the Birth of American Finance* (Chicago: University of Chicago Press, 2005). The best general account from a critical perspective is William Hogeland, *Founding Finance: How Debt, Speculation, Foreclosures, Protests, and Crackdowns Made Us a Nation* (Austin: University of Texas Press, 2012).

9. This historiography is rooted in a long tradition analyzing social conflict in revolutionary America. Its early reference points were Charles Beard, *An Economic Interpretation of the Constitution of the United States* (New York: Free Press, 1913); and J. Franklin Jameson, *The American Revolution Considered as a Social Movement* (Princeton: Princeton University Press, 1926). The most important recent works are Woody Holton, *Unruly Americans and the Origins of the Constitution* (New York: Hill & Wang, 2007); Terry Bouton, *Taming Democracy: "The People," the Founders, and the Troubled Ending of the American Revolution* (New York: Oxford University Press, 2007); and Gary Nash, *The Unknown American Revolution: The Unruly Birth of Democracy and the Struggle to Create America* (New York: Viking, 2005); but see also Larry Tise, *The American Counterrevolution: A Retreat from Liberty, 1783–1800* (Mechanicsburg, PA: Stackpole Books, 1998); and Robert Martin, *Government by Dissent: Protest, Resistance, and Radical Democratic Thought in the Early American Republic* (New York: New York University Press, 2013).

10. Attempts to recover the intellectual tradition of American popular movements have often drawn on the example of E. P. Thompson, *The Making of the English Working Class* (London: Victor Gollancz, 1963). See Staughton Lynd, *Intellectual Origins of American Radicalism* (New York: Pantheon Books, 1968); and Lynd, *Class Conflict, Slavery,*

and the United States Constitution (Indianapolis, IN: Bobbs-Merrill, 1967). More recently, see Saul Cornell, *The Other Founders: Anti-federalism and the Dissenting Tradition in America, 1788–1828* (Chapel Hill: University of North Carolina Press, 1999). For the race and gender politics of white male solidarity, see Mark Kann, *A Republic of Men: The American Founders, Gendered Language, and Patriarchal Politics* (New York: New York University Press, 1998); and for the extension of slavery, see Rachel Klein, *Unification of a Slave State: The Rise of the Planter Class in the South Carolina Backcountry, 1760–1808* (Chapel Hill: University of North Carolina Press, 1990).

11. Woody Holton, "An 'Excess of Democracy'—or a Shortage?: The Federalists' Earliest Adversaries," *Journal of the Early Republic* 25 (Fall 2005): 339–382. On the word "democracy" and associated practices, see Joanna Innes and Mark Philp, eds., *Re-imagining Democracy in the Age of Democratic Revolutions: America, France, Britain, Ireland, 1750–1850* (Oxford: Oxford University Press, 2013).

12. While they rarely feature prominently in historians' accounts of this period, the Cincinnati mattered both as an organization that helped knit together a nationwide network of gentlemen and mobilize them in defense of political goals, and as the spur to a debate about the role of inheritance and hierarchy in republican society. This is not a book about the Cincinnati, but it is about events and ideas in which the Society played a significant part. See Tom Cutterham, "'What ought to belong *to merit only*': Debating Status and Heredity in the New American Republic," *Journal for Eighteenth Century Studies* 39.4 (2016).

13. On the problem of building a republican society through law and constitution making, see Eric Slauter, *The State as a Work of Art: The Cultural Origins of the Constitution* (Chicago: University of Chicago Press, 2009). Americans in the 1780s struggled to grasp the implications of the question: does society reflect the form of its government institutions, or vice versa? For the religious establishment especially, the fundamental goal was to reform the individual person: then society and government would follow.

14. Recent works that focus on the Convention and ratification process include Edling, *Revolution in Favor of Government*; Richard Beeman, *Plain, Honest Men: The Making of the American Constitution* (New York: Random House, 2009); Calvin Johnson, *Righteous Anger at the Wicked States: The Meaning of the Founders' Constitution* (Cambridge: Cambridge University Press, 2009); Pauline Maier, *Ratification: The People Debate the Constitution, 1787–1788* (New York: Simon and Schuster, 2010).

Chapter One. Inheritance

1. The three crucial works on republicanism in the American Revolution are Bailyn, *Ideological Origins of the American Revolution*; Gordon S. Wood, *The Creation of the American Republic, 1776-1787* (Chapel Hill: University of North Carolina Press, 1969); J.G.A. Pocock, *The Machiavellian Moment: Florentine Political Thought and the Atlantic Republican Tradition* (Princeton: Princeton University Press, 1975). On classical influences, see Carl J. Richard, *The Founders and the Classics: Greece, Rome, and the American enlightenment* (Cambridge: Harvard University Press, 1994); and Caroline Winterer, *The Culture of Classicism: Ancient Greece and Rome in American Intellectual Life, 1780–1910* (Baltimore: Johns Hopkins University Press, 2002).

2. For exegeses of the Declaration of Independence, see Carl Becker, *The Declaration of Independence: A Study in the History of Political Ideas* (New York: Harcourt, Brace, 1922); Garry Wills, *Inventing America: Jefferson's Declaration of Independence* (Garden City, NY: Doubleday, 1978); David Armitage, *The Declaration of Independence: a global history* (Cambridge: Harvard University Press, 2007); and especially Danielle Allen, *Our*

Declaration: A Reading of the Declaration of Independence in Defense of Equality (New York: W.W. Norton, 2014).

3. On slavery and the constitution, see Staughton Lynd, *Class Conflict, Slavery, and the United States Constitution* (Indianapolis, IN: Bobbs-Merrill, 1967); David Waldstreicher, *Slavery's Constitution: From Revolution to Ratification* (New York: Hill and Wang, 2009); George Van Cleve, *A Slaveholders' Union: Slavery, Politics, and the Constitution in the Early Republic* (Chicago: University of Chicago Press, 2010).

4. Before and after the revolution, American society was racist and patriarchal as well as divided by wealth. See Smith-Rosenberg, *This Violent Empire*; Kann, *Republic of Men*; and for powerful local studies, see Woody Holton, *Forced Founders: Indians, Debtors, Slaves, and the Making of the American Revolution in Virginia* (Chapel Hill: University of North Carolina Press, 1999); and Michael McDonnell, *The Politics of War: Race, Class, and Conflict in Revolutionary Virginia* (Chapel Hill: University of North Carolina Press, 2007).

5. For Laurens, see Gregory Massey, *John Laurens and the American Revolution* (Columbia: University of South Carolina Press, 2000); and Sara Townshend, *An American Soldier: The Life of John Laurens Drawn Largely from Correspondence between His Father and Himself* (Raleigh, NC, Edwards & Broughton, 1958). There are many biographies of Hamilton, but among the best are Broadus Mitchell, *Alexander Hamilton: Youth to Maturity, 1755-1788* (New York: Macmillan, 1957); Jacob Cooke, *Alexander Hamilton* (New York: Scribners, 1982); and Ron Chernow, *Alexander Hamilton* (New York: Penguin, 2004). Their friendship is examined in Massey, *John Laurens*, 80–82; and Richard Godbeer, *The Overflowing of Friendship: Love between Men and the Creation of the American Republic* (Baltimore: Johns Hopkins University Press, 2009), 126–138.

6. Alexander Hamilton to John Laurens, April 1779, in Harold C. Syrett ed., *The Papers of Alexander Hamilton*. 27 vols. New York: Columbia University Press, 1961–1987), II, 34–35.

7. Sarah Knott details the culture of sensibility, and its role in fostering elite "accommodation" of the middling sort, in Knott, *Sensibility and the American Revolution* (Chapel Hill: University of North Carolina Press, 2009), 1, 18, 201, *passim*; for Hamilton and Laurens, see 162–163; see also Knott, "Sensibility and the American War for Independence," *American Historical Review* 109 (Feb. 2004): 19–40; Godbeer, *Overflowing of Friendship*, 10–13; and Andrew Burstein, "The Political Character of Sympathy," *Journal of the Early Republic* 21 (Winter 2001): 601–632.

8. Hamilton to Laurens, April 1779, 8 January 1780, 30 March 1780, and 22 May 1779, in Syrett, ed., *Papers of Alexander Hamilton*, II, 38, 255, 304, 53.

9. Hamilton to Laurens, April 1779, in Syrett, ed., *Papers of Alexander Hamilton*, II, 36. On the Continental Army as a source of social opportunity for young men, see John Ruddiman, *Becoming Men of Some Consequence: Youth and Military Service in the Revolutionary War* (Charlottesville: University of Virginia Press, 2014).

10. Hamilton to Laurens, 8 January 1780, in Syrett, ed., *Papers of Alexander Hamilton*, II,, 38.

11. Hamilton to Laurens, April 1779, in ibid., 37.

12. Hamilton to Laurens, 8 January 1780, in ibid., 255.

13. Hamilton to Elizabeth Schuyler, June-October 170, in ibid., 350. On Elizabeth's father, see Don R. Gerlach, *Proud Patriot: Philip Schuyler and the War for Independence, 1775-1783* (Syracuse, NY: Syracuse University Press, 1987); and Gerlach, *Philip Schuyler and the American Revolution in New York, 1733-1777* (Lincoln: University of Nebraska Press, 1964). On her mother, see Mary Gay Humphreys, *Catherine Schuyler* (New York: C. Scribner's Sons, 1897).

14. Hamilton to Elizabeth Schuyler, 17 March, 2–4 July 1780, in Syrett, ed., *Papers of Alexander Hamilton*, II, 285–286, 350. For their engagement, see Philip Schuyler to Alexander Hamilton, 8 April 1780, in ibid., 305–307.

15. Marquis de Fleury to Hamilton, 20 October 1780, in Syrett, ed., *Papers of Alexander Hamilton*, II, 482.

16. Hamilton to Laurens, 16 September 1780, in ibid., 431.

17. Hamilton to Elizabeth Schuyler, August 1780, in ibid., 397–399.

18. Ibid.

19. Quoted in Chernow, *Alexander Hamilton*, 131.On gender roles, see Linda Kerber, "The Republican Mother: Women and the Enlightenment—An American Perspective," *American Quarterly* 28.2 (Summer 1976): 187–205; Kerber, *Women of the Republic: Intellect and Ideology in Revolutionary America* (Chapel Hill: University of North Carolina Press, 1980); Mary Beth Norton, *Liberty's Daughters: The Revolutionary Experience of American women, 1750–1800* (Ithaca, NY: Cornell University Press, 1980); Rosemarie Zagarri, "Morals, Manners, and the Republican Mother," *American Quarterly* 44.2 (June 1992): 192–215.

20. Accounts of the wedding appear in Mitchell, *Alexander Hamilton*, 206, and Chernow, *Alexander Hamilton*, 148; the house is photographed in Hugh Howard, *Homes of the Founding Fathers* (New York: Artisan, 2007), 156–163.

21. Washington to Jonathan Trumbull, 26 May 1780, in John Clement Fitzpatrick, ed., *The Writings of George Washington: from the Original Manuscript Sources, 1749–1799*. 39 vols. (Washington, DC: Government Printing Office, 1931–1944), XVIII, 425–6; Washington to Gouverneur Morris, 10 December 1780, in ibid, XX, 459.

22. The problems of supply for the American forces in the revolutionary war are detailed in Wayne E. Carp, *To Starve the Army at Pleasure: Continental Army Administration and American Political Culture, 1775–1783* (Chapel Hill: University of North Carolina Press, 1983); and see Charles Royster, *A Revolutionary People at War: The Army and the American Character, 1775–1783* (Chapel Hill: University of North Carolina Press, 1979); Ronald Higginbotham and Peter J. Albert, *Arms and Independence: The Military Character of the American Revolution* (Charlottesville: University Press of Virginia, 1984); and James A. Huston, *Logistics of Liberty: American Services of Supply in the Revolutionary War and After* (Newark: University of Delaware Press, 1991).

23. George Washington to John Laurens, 15 January 1781, in W. C. Ford, ed., *The Writings of George Washington*, 14 vols., (New York: G. P. Putnam's and Sons, 1891), IX, 102–109.

24. Alexander Hamilton to John Laurens, 4 February 1781, in Syrett, ed., *Papers of Alexander Hamilton*, II, 549–550; Washington to Colonel Frederick Frelinghuysen, 21 January 1781, Fitzpatrick, ed., *The Writings of George Washington*, XXI, 125; Washington to President of Congress, 15 Jan 1781, Fitzpatrick, ed., *The Writings of George Washington*, XXI, 102.

25. Joseph Reed to Nathanael Greene, 1 Nov 1781, quoted in E. James Ferguson ed., *The Papers of Robert Morris, 1781–1784* (Pittsburgh: University of Pittsburgh Press, 1973), I, 21.

26. For the most thorough account of Morris's official activities during the 1780s, and of congressional finance more generally, see Ferguson, *The Power of the Purse: A History of American Public Finance, 1776–1790* (Chapel Hill: University of North Carolina Press, 1961). On Morris himself, see Clarence Lester Ver Steeg, *Robert Morris: Revolutionary Financier* (Philadelphia: University of Pennsylvania Press, 1954); Charles Rappleye, *Robert Morris: Financier of the American Revolution* (New York: Simon & Schuster, 2010).

27. Robert Morris to a Committee of Congress (Thomas Burke, William Churchill Houston, and Oliver Wolcott), 26 March 1781, in E. James Ferguson ed., *The Papers of*

Robert Morris, 1781–1784 (Pittsburgh: University of Pittsburgh Press, 1973), I, 22; Joseph Reed to Nathanael Greene, 1 Nov 1781, quoted in ibid., 21. Hamilton to Robert Morris, 30 April 1781, in Syrett, ed., *Papers of Alexander Hamilton*, II, 606.

28. On Yorktown, see Richard Ketchum, *Victory at Yorktown: The Campaign That Won the Revolution* (New York: Henry Holt, 2004); and Jerome Greene, *The Guns of Independence: the siege of Yorktown, 1781* (New York: Savas Beattie, 2005).

29. Alexander Hamilton to Elizabeth Hamilton, 16 October 1781, in Syrett, ed., *Papers of Alexander Hamilton*, II, 682.

30. Henry Knox to John Jay, 21 October 1781, quoted in Mark Puls, *Henry Knox: Visionary General of the American Revolution* (New York: Palgrave Macmillan, 2008), 167–168.

31. This issue of respectability within the army, and its relationship to politics in the new nation, is addressed by Richard Kohn, *Eagle and Sword: The Federalists and the Creation of the Military Establishment in America, 1783–1802* (New York: Free Press, 1975); and James Kirby Martin and Mark Edward Lender, *A Respectable Army: The Military Origins of the Republic, 1763–1782.* 2nd ed. (Wheeling, IL: Harlan Davidson, 2006,). For the important effects of wartime experience on American ideology more broadly, see John Shy, *A People Numerous and Armed: Reflections on the Struggle for American Independence.* Rev. ed. (Ann Arbor: University of Michigan Press, 1990).

32. For Henry Knox, see Puls, *Henry Knox*; and Alan Taylor, *Liberty Men and the Great Proprietors: The Revolutionary Settlement on the Maine Frontier, 1760–1820* (Chapel Hill: University of North Carolina Press, 1990), 37–47.

33. Henry Knox et al. to Congress, December 1782, in Gaillard Hunt, ed., *Journals of the Continental Congress, 1774–1789* (Washington, DC: Government Printing Office, 1922), XXIV, 291–293.

34. Alexander to Elizabeth Hamilton, 18 November 1782, in Syrett, ed., *Papers of Alexander Hamilton*, III, 198.

35. Those who sought greater centralized powers for Congress are often called "nationalists" by historians, though the coherence and exact membership of the nationalist group is disputed. See Ferguson, *Power of the Purse*; but also Jack Rakove, *The Beginnings of National Politics: An Interpretive History of the Continental Congress* (New York: Knopf, 1979), esp. 323–324. More recently, see Rakove, *Revolutionaries: A New History of the Invention of America* (Boston: Houghton Mifflin Harcourt, 2010); and Joseph J. Ellis, *The Quartet: Orchestrating the Second American Revolution, 1783–1789* (New York: Knopf, 2015).

36. Knox to McDougall, 21 February 1782, quoted in Richard Kohn, *Eagle and Sword: The Federalists and the Creation of the Military Establishment in America, 1783–1802* (New York: Free Press, 1975), 27.

37. *Journals of the Continental Congress*, XXIV, 295–297.

38. Ibid., 306–310.

39. The best account of the Newburgh Conspiracy is still Kohn, *Eagle and Sword*, 17–39; and see Chernow, *Alexander Hamilton*, 176–180.

40. Washington to Hamilton, 4 April 1783, in Syrett, ed., *Papers of Alexander Hamilton*, III, 315–316.

41. There are two book-length accounts of the Society: Minor Myers, *Liberty Without Anarchy: A History of the Society of the Cincinnati* (Charlottesville: University Press of Virginia, 1983); and Marcus Hünemörder, *The Society of the Cincinnati: Conspiracy and Distrust in Early America* (New York: Berghahn Books, 2006). See also William Doyle, *Aristocracy and Its Enemies in the Age of Revolutions* (New York: Oxford University Press, 2009), chapter 4.

42. Myers, *Liberty without Anarchy*, 263.

43. Ibid., 259.

44. Ibid.

45. A similar dynamic took place in Freemasonry, which increased in popularity during the revolution: see Steven Bullock, *Revolutionary Brotherhood: Freemasonry and the Transformation of the American Social Order, 1730–1840* (Chapel Hill: University of North Carolina Press, 1998).

46. Hamilton to Jay, 14 March 1779, in Syrett, ed., *Papers of Alexander Hamilton*, II, 17.

47. Hünemörder, *Society of the Cincinnati*, 18; Myers, *Liberty Without Anarchy*, 38.

48. Henry Knox to Benjamin Lincoln, May 1783, quoted in Hünemörder, *Society of the Cincinnati*, 25; Alexander Moore, *The Fabric of Liberty: the Society of the Cincinnati of the State of South Carolina* (Home House Press: Charleston, 2012), 39.

49. Moore, *Fabric of Liberty*, 42.

50. Cassius [Aedanus Burke], *Considerations on the Society or Order of the Cincinnati* (Charleston, 1783), 1, 8.

51. On Burke, see John C. Meleney, *The Public Life of Aedanus Burke: Revolutionary Republican in Post-Revolutionary South Carolina* (Columbia: University of South Carolina Press, 1989).

52. Elbridge Gerry to John Adams, 23 Nov 1783, in Gregg Lint et al., eds., *Papers of John Adams*, 16 vols. (Cambridge, MA: Belknap Press, 2010), XV, 372–373, and 375, note 8. See also the extravagant suspicions of intrigue involving French influence on the officers of Congress, especially Robert Morris, in Samuel Osgood to John Adams, 7 December 1784, in ibid., 400–402.

53. Elbridge Gerry to John Adams, 23 November 1783, in Lint et al., eds., *Papers of John Adams*, XV, 373.

54. Adam Boyd to Henry Knox, 29 December 1783, Archives of the Society of the Cincinnati, Anderson House, Washington, D.C.

55. Henry Knox to George Washington, 21 February 1784, in W. W. Abbot et al., eds., *The Papers of George Washington, Confederation Series*. 6 vols.(Charlottesville: University of Virginia Press, 1992–1997), I, 142–143.

56. Benjamin Franklin to Sarah Bache, 26 January 1784, in J.A. Leo Lemay ed., *Benjamin Franklin: Writings* (New York: Library of America, 1987), 1084–1085.

57. Ibid., 1085.

58. Marquis de Lafayette to Washington, 9 March 1784, in Abbot et al., eds., *Papers of George Washington*, I, 181.

59. George Washington to Thomas Jefferson, 8 April 1784, in ibid., 275–276.

60. Jefferson to Washington, 16 April 1784, in ibid., 287–290.

61. Washington, Observations on the Institution of the Cincinnati, in ibid., 330–31; Winthrop Sargent's Journal, in ibid., 335.

62. Ibid., 341, 336.

63. To the State Societies of the Cincinnati, 15 May 1784, in ibid., 361, 364.

64. Farewell Orders to the Armies of the United States, 2 November 1783, in Fitzpatrick, ed., *Writings of George Washington*, XXVII, 226.

65. On Moylan's life, see U.S. Army Quartermaster Foundation, http://old.qmfound.com/COL_Stephen_Moylan.htm, accessed 12 December 2016.

66. An Obscure Individual [Stephen Moylan], *Observations on a Late Pamphlet, entitled Considerations upon the Society or Order of the Cincinnati* (Robert Bell: Philadelphia, 1783), 20.

67. [Moylan], *Observations on a Late Pamphlet*, 19–20, emphasis in original.

68. *The Institution and Records of the New Hampshire Society of the Cincinnati, 1783–1823* (Concord, NH: I. C. Evans, 1893), 27.

69. Ibid., 27–28.

70. Ibid., 28–29.

71. *The Institution of the Society of the Cincinnati ... Together with Some of the Proceedings of the General Society, and of the New-York Society* (New York, 1851), 40, Archives of the Society of the Cincinnati, Anderson House, Washington, D.C.

72. Report of a Committee of the New York State Society of the Society of the Cincinnati, 6 July 1786, in Syrett, ed., *Papers of Alexander Hamilton*, III, 675–76.

73. Ibid.

74. From the beginning of the revolution, some Americans had recognized primogeniture as a key feature of the old regime to be eliminated. Thomas Jefferson was foremost among them; see Holly Brewer, "Entailing Aristocracy in Colonial Virginia: 'Ancient Feudal Restraints' and Revolutionary Reform," *William & Mary Quarterly* 54.2 (Apr. 1997): 307–346.

75. Report of a Committee of the New York State Society of the Society of the Cincinnati, 6 July 1786, in Syrett, ed., *Papers of Alexander Hamilton*, III, 675–676.

76. Address of the Annapolis Convention, 14 September 1786, in ibid., 689; Circular Letter to the State Societies of the Cincinnati, 1 November 1786, in ibid., 695.

Chapter Two. Obedience

1. Quite which of these two institutions revolutionaries most meant to rebel against has been a topic of dispute in recent historiography: see Brendan McConville, *The King's Three Faces: The Rise and Fall of Royal America, 1688–1776* (Chapel Hill: University of North Carolina Press, 2006); Eric Nelson, *The Royalist Revolution: Monarchy and the American Founding* (Cambridge: Harvard University Press, 2014); but for a different perspective, Winthrop Jordan, "Familial Politics: Thomas Paine and the Killing of the King, 1776," *Journal of American History* 60.2 (Sept., 1973): 294–308. For further Freud-inflected interpretations of revolutionary disobedience, see Jay Fliegelman, *Prodigals and Pilgrims: The American Revolution against Patriarchal Authority, 1750–1800* (Cambridge: Cambridge University Press, 1982); Melvin Yazawa, *From Colonies to Commonwealth: Familial Ideology and the Beginnings of the American Republic* (Baltimore: Johns Hopkins University Press, 1985). On the deeper history of obedience and consent, see Holly Brewer, *By Birth or Consent: Children, Law, and the Anglo-American Revolution in Authority* (Chapel Hill: University of North Carolina Press, 2007).

2. John Adams to Abigail Adams, 14 April 1776, *Adams Family Papers: An Electronic Archive*, Massachusetts Historical Society. http://www.masshist.org/digitaladams/

3. On class and social dynamics in revolutionary America, see Keith Wrightson, "Class," in David Armitage and Michael Braddick eds., *The British Atlantic World, 1500–1800* (Basingstoke: Palgrave Macmillan, 2002); Simon Middleton and Billy G. Smith, *Class Matters: Early North America and the Atlantic World* (Philadelphia: University of Pennsylvania Press, 2008); and for a local study, Stephen Rosswurm, *Arms, Country, and Class: The Philadelphia Militia and the "Lower Sort" During the American Revolution, 1775–1783* (New Brunswick, NJ: Rutgers University Press, 1987).

4. For Barlow's life, see Richard Buel, *Joel Barlow: American Citizen in a Revolutionary World* (Baltimore: Johns Hopkins University Press, 2011); and Peter Hill, *Joel Barlow: American Diplomat and Nation Builder* (Washington, DC: Potomac Books, 2012).

5. From Joel Barlow, *The Prospect of Peace* (New Haven, 1778), Evans #15729, 4.

6. Barlow to Noah Webster, 30 January 1779, quoted in Hill, *Joel Barlow*, 1.

7. On this establishment in the era of the revolution, especially in relation to the clergy, see Peter Field, *The Crisis of the Standing Order: Clerical Intellectuals and Cultural Authority in Massachusetts, 1780–1833* (Amherst: University of Massachusetts Press, 1998);

Christopher Grasso, *A Speaking Aristocracy: Transforming Public Discourse in Eighteenth Century Connecticut* (Chapel Hill: University of North Carolina Press, 1999); and Jonathan Sassi, *A Republic of Righteousness: The Public Christianity of the Post-Revolutionary New England Clergy* (New York: Oxford University Press, 2001).

8. John Adams to Richard Cranch, 2 September 1755, in *The Adams Papers Digital Edition*, ed. C. James Taylor (Charlottesville: University of Virginia Press, Rotunda, 2008).

9. Abraham Baldwin to Barlow, 1780, quoted in Theodore Albert Zunder, *The Early Days of Joel Barlow, A Connecticut Wit* (New Haven: Yale University Press, 1934), 99.

10. From "The Progress of Dulness, Part One, Or the Adventures of Tom Brainless," in Vernon Parrington ed., *The Connecticut Wits* (Hamden, CT: Archon Books, 1963), 11–12.

11. Barlow to Ruth Baldwin, October 1780, quoted in Zunder, *Early Days of Joel Barlow*, 113.

12. Charles Chauncy, *The Accursed Thing* (Boston: Thomas & John Fleet, 1778), Evans #15759, 20, 14.

13. Samuel Adams to James Warren, 4 November 1775, quoted in Richard D. Brown, *The Strength of a People: The Idea of an Informed Citizenry in America, 1650–1870* (Chapel Hill: University of North Carolina Press, 1996), 100; Field, *Crisis of the Standing Order*, 45; Mary Handlin and Oscar Handlin, eds., *The Popular Sources of Political Authority: Documents on the Massachusetts Constitution of 1780* (Cambridge: Harvard University Press, 1966), 202. For the Baptist revival in Massachusetts, 1778–1782, see John L. Brooke, *The Heart of the Commonwealth: Society and Political Culture in Worcester County, Massachusetts, 1713–1861* (Cambridge: Cambridge University Press, 1989), 176.

14. Peter Thacker, *Observations Upon the Present State of the Clergy* (Boston: Norman & White, 1783), Evans #18206, 4.

15. William B. Weeden, ed., "Diary of Enos Hitchcock, D. D., A Chaplain in the Revolutionary Army," *Publications of the Rhode Island Historical Society* 7 (July 1899), 90.

16. Ibid.

17. Ezra Stiles to Enos Hitchcock, 12 July 1780, in ibid., 93; Joel Barlow to Ruth Barlow, 12 November 1782, quoted in Hill, *Joel Barlow*, 6.

18. For Franklin's creation as an American icon, see Gordon Wood, *The Americanization of Benjamin Franklin* (New York: Penguin, 2004); and for his relationship with the laboring class, see Simon Newman, "Benjamin Franklin and the Leather Apron Men: The Politics of Class in Eighteenth-Century Philadelphia," *Journal of American Studies* 43 (2009): 161–175.

19. Barlow, "Prospect of Peace," 7; "The Post-Boy's Present to his Customers," quoted in Theodore A. Zunder, *The Early Years of Joel Barlow (New Haven: Yale University Press, 1934)*, 65.

20. Weeden, ed., "Diary of Enos Hitchcock," 93–98.

21. It is difficult to determine how many potential voters were excluded by this provision, but most scholars agree that its effect was tangible. For some data on local incomes see Van Beck Hall, *Politics Without Parties: Massachusetts, 1781–1791* (Pittsburgh: University of Pittsburgh Press, 1972), 61 n. 77.

22. Zabdiel Adams, "An Election Sermon," in Charles Hyneman and Donald Lutz, eds., *American Political Writing During the Founding Era, 1760–1805* (Indianapolis, IN: Liberty Fund, 1983), 544.

23. Ibid., 555; Adams, The Evil Designs of Men (Boston: Edes and Sons, 1783), Evans #17807, 25; Thacker, *Present State of the Clergy*, 4.

24. Samuel McClintock, "On the Commencement of the New Hampshire Constitution," in Ellis Sandoz, *Political Sermons of the American Founding Era, 1730–1805* (Indianapolis, IN: Liberty Fund, 1998), 805–809; Samuel Wales, "The Dangers of Our National Prosperity," ibid., 852, 861.

25. Enos Hitchcock, "A Discourse on Education" (Providence: Wheeler, 1785), Evans #19040, 11.

26. For educational thought in the revolutionary era, see Lawrence Cremin, *American Education*. 2 vols. (New York: Harper & Row, 1970–1980); Brown, *Strength of a People*; and John Yolton, *John Locke and Education* (New York: Random House, 1971).

27. Hitchcock, "Discourse on Education," 4–8; see John Locke, *Some Thoughts Concerning Education*, eds. John Yolton and Jean Yolton (Oxford: Clarendon Press, 1989), 83–84.

28. Hitchcock, "Discourse on Education," 9–13; see Jean-Jacques Burlamaqui, *The Principles of Natural and Politic Law* (Cambridge, MA, 1807 [1747]), II, 105.

29. Hitchcock, "Discourse on Education," 15–16.

30. Noah Webster, "Memoir of Noah Webster, Ll. D.," No. 5, in Richard M. Rollins, ed., *The Autobiographies of Noah Webster: From the Letters and Essays, Memoir, and Diary* (Columbia: University of South Carolina Press, 1989), 133. On Webster's life, see also Harry Warfel, *Noah Webster: Schoolmaster to America* (New York: Octagon Books:, 1966 [1936]); Rollins, *The Long Journey of Noah Webster* (Philadelphia: University of Pennsylvania Press, 1980); and Joshua Kendall, *The Forgotten Founding Father: Noah Webster's Obsession and the Creation of an American Culture* (New York: G.P. Putnam's Sons, 2010).

31. David Micklethwait, *Noah Webster and the American Dictionary* (Jefferson, NC: McFarland and Co., 2000), 20. For the school and its legacy, see Mark Boonshoft, "The Litchfield Network: Education, Social Capital, and the Rise and Fall of a Political Dynasty, 1784–1833," *Journal of the Early Republic* 34.4 (Winter 2014): 561–595.

32. Micklethwait, *Noah Webster*, 20.

33. Webster, "Memoirs of Noah Webster," 135–136. Placing Webster's textbooks in the context of American education and literary culture, see E. Jennifer Monaghan, *A Common Heritage: Noah Webster's Blue-Backed Speller* (Hamden, CT: Archon Books, 1983).

34. Joel Barlow to Noah Webster, 31 August 1782, in Emily Ellsworth Ford Skeel, ed., *Notes on the Life of Noah Webster* (New York: Privately printed, 1912), I, 54–55.

35. Ibid., 55.

36. Webster, "Introduction to the Blue-Backed Speller," in Rollins, ed., *Autobiographies of Noah Webster*, 69.

37. Ibid. For this psychological aspect of the revolution, see Jay Fliegelman, *Prodigals and Pilgrims: The American Revolution Against Patriarchal Authority* (Cambridge: Cambridge University Press, 1982).

38. Webster, "Introduction to the Blue-Backed Speller," 70, 79.

39. Ibid., 70–71, 79.

40. Ibid., 72.

41. Micklethwait, *Noah Webster*, 75, and see 310, note 6.

42. Webster, "Memoir of Noah Webster," 139; Buel, *Joel Barlow*, 68–69.

43. Micklethwait, *Noah Webster*, 93–94.

44. Ibid., 95.

45. *Massachusetts Centinel*, 12 July 1786, quoted in ibid., 96.

46. Webster, Diary for 13 February 1786, in Rollins, ed., *Autobiographies of Noah Webster*, 223.

47. Noah Webster, "On the Education of Youth in America," in Frederick Rudolph, ed., *Essay in Education in the Early Republic* (Cambridge: Harvard University Press, 1965), 53–54.

48. Ibid., 54–56.

49. Ibid., 57–59.

50. Ibid., 59–61.

51. Ibid., 64, 77.

52. Thomas Jefferson, "A Bill for the More General Diffusion of Knowledge," in Merrill Peterson, ed., *Thomas Jefferson: Writings* (New York: Library of America, 1984), 365. Much has been written on Jefferson's educational thought. See, especially, James Gilreath ed., *Thomas Jefferson and the Education of a Citizen* (Washington, DC: Library of Congress, 1999); Michael Zuckerman, "Founding Fathers: Franklin, Jefferson, and the Educability of Americans," in John Pollack ed., *The Good Education of Youth: Worlds of Learning in the Age of Franklin* (Philadelphia: Oak Knoll Press, 2009); and for an alternative, unduly generous account, Onuf, *The Mind of Thomas Jefferson* (Charlottesville: University of Virginia Press, 2007), 169–178.

53. See David Tyack, "Forming the National Character: Paradox in the Educational Thought of the Revolutionary Generation," *Harvard Educational Review* 36 (1966); and Peter Onuf, "State Politics and Republican Virtue: Religion, Education, and Morality in Early American Federalism", in Paul Finkelman and Stephen Gottlieb, eds., *Toward a Usable Past: Liberty under State Constitutions* (Athens: University of Georgia Press, 1991), 91–116. As Rhys Isaac has put it, "at this time the symbolism of learning communicated most directly the principle of due subordination within the society of free persons. Learning was one aspect of hierarchical social structure that could readily be republicanized." Isaac, *The Transformation of Virginia, 1740-1790* (Chapel Hill: University of North Carolina Press, 1982), 289.

54. Peterson, ed., *Thomas Jefferson*, 365, 371.

55. Ibid., 365.

56. Jefferson, *Notes on the State of Virginia*, in Peterson, ed., *Thomas Jefferson: Writings*, 273–275.

57. Jefferson to Washington, 4 January 1786, Founders Online, National Archive, http://founders.archives.gov/documents/Washington/04-03-02-0419.

58. John Adams to John Jebb, 10 September 1785, Founders Online, National Archive, http://founders.archives.gov/documents/Adams/06-17-02-0232.

59. Charles Francis Adams, ed., *The Works of John Adams, Second President of the United States,* 10 vols. (Boston: Charles C. Little and James Brown:, 1851), VI, 198.

60. On political economy and the turbulence in western Pennsylvania, see Terry Bouton, *Taming Democracy: "The People," the Founders, and the Troubled Ending of the American Revolution* (Oxford: Oxford University Press, 2007), 88–104.

61. Surprisingly, the best biography of Rush remains David Freeman Hawke, *Benjamin Rush: Revolutionary Gadfly* (Indianapolis, IN: Bobbs-Merrill, 1971). See also Donald D'Elia, *Benjamin Rush: Philosopher of the American Revolution* (Philadelphia: American Philosophical Society, 1974); and Nathan Goodman, *Benjamin Rush: Physician and Citizen, 1746-1813* (Philadelphia: University of Pennsylvania Press , 1934).

62. Hawke, *Benjamin Rush*, 283–298.

63. Benjamin Rush to Charles Nisbet, 27 August 1784, quoted in Hawke, *Benjamin Rush*, 286.

64. Rush to John Montgomery, 7 July 1783; John King to Rush, 24 March 1783; quoted in ibid., 288–289.

65. Benjamin Rush, "Thoughts Upon the Mode of Education Proper in a Republic," in Rudolph, ed., *Essays on Education*, 9–23, quotations at 9, 22.

66. Ibid., 10–12, 16.

67. Ibid., 10, 17–18, 22–23.

68. Ibid., 14, 21–22.

69. Description of Moyes in Webster, Diary for 15 May 1785, 212; for meeting with Rush, see Diary for 21 February 1786, 224.

70. A. D. Morrison-Low, "Moyes, Henry (1749/50–1807)," *Oxford Dictionary of National Biography* (Oxford: Oxford University Press, 2004).

71. See Alexander Broadie, ed., *The Cambridge Companion to the Scottish Enlightenment* (Cambridge: Cambridge University Press, 2003); Arthur Herman, *The Scottish Enlightenment: The Scots' Invention of the Modern World* (London: Fourth Estate, 2001).

72. Benjamin Rush, "Thoughts Upon the Mode of Education Proper in a Republic," in Rudolph, ed., *Essays on Education*, 21.

73. Ibid., 19. For the relationship of education to capitalism in the early republic, see Nancy Beadie, *Education and the Creation of Capital in the Early American Republic* (New York: Cambridge University Press, 2010).

74. Adam Smith, *An Enquiry Concerning the Origins of the Wealth of Nations* (London: W. Strahan & T. Cadell, 1776), II, 373.

75. James Madison, Federalist #10, in Lawrence Goldman, ed., *The Federalist Papers* (Oxford: Oxford University Press, 2008), 55.

76. Webster, "Education of Youth," 66–67.

Chapter Three. Justice

1. On this debate, see Wood, *Creation of the American Republic*, chap. 9; Edmund S. Morgan, *Inventing the People: The Rise of Popular Sovereignty in England and America* (New York: W.W. Norton, 1989); Bruce Ackerman, *We the People*. Volume 1, *Foundations* (Cambridge: Harvard University Press, 1993); Christian Fritz, *American Sovereigns: The People and America's Constitutional Tradition before the Civil War* (Cambridge: Cambridge University Press, 2008); Jason Frank, *Constituent Moments: Enacting the People in Postrevolutionary America* (Durham, NC: Duke University Press, 2010).

2. Robert Dinkin, *Voting in Revolutionary America: A Study of Elections in the Original Thirteen States, 1776–1789* (Westport, CT: Greenwood Press, 1982); Sean Wilentz, *The Rise of American Democracy: Jefferson to Lincoln* (New York: W.W. Norton, 2005); Donald Ratcliffe, "The Right to Vote and the Rise of Democracy, 1787–1828," *Journal of the Early Republic* 33 (Summer 2013): 219–254.

3. For historical considerations of American property rights, see Jennifer Nedlesky, *Private Property and the Limits of American Constitutionalism: The Madisonian Framework and Its Legacy* (Chicago University Press: Chicago, 1990); James W. Ely, *The Guardian of Every Other Right: A Constitutional History of Property Rights* (New York: Oxford University Press, 1992); Christopher Tomlins, *Law, Labor, and Ideology in the Early American Republic* (Cambridge: Cambridge University Press, 1993); Gregory Alexander, *Commodity and Propriety: Competing Visions of Property in American Legal Thought* (Chicago: University of Chicago Press, 1997); James M. Banner, *American Property: A History of How, Why, and What We Own* (Cambridge: Harvard University Press, 2011).

4. Massey, *John Laurens*, 162.

5. Laurens to Richard Kidder Meade, 22 October 1781, in ibid., 200.

6. The best account of the American Revolution in South Carolina is Jerome Nadelhaft, *The Disorders of War: The Revolution in South Carolina* (Orono: University of Maine at Orono Press, 1981); see also Henry Lumpkin, *From Savannah to Yorktown: The American Revolution in the South* (Columbia: University of South Carolina Press, 1981); Ronald Hoffman, Peter J. Albert, and Thad W. Tate, *An Uncivil War: The Southern Backcountry during the American Revolution* (Charlottesville: University Press of Virginia, 1985); John Buchanan, *The Road to Guildford Courthouse: The American Revolution in the Carolinas* (New York: John Wiley and Sons, 1997). For Greene, see Theodore Thayer, *Nathanael Greene: Strategist of the American Revolution* (New York: Twayne Publishers, 1960); Greg-

NOTES TO CHAPTER THREE [173]

ory Massey, *Nathanael Greene and the American Revolution in the South* (Columbia: University of South Carolina Press, 2012).

7. On the role of African-Americans and slavery in the revolution, see, among much else, Benjamin Quarles, *The Negro in the American Revolution* (Chapel Hill: University of North Carolina Press, 1961); Sylvia Frey, *Water from the Rock: Black Resistance in a Revolutionary Age* (Princeton: Princeton University Press, 1991); Cassandra Pybus, *Epic Journeys of Freedom: Runaway Slaves of the American Revolution and Their Global Quest for Liberty* (Boston: Beacon Press, 2006); Gary Nash, *The Forgotten Fifth: African Americans in the Age of Revolution* (Cambridge: Harvard University Press, 2006); Douglas Egerton, *Death or Liberty: African Americans and Revolutionary America* (New York: Oxford University Press, 2009); Alan Gilbert, *Black Patriots and Loyalists: Fighting for Emancipation in the War for Independence* (Chicago: University of Chicago Press, 2012).

8. Quoted in Nadelhaft, *Disorders of War*, 87.

9. Massey, *John Laurens*, 93.

10. Hamilton to Jay, 14 March 1779, in Syrett, ed., *Papers of Alexander Hamilton*, II, 18.

11. Massey, 131.

12. Greene to John Rutledge, Papers of Nathanael Greene, X, 22.

13. Aedanus Burke to Arthur Middleton, 25 January 1782, "Correspondence of Hon. Arthur Middleton," 193.

14. Edward Rutledge to Arthur Middleton, 12 December 1781, in ibid., 208.

15. Quoted in John Meleney, *The Public Life of Aedanus Burke: Revolutionary Republican in Post-Revolutionary South Carolina* (Columbia: University of South Carolina Press, 1989), 65.

16. Robert Wilson Gibbes, ed., *Documentary History of the American Revolution*, 3 vols. (Columbia, SC: Banner Steam-Power Press, 1853), II, 233–237.

17. *JCC*, vol. 9, 971.

18. See, for example, Harry Yoshpe, *The Disposition of Loyalist Estates in the Southern District of the State of New York* (New York: Columbia University Press, 1939); and Richard D. Brown, "The Confiscation and Disposition of Loyalists' Estates in Suffolk County, Massachusetts," *William and Mary Quarterly*, 3rd ser., 21 (October 1964): 534–550.

19. Thomas Cooper, ed., *The Statutes at Large of South Carolina: Acts from 1752 to 1786* (Columbia, SC: A.S. Johnston:, 1838), IV, 517.

20. Edward Rutledge to Arthur Middleton, 28 January 1782, "Correspondence of Hon. Arthur Middleton," 212.

21. Gregory Massey, *John Laurens and the American Revolution* (Columbia: University of South Carolina Press, 2000), 209–210.

22. Burke to Middleton, 25 January 1782, "Correspondence of Hon. Arthur Middleton," 193.

23. Ibid., 192.

24. There were 237 people named in the Confiscation Act, "plus about 140 more who fell into general categories specified in the law"; 47 named in the Amercement Act, "and about the same number who came under its general provisions"; James Haw, *John and Edward Rutledge of South Carolina* (Athens: University of Georgia Press, 1997), 163–164.

25. Robert M. Weir, "'The Violent Spirit,' the Reestablishment of Order, and the Continuity of Leadership in Post-Revolutionary South Carolina', in *An Uncivil War*, ed. Hoffman et al., 83–98, esp. 86–88.

26. A. S. Salley Jr., ed., *Journal of the House of Representatives of South Carolina* (Columbia, SC: The State Company, 1916), 56.

27. Aedanus Burke to Arthur Middleton, 25 January 1782, "Correspondence of Hon. Arthur Middleton," 194.

28. Rutledge to Middleton, 8 February 1782, "Correspondence of Hon. Arthur Middleton," 4.

29. Laurens to Hamilton, July 1782, in Syrett, ed., *Papers of Alexander Hamilton*, III, 121.

30. On the role of slavery in the consolidation of a white republic in South Carolina, see especially Rachel Klein, *Unification of a Slave State: The Rise of the Planter Class in the South Carolina Backcountry, 1760–1808* (Chapel Hill: University of North Carolina Press, 1990).

31. Quoted in Nadelhaft, *Disorders of War*, 84.

32. Chistopher Gadsden to Governor John Mathews, 16 October 1782, in Richard Walsh ed., *The Writings of Christopher Gadsden, 1746–1805* (Columbia: University of South Carolina Press, 1966), 182.

33. Hamilton to the Marquis de Lafayette, 3 November 1782, in Syrett, ed., *Papers of Alexander Hamilton*, III, 193.

34. Quarles, *Negro in the American Revolution*, 166–167. On the fate of those who sailed out with the British, see also Pybus, *Epic Journeys of Freedom*; and Maya Jasanoff, *Liberty's Exiles: American Loyalists in the Revolutionary World* (New York: Knopf, 2011). But for loyalists who brought enslaved men and women to Canada, see Harvey Amani Whitfield, *North to Bondage: Loyalist Slavery in the Maritimes* (Vancouver: University of British Columbia Press, 2016).

35. David Ramsay, *History of the Revolution of South-Carolina*, (Trenton: NJ:, Isaac Collins, 1785), II, 384, 383.

36. Gadsden to Marion, 17 November 1782, in Richard Walsh, ed., *The Writings of Christopher Gadsden, 1746-1805 (Columbia: University of South Carolina Press, 1966)*, 194, 196–197.

37. Meleney, *Aedanus Burke*, 17–24.

38. Meleney, *Aedanus Burke*, 82; Burke was, however, elected to fill a vacancy a month later.

39. Cassius [Burke], *An Address to the Freemen*, 77.

40. On the important role of the law of nations in American thought, see Peter Onuf and Nicholas Onuf, *Federal Union, Modern World: The Law of Nations in an Age of Revolutions, 1776-1814* (Madison, WI: Madison House, 1993); Mark Janis, *America and the Law of Nations, 1776-1939* (New York: Oxford University Press, 2010), esp. chapter 2; and Gould, *Among the Powers*.

41. Cassius [Burke], *An Address to the Freemen*, 19.

42. Ibid., 5–7.

43. Ibid., 24–5.

44. Ibid., 26–28, 20.

45. John Sandford Dart to Ralph Izard, 11 July 1783, quoted in Nadelhaft, *Disorders of War*, 97; see Emma Hart, *Building Charleston: Town and Society in the Eighteenth Century British Atlantic World* (Charlottesville: University of Virginia Press, 2010), 191.

46. *Ordinances of Charleston Passed in the First Year of Incorporation of the City*, quoted in Hart, *Building Charleston*, 103.

47. For accounts of the diplomacy behind the Peace of Paris, see Jonathan Dull, *A Diplomatic History of the American Revolution* (New Haven: Yale University Press, 1985); and Richard B. Morris, *The Peacemakers: The Great Powers and American Independence* (New York: Harper & Row, 1965).

48. Mary Giunta, ed., *The Emerging Nation: A Documentary History of the Foreign Relations of the United States under the Articles of Confederation, 3 vols.* (Washington, DC: National Historical Publications and Records Commission, 1996), I, 111.

49. Ibid.., 111.

50. Henry Strachey to Alleyne Fitzherbert 10 February 1783, and Strachey to Thomas Townshend, 29 November 1782, quoted in Andrew Stockley, *Britain and France at the Birth of America: The European Powers and the Peace Negotiations of 1782-1783* (Exeter: University of Exeter Press, 2001), 65.

51. Ibid., 46, emphasis in original.

52. Treaty of Paris, 1783, in Hunter Miller, ed., *Treaties and Other International Acts of the United States of America* (Washington, DC: Government Printing Office, 1931).

53. John Jay to George Clinton, 6 May 1780, Papers of John Jay, Columbia University, Butler Library.

54. Circular Letter from Congress to their Constituents, 13 September 1779, *PJJ*, I, 235-6.

55. Memorial by American Loyalists, presented by Samuel Hayke and Mr. Lydekker, 18 December 1782, quoted in Ruma Chopra, *Unnatural Rebellion: Loyalists in New York City during the Revolution* (Charlottesville: University of Virginia Press, 2011), 209.

56. New Yorker to a friend in London, 6 April 1783, quoted ibid. See also Judith Van Buskirk, *Generous Enemies: Patriots and Loyalists in Revolutionary New York* (Philadelphia: University of Pennsylvania Press, 2002), 165.

57. Brutus, *To All Adherents to the British Government . . .* , (Poughkeepsie, NY: Morton and Horner, 1783), Evans #44464, emphasis in original.

58. Edwin Burrows and Mike Wallace, *Gotham: A History of New York to 1898* (New York: Oxford University Press, 1999), 261.

59. Hezekiah Niles, ed., *Principles and Acts of the Revolution in America* (Baltimore: William Ogden Niles, 1822), 479.

60. Chernow, *Alexander Hamilton*, 185–186.

61. Alexander Hamilton to George Clinton, 14 May 1784, in Syrett, ed., *Papers of Alexander Hamilton*, III, 356.

62. Phocion [Alexander Hamilton], "A Letter from Phocion to the Considerate Citizens of New York," (New York: Samuel Loudon, 1784), in ibid., II, 483–484.

63. Constitution of the State of New York, 1777, in *The Federal and State Constitutions, Colonial Charters, and Other Organic Laws of the States, Territories, and Colonies Now or Heretofore Forming the United States of America*, ed. Francis Newton Thorpe (Washington, DC: Government Printing Office, 1909), II, 1332.

64. *The Speeches of the Different Governors, to the Legislature of the State of New York* (New York: J. B. Van Steenburgh, 1825), 22.

65. Hamilton, "Letter from Phocion."

66. Ibid.

67. Ed. note in Syrett, *Papers of Alexander Hamilton*, 484.

68. Hamilton to Gouverneur Morris, 21 February 1784, in ibid., 512.

69. Second Letter of Phocion, 10.

70. Phocion [Alexander Hamilton], "A Second Letter from Phocion to the Considerate Citizens of New York, Containing Remarks on Mentor's Reply," Syrett, ed., *Papers of Alexander Hamilton*, III, 549–551.

71. For Duane, see Edward Alexander, *A Revolutionary Conservative: James Duane of New York* (New York: Columbia University Press, 1938). On the trial, see ibid., 162–163; Julius Goebel, ed., *The Law Practice of Alexander Hamilton: Documents and Commentary* (New York: Columbia University Press, 1964–1981), I, 291–419; Daniel Hulsebosch, *Constituting Empire: New York and the Transformation of Constitutionalism in the Atlantic World, 1664–1830* (Chapel Hill: University of North Carolina Press, 2005), 194–202.

72. Quoted in Mitchell, *Alexander Hamilton*, I, 342.

73. Alexander, *Revolutionary Conservative*, 163.

74. Quoted in ibid., 345.

75. James Duane to George Washington, 16 December 1784, Founders Online, National Archive, http://founders.archives.gov/documents/Washington/04-02-02-0152.

76. Niles, ed., *Principles and Acts*, 187.

77. An Act for the Gradual Abolition of Slavery, Pennsylvania, 1780, Avalon Project. On abolition in the north, see Arthur Zilversmit, *The First Emancipation: The Abolition of Slavery in the North* (Chicago: Chicago University Press, 1967); Joan Pope Melish, *Disowning Slavery: Gradual Emancipation and "Race" in New England, 1780–1860* (Ithaca, NY: Cornell University Press, 1998); Ira Berlin, *Many Thousands Gone: The First Two Centuries of Slavery in North America* (Cambridge: Harvard University Press, 1998), 228–255; David Gellman, *Emancipating New York: The Politics of Slavery and Freedom, 1777–1827* (Baton Rouge: Louisiana State University Press, 2006).

78. Gellman, *Emancipating New York*, 45.

79. John Jay to Benjamin Rush, 24 March 1785, in Henry P. Johnston, ed., *The Correspondence and Public Papers of John Jay* (New York: G. P. Putnam's Sons, 4 vols., 1890-93), III, 139.

80. Gellman, *Emancipating New York*, 49.

81. New York Council of Revision, Veto Message, 1785, in Gellman, ed., *Jim Crow New York: A Documentary History of Race and Citizenship, 1777–1877* (New York: New York University Press, 2003), 31–32.

82. Gellman, *Emancipating New York*, 52, and quotation at 60.

83. "Liberal principles" were a core element of gentility. As Rhys Isaac has put it, "the quality that most nearly epitomized what was needed to make a gentleman was 'liberality.'" Isaac, *Transformation of Virginia*, 131.

84. Gellman, *Emancipating New York*, 63.

85. Ezra Stiles, "The United States Elevated to Glory and Honor," 49–50, 85; see Onuf and Onuf, *Federal Union, Modern World*.

86. Marshall, *Remaking the British Atlantic*, 107–108.

87. Lord Sheffield, *Observations on the Commerce of the American States* (London: J. Debrett, 1783), 109.

88. John Adams to Robert R. Livingston, 15 July 1783, Founders Online, National Archives, https://founders.archives.gov/documents/Adams/06-15-02-0059.

89. Robert Morris to John Jay, 27 November 1783, in E. James Ferguson, *The Papers of Robert Morris* (Pittsburgh: University of Pittsburgh Press, 9 vols., 1973-1999) VIII, 785–786; and see John Jay to Robert Morris, 12 September 1783, ibid., 506–507.

90. For the postwar depression, see Cathy Matson, "Revolution, Constitution, and the New Nation," in Stanley Engerman and Robert Gallman, eds., *Cambridge Economic History of the United States* (Cambridge: Cambridge University Press, 1996), 363–402; P. J. Marshall, *Remaking the British Atlantic: The United States and the British Empire after American Independence* (Oxford: Oxford University Press, 2012), 97–117.

91. Richard Henry Lee to George Washington, 20 November 1784, Founders Online, National Archive, http://founders.archives.gov/documents/Washington/04-02-02-0119.

92. William Bingham, *A Letter from an American, Now Resident in London* (Philadelphia, 1784), 4.

93. John Jay to Charles Thomson, 7 April 1784, in Henry Johnston, ed., *The Correspondence and Public Papers of John Jay,* (New York: G.P. Putnam's Sons, 1890–1893), III, 125.

94. Richard Price, *Observations on the Importance of the American Revolution* (Hartford, CT: Barlow and Babcock, 1785) 52, 54–55, 58.

95. John Jay to John Adams, 5 February 1785, in Mary Giunta, ed., *The Emerging Nation: A Documentary History of the Foreign Relations of the United States under the*

Articles of Confederation (Washington, DC: National Historical Publications and Records Commission, 1996), II, 541.

96. Ibid., 587.

97. David Ramsay, *History of South Carolina* (Spartanburg, SC: The Reprint Company:, 1962 [1809]), II, 133.

98. John Lewis Gervais to Henry Laurens, 16 December 1783, quoted in Nadelhaft, *Disorders of War*, 160.

99. [Aedanus Burke], A Few Salutary Hints (New York, 1785 [1784]), 4–5.

100. Ibid., 7, 6, 14.

101. *Journals of the House of Representatives 1785-1786*, eds. Lark Adams et al. (Columbia: University of South Carolina Press, 1979), 313–314.

102. Ralph Izard to Thomas Jefferson, 1 July 1786, *The Papers of Thomas Jefferson Digital Edition*, eds. Barbara Oberg and J. Jefferson Looney (Charlottesville: University of Virginia Press, Rotunda, 2008).

103. Giunta, *Emerging Nation*, 541

104. Ibid.

105. Debate in the House of Representatives, 16 February 1787, quoted in Nadelhaft, *Disorders of War*, 171.

106. David Ramsay to Thomas Jefferson, 7 April 1787, *The Papers of Thomas Jefferson Digital Edition*, eds. Barbara Oberg and J. Jefferson Looney (Charlottesville: University of Virginia Press, Rotunda, 2008).

Chapter Four. Capital

1. Of course, having access to capital does not mean exactly the same thing as having lots of money. Some gentlemen, lawyers like Alexander Hamilton or physicians like Benjamin Rush for example, possessed little property compared to the wealthiest Americans; yet through social and institutional connections they had influence over flows of capital. Other very wealthy gentlemen, like Robert Morris, were in fact heavily indebted. That did not make them poor. What mattered was their access to credit and their ability to negotiate their debts—resources that indebted farmers mostly did not have. Capital, in other words, is a relational phenomenon. See David Harvey, *The Limits to Capital* (Oxford: Blackwell, 1982).

2. On corporations, see Terry Bouton, "Moneyless in Pennsylvania: Privatization and the Depression of the 1780s," in Cathy Matson, ed., *The Economy of Early America: historical perspectives and new directions* (College Park: Pennsylvania State University Press, 2006); Andrew Schocket, *Founding Corporate Power in Early National Philadelphia* (DeKalb: Northern Illinois University Press, 2007); Robert E. Wright, "Rise of the Corporation Nation," in Douglas A. Irwin and Richard Sylla, eds., *Founding Choices: American Political Economy in the 1790s* (Chicago: University of Chicago Press, 2011); idem., "Capitalism and the Rise of the Corporation Nation," in Michael Zakim and Gary J. Kornblith, *Capitalism Takes Command: The Social Transformation of Nineteenth-Century America* (Chicago: University of Chicago Press, 2011).

3. The impact of capital in the countryside has been the subject of long-running debate among historians. See footnote 38 below. More generally on capitalism's transformative power, see Ellen Meiksins Wood, *The Origin of Capitalism: A Longer View* (London: Verso, 2002); and Joyce Appleby, *The Relentless Revolution: A History of Capitalism* (New York: W.W. Norton, 2011).

4. The best summary of these movements across the United States as a whole is Woody Holton, *Unruly Americans and the Origins of the Constitution* (New York: Hill & Wang, 2007).

5. George Washington to John Augustine Washington, 15 June 1783, *WGW*, XXVII, 11–13.

6. Ibid.

7. Circular Letter from Congress to their Constituents, 13 September 1779, *PJJ*, I, 232–3.

8. Washington to John Augustine Washington, 15 June 1783, *WGW*, XXVII, 11–13.

9. Washington to Elias Boudinot, 17 June 1783, ibid., 16–18.

10. These disputes among states are analyzed in Peter Onuf, *The Origins of the Federal Republic: Jurisdictional Controversies in the United States, 1775–1787* (Philadelphia: University of Pennsylvania Press , 1983).

11. On Native Americans' involvement with the American Revolution, see James H. O'Donnell III, *Southern Indians in the American Revolution* (Knoxville: University of Tennessee Press, 1973); Gregory Evans Dowd, *A Spirited Resistance: The North American Indian Struggle for Unity, 1745–1815* (Baltimore: Johns Hopkins University Press, 1992); Tom Hatley, *The Dividing Paths: Cherokees and South Carolinians Through the Era of Revolution* (New York: Oxford University Press, 1993); Colin Calloway, *The American Revolution in Indian Country: Crisis and Diversity in Native American Communities* (Cambridge: Cambridge University Press, 1995); Alan Taylor, *The Divided Ground: Indians, Settlers, and the Northern Borderland of the American Revolution* (New York: Knopf, 2006).

12. Washington to James Duane, 7 September 1783, *WGW*, XXVII, 133–137.

13. Ibid.

14. Stuart Banner, *How the Indians Lost Their Land: Law and Power on the Frontier* (Cambridge: Harvard University Press, 2007), 112.

15. Douglas Southall Freeman, *George Washington: A Biography* 7 vols. (London: Eyre and Spotiswood,1954), VI, 4.

16. George Washington to Benjamin Harrison, 10 October 1784, in *PGW*, II, 89–96.

17. George Washington to Benjamin Harrison, 10 October 1784, in *PGW*, II, 89–96.

18. George Washington, Diary Entry, 4 October 1784, Founders Online, National Archive, http://founders.archives.gov/documents/Washington/01-04-02-0001-0002-0004.

19. Washington to Harrison, 10 October 1784, in *PGW*, II, 92.

20. For Kentucky and Franklin, see Joan Coward, *Kentucky in the New Republic: The Process of Constitution Making* (Lexington: University Press of Kentucky, 1979); Fredrika Teute, "Land, Liberty, and Labor in the Post-Revolutionary Era: Kentucky as the Promised Land" (Ph.D. Diss., Johns Hopkins University, 1988); Kevin Barksdale, *The Lost State of Franklin: America's First Secession* (Lexington: University Press of Kentucky, 2009). More generally, the problematic relationship between the early United States and western settlers is analyzed in Eric Hinderaker, *Elusive Empires: Constructing Colonialism in the Ohio Valley, 1673–1800* (Cambridge: Cambridge University Press, 1997); and Patrick Griffin, *American Leviathan: Empire, Nation, and the Revolutionary Frontier* (New York: Hill & Wang, 2007).

21. Jefferson to Washington, 15 March 1784, Founders Online, National Archive, http://founders.archives.gov/documents/Washington/04-01-02-0159.

22. Washington to Jefferson, 29 March 1784, Founders Online, National Archive, http://founders.archives.gov/documents/Washington/04-01-02-0179.

23. On the canal project, see Stuart Leibiger, *Founding Friendship: George Washington, James Madison, and the Creation of the American Republic* (Charlottesville: University of Virginia Press, 1999), chap. 2; Jon Lauritz Larson, *Internal Improvement: National Public Works and the Promise of Popular Government in the Early United States* (Chapel Hill: University of North Carolina Press, 2001), 11–37; Joel Achenbach, *The Grand Idea: George Washington's Potomac and the Race to the West* (New York: Simon & Schuster, 2004).

24. Washington to Harrison, 10 October 1784, Founders Online, National Archive, http://founders.archives.gov/documents/Washington/04-02-02-0082.

25. Washington to Jefferson, 29 March 1784, *PGW*, vol. 1, 237.

26. Washington to Harrison, 10 October 1784, Founders Online, National Archive, http://founders.archives.gov/documents/Washington/04-02-02-0082.

27. Washington to James Madison, 3 December 1784, *PGW*, II, 166.

28. Gordon Wood, "Interests and Disinterestedness in the Making of the Constitution," in Richard Beeman, et al., eds., *Beyond Confederation: Origins of the Constitution and American National Identity* (Chapel Hill: University of North Carolina Press, 1987), 69–110, argues that Washington's ideas—and those of other gentlemen in the new republic—were defined by the notion of disinterested virtue. But Washington's actions, and his writing, show how deeply engaged he was with the commercial world and its idea of justice.

29. Ibid.

30. Richard Henry Lee to George Washington, 20 November 1784, Founders Online, National Archive, http://founders.archives.gov/documents/Washington/04-02-02-0119.

31. Washington to Richard Henry Lee, 15 March 1785, Founders Online, National Archive, http://founders.archives.gov/documents/Washington/04-02-02-0298.

32. George Washington to Hugh Williamson, 15 March 1785, Founders Online, National Archive http://founders.archives.gov/documents/Washington/04-02-02-0301.

33. William Grayson to George Washington, 4–8 May 1785, Founders Online, National Archive, http://founders.archives.gov/documents/Washington/04-02-02-0390.

34. Norman B. Wilkinson, "Land Policy and Speculation in Pennsylvania, 1779–1800" (Ph.D. Dissertation, University of Pennsylvania, 1958), 89–92.

35. Bergmann, *The American National State and the Early West (Cambridge: Cambridge University Press, 2012)*, 28–29.

36. Bouton, *Taming Democracy*, 122.

37. Bouton, "A Road Closed: Rural Insurgency in Post-Independence Pennsylvania," *Journal of American History* 87.3 (Dec. 2000): 855–887, 860.

38. There is a storied historiography regarding the expansion and adoption of markets in eighteenth- and nineteenth-century North America. See Joyce Appleby, *Capitalism and a New Social Order: The Republican Vision of the 1790s* (New York: New York University Press, 1984); Christopher Clark, *The Roots of Rural Capitalism: Western Massachusetts, 1780–1860* (Ithaca, NY: Cornell University Press, 1990); Winifred Barr Rothenberg, *From Market-Places to a Market Economy: The Transformation of Rural Massachusetts, 1750–1850* (Chicago: University of Chicago Press, 1992); Alan Kulikoff, *The Agrarian Origins of American Capitalism* (Charlottesville: University of Virginia Press, 1997); John Lauritz Larson, *The Market Revolution in America: Liberty, Ambition, and the Eclipse of the Common Good* (Cambridge: Cambridge University Press, 2010); Charles Post, *The American Road to Capitalism: Studies in Class-Structure, Economic Development, and Political Conflict, 1620–1877* (Boston: Brill, 2011).

39. Syrett, ed., *Papers of Alexander Hamilton*, II, 617.

40. Accounts of the Bank of North America include Bray Hammond, *Banks and Politics in America: From Revolution to Civil War* (Princeton: Princeton University Press, 1957), chap. 2; Robert E. Wright, *The Origins of Commercial Banking in America, 1750–1800* (Lanham, MD: Rowman & Littlefield, 2001); Howard Bodenhorn, *State Banking in Early America: A New Economic History* (Oxford: Oxford University Press, 2002), chap. 6; Wright, *The First Wall Street: Chestnut Street, Philadelphia, and the Birth of American Finance* (Chicago: University of Chicago Press, 2005); Andrew Schocket, *Founding Corporate Power in Early National Philadelphia* (DeKalb: Northern Illinois University Press, 2007), chap. 3.

41. John Keane, *Tom Paine: A Political Life* (London: Bloomsbury, 1995), 212–213.

42. Robert Morris, "To the Public," *Pennsylvania Packet* 28 May 1781, in Ferguson, *Papers of Robert Morris*, I, 85–86.

43. Alexander Hamilton to John Barker Church, 10 March 1784, *PAH*, III, 521.

44. For the Bank of New York, see Allan Nevins, History of the Bank of New York and Trust Company, 1784–1934 (New York: Privately printed, 1934); Hammond, *Banks and Politics*, chap. 3; Wright, *Origins of Commercial Banking*.

45. N.S.B. Gras, *The Massachusetts First National Bank of Boston, 1784–1934* (Cambridge: Harvard University Press, 1937).

46. Quoted in Mitchell, *Alexander Hamilton*, 352.

47. On the importance of personal networks in early banking practice, see Naomi Lamoreaux, *Insider Lending: Banks, Personal Connections, and Economic Development in Industrial New England* (Cambridge: Cambridge University Press, 1994); and see Ta-Chen Wang, "Banks, Credit Markets, and Early American Development: A Case Study of Entry and Competition," *Journal of Economic History* 68.2 (June 2008): 438–461. "The gentry's ability to secure deference and compliance was reinforced by their share in the social power that was inherent in the control of credit," Rhys Isaac, *Transformation of Virginia*, 133.

48. George Washington to Robert Morris, 1 February 1785, *PGW*, II, 315.

49. Morris to Washington, 17 April 1785, Founders Online, National Archive, http://founders.archives.gov/documents/Washington/04-02-02-0364.

50. Benjamin Rush to Charles Nisbet, 27 August 1784, quoted in Hawke, *Benjamin Rush*, 286.

51. Quoted in Bouton, *Taming Democracy*, 159.

52. Bouton, "Tying up the Revolution: Money, Power, and Regulation in Pennsylvania, 1765–1800," PhD. Diss. (Duke University, 1996) 175–176.

53. Bouton, *Taming Democracy*, 113.

54. Ibid., 114, 123.

55. Bouton, "Tying up the Revolution," 194.

56. *Freeman's Journal*, 23 February 1785.

57. On Findley, see John Caldwell, *William Findley from West of the Mountains: A Politician in Pennsylvania, 1783–1791* (Gig Harbor, WA: Red Apple Publishing, 2000); Gordon Wood, *Empire of Liberty: A History of the Early Republic, 1789–1815* (New York: Oxford University Press, 2009), 218–23.

58. Bouton, "Tying up the Revolution," 132–133, 181–182.

59. Ibid., 182–183.

60. Ibid., 187.

61. *Pennsylvania Gazette*, 30 March 1785.

62. *Pennsylvania Gazette*, 6 April 1785.

63. For the struggle over charter repeal, see Janet Wilson, "The Bank of North America and Pennsylvania Politics, 1781–1787," *Pennsylvania Magazine of History and Biography* 66.1 (1942): 3–28; Gordon Wood, *Radicalism of the American Revolution*, 256–258.

64. Minutes of the Directors, 12 May 1785, quoted in Wilson, "Bank of North America", 10.

65. Ibid., 11.

66. Thomas Willing to William Bingham, 29 August 1785, quoted in ibid., 12.

67. Minutes of the Directors, 1 September 1785, quoted in ibid., 11.

68. James Wilson, *Considerations on the Bank of North America* (Philadelphia: Hall & Sellers, 1785), Evans #19388, 10–13.

69. Ibid., 20–21.

70. Ibid., 17.

71. Ibid., 16–17.

72. Ibid., 8.

73. Ibid., 17–19.

74. *Pennsylvania Evening Herald*, 7 September 1785.

75. Pieter Johan Van Berckel, William Edgar, Sampson Fleming, William Denning, and Alexander Hamilton (for John Church) to Jeremiah Wadsworth, 3 January 1786, *PAH*, III, 643–4.

76. Jeremiah Wadsworth to Alexander Hamilton, 9 January 1786, ibid., 645–6.

77. John Barker Church to Hamilton, 5 April 1786, ibid., 657.

78. Berckel et al. to Wadsworth, 3 January 1786, ibid., 644.

79. Wadsworth to Hamilton, 9 January 1786, ibid., 645.

80. Bouton, *Taming Democracy*, 137.

81. John Keane, *Tom Paine: A Political Life* (London: Bloomsbury, 1995), 259, 262.

82. Diary of Robert Morris, 18 September 1781, in Ferguson, *Papers of Robert Morris*, 290.

83. "On the Advantages of a Public Bank," *Pennsylvania Packet*, 20 June 1786.

84. For Paine, see Eric Foner, *Tom Paine and Revolutionary America* (New York: Oxford University Press, 1976); John Keane, *Tom Paine: A Political Life* (London: Bloomsbury, 1995); Mark Philp, *Thomas Paine* (Oxford: Oxford University Press, 2007).

85. [Thomas Paine], *Dissertations on Government, the Affairs of the Bank, and Paper Money* (Philadelphia: Cist, 1786), Evans #19880, 39, 42.

86. Ibid., 1–3, 5–6.

87. Ibid., 6–8.

88. Ibid., 9.

89. Ibid., 53.

90. Ibid., 10, 14.

91. See Hannis Taylor, "The Designer of the Constitution of the United States," *North American Review*, 185.621 (16 August, 1907): 813–824.

92. Pelatiah Webster, "An Essay on Credit," 10 February 1786, in Webster, *Political Essays*, 455.

93. Ibid., 427.

94. Ibid., 435, 438.

95. Ibid., 439.

96. Ibid., 443.

97. Ibid., 459.

98. Ibid.

99. Quoted in Wilson, "Bank of North America," 16.

100. *Pennsylvania Gazette*, 15 March 1786, quoted ibid.

101. *Pennsylvania Gazette*, 5 April 1786, quoted ibid., 17.

102. Mathew Carey, *Debates and Proceedings of the General Assembly on Pennsylvania, on the memorials praying a repeal or suspension of the law annulling the charter of the bank* (Philadelphia: Carey & Co., 1786), Evans #19884, 53.

103. Thomas Willing to P. J. Van Berckel, William Edgar, John Barker Church, and Sampson Fleming, 13 June 1786, quoted in Wilson, "Bank of North America," 26.

104. *Pittsburgh Gazette*, 30 September 1786, in Claude Milton Newlin ed., *The Life and Writings of Hugh Henry Brackenridge* (Princeton: Princeton University Press, 1932), 75.

105. *Pittsburgh Gazette*, 9 September 1786, in ibid., 73.

106. *Pittsburgh Gazette*, 21 April 1787, quoted in Newlin, *Hugh Henry Brackenridge*, 83.

107. *Pittsburgh Gazette*, 21 April 1787, quoted in Bouton, *Taming Democracy*, 139.

108. Alexander Fowler, quoted in ibid.

109. *Pittsburgh Gazette*, 20 January 1787, quoted in Newlin, *Hugh Henry Brackenridge*, 79.

110. William Findley, *Pittsburgh Gazette*, 10 February 1787, quoted in Newlin, *Hugh Henry Brackenridge*, 80.

111. Newlin, *Hugh Henry Brackenridge*, 78.

112. Ibid., 85.

113. Wilson, "Bank of North America," 27–28.

114. George Washington to Bushrod Washington, 15 November 1786, *PGW*, IV, 368–369.

115. George Washington to Bushrod Washington, 30 September 1786, ibid., 278.

116. Hugh Henry Brackenridge, *Modern Chivalry* (Philadelphia, 1792), in Claude Milton Newlin, ed., *The Life and Writings of Hugh Henry Brackenridge* (Princeton: Princeton University Press, 1932), 119.

Chapter Five. Rebellion

1. David Ramsay to Thomas Jefferson, 7 April 1787.

2. There is, of course, a long historiography of class conflict in the American Revolution. See footnote 9 in the Introduction, and for an overview, Alfred F. Young and Gregory H. Nobles, *Whose American Revolution Was It?: Historians Interpret the Founding* (New York: Oxford University Press, 2011). My understanding of how class struggle occurred in the 1780s United States, despite the complexity and ambiguity of class identities at that time, is drawn from E.P. Thompson's classic essay, "Eighteenth Century English Society: class struggle without class," *Social History* 3.2 (May, 1978): 133–165.

3. The idea of a balanced constitution, in which different elements represented the popular and aristocratic elements of society, went back to ancient Greece. See Gordon Wood, *The Creation of the American Republic, 1776–1787* (Chapel Hill: University of North Carolina Press, 1969), esp. chap. 14.

4. Robert Taylor, *Western Massachusetts in the Revolution* (Providence: Brown University Press, 1954), 109.

5. Ibid., 111, 120–122.

6. Samuel Adams to John Adams, 4 November 1783, in Henry Cushing ed., *The Writings of Samuel Adams*, 4 vols. (New York: G.P. Putnam and Sons, 1908), IV, 288.

7. Samuel Adams to Noah Webster, 30 April 1784, in ibid, 305–306.

8. Taylor, *Western Massachusetts*, 117, 126.

9. Samuel Adams to John Adams, 2 July 1785, in Cushing, *Writings of Samuel Adams*, IV, 315–316.

10. *Massachusetts Centinel*, 15 January 1785.

11. For Samuel Adams and his generation, see Pauline Maier, *The Old Revolutionaries: Political Lives in the Age of Samuel Adams* (New York: Knopf, 1980); John Alexander, *Samuel Adams: America's Revolutionary Politician* (Lanham, MD: Rowman & Littlefield, 2002); Ira Stoll, *Samuel Adams: A Life* (New York: Free Press, 2008). See also Gregory Nobles, "Yet the Old Republicans Still Persevere: Samuel Adams, John Hancock, and the Crisis of Popular Leadership in Revolutionary Massachusetts, 1775–90," in Ronald Hoffman and Peter J. Albert, eds., *The Transforming Hand of Revolution: Reconsidering the American Revolution as a Social Movement.* (Charlottesville: University Press of Virginia, 1995).

12. *Boston Gazette*, 24 January 1785; and see Charles Warren, "Samuel Adams and the Sans Souci Club in 1785," *Proceedings of the Massachusetts Historical Society*, 60 (1927): 321.

13. William M. Fowler, *The Baron of Beacon Hill: A Biography of John Hancock* (Boston: Houghton Mifflin, 1979); Harlow Giles Unger, *John Hancock: Merchant King and American Patriot* (New York: Wiley & Sons, 2000).

14. Samuel Adams to John Adams, 2 July 1785, Cushing, *Writings of Samuel Adams*, IV, 316.

15. [James Bowdoin], *A Proclamation for the Encouragement of Piety* ... (Boston: Adams and Nourse, 1785), Evans #19085.

16. Taylor, *Western Massachusetts*, 130–132; Hall, *Politics Without Parties*, 138.

17. Roger H. Brown, *Redeeming the Republic: Federalists, Taxation, and the Origins of the Constitution* (Baltimore: Johns Hopkins University Press, 1993), 90.

18. *Newport Mercury*, 21 January 1786.

19. Brown, *Redeeming the Republic*, 91–92. On Rhode Island politics during this period, see Irwin Polishook, *Rhode Island and the Union, 1774–1795* (Evanston, IL: Northwestern University Press, 1969).

20. Brown, *Redeeming the Republic*, 94.

21. Polishook, *Rhode Island*, 126.

22. Brown, *Redeeming the Republic*, 95.

23. Polishook, *Rhode Island*, quotations on 128–129.

24. Ibid.

25. Timothy Bloodwell to Richard Caswell, 28 July 1786, in Smith, *Letters of the Delegates*, XXIII, 421.

26. Enos Hitchcock, *A Discourse on the Causes of National Prosperity* (Providence: Wheeler, 1786), Evans #19713, 14–15.

27. Edward Carrington to James Mercer, 1 September 1786, in Smith, *Letters of the Delegates*, XXIII, 538.

28. Samuel Adams to John Adams, 21 July 1786, Cushing, *Writings of Samuel Adams*, IV, 322–323.

29. *Worcester Magazine*, quoted in ibid., 141–2.

30. The events that emerged from this strategy in the summer of 1786, through to the beginning of 1787, later became known as Shays' Rebellion. See David Szatmary, *Shays' Rebellion: The Making of an Agrarian Insurgency* (Amherst: University of Massachusetts Press, 1980); Martin Kaufman, ed., *Shays' Rebellion: Selected Essays* (Westfield: Institute for Massachusetts Studies, 1987); Robert A. Gross, ed., *In Debt to Shays: The Bicentennial of an Agrarian Rebellion* (Charlottesville: University Press of Virginia, 1993); Leonard Richards, *Shays' Rebellion: The American Revolution's Final Battle* (Philadelphia: University of Pennsylvania Press, 2002); Sean Condon, *Shays' Rebellion: Authority and Distress in Post-Revolutionary America* (Baltimore: Johns Hopkins University Press, 2015).

31. *By His Excellency James Bowdoin ... A Proclamation, 2nd September* (Boston, 1786), Evans #19789.

32. Stephen Riley, "Dr William Whiting and Shays' Rebellion," *Proceedings of the American Antiquarian Society* 66.2 (1957): 119–124, quotations at 131–132.

33. Szartmary, *Shays' Rebellion*, 58–59, 65, quotation at 77.

34. Henry Lee to George Washington, 8 September 1786, in Paul H. Smith ed., *Letters of the Delegates to the Continental Congress* (Washington, DC: Library of Congress, 1995), XXIII, 553.

35. Lee to Washington, 1 October 1786, *PGW*, IV, 281.

36. James Mitchell Varnum, *The Case, Trevett against Weeden* (Providence: Carter, 1787), Evans #20825, iii.

37. Varnum, *Trevett against Weeden*, 11.

38. Ibid., 21–22.

39. Ibid., 23, 29.

40. Ibid., 36; see Polishook, *Rhode Island*, 138.

41. Ibid., 138–139.

42. Washington to Humphreys, 22 October 1786, in Abbot, ed., *Papers of George Washington*, IV, 297.

43. Humphreys to Washington, 24 September 1786, Founders Online, National Archive, http://founders.archives.gov/documents/Washington/04-04-02-0245.

44. Henry Knox to Washington, 23 October 1786, Abbot, ed., *Papers of George Washington*, IV, 300.

45. Ibid.

46. Ibid.

47. Ibid., 300–301.

48. Rufus King to Theodore Sedgwick, 26 October 1786, in Smith, *Letters of the Delegates*, vol. 23, 612.

49. King to Elbridge Gerry, 5 November 1786, ibid., 636.

50. Knox to Bowdoin, 1 October 1786; Knox to John Jay, 3 October 1786; quoted in North Callahan, *Henry Knox: General Washington's General* (New York, 1958), 244-245.

51. Joseph Parker Warren, "The Confederation and the Shays Rebellion," *American Historical Review* 11.1 (Oct. 1905): 42–67, 47.

52. Callahan, *Henry Knox*, 245; Warren, "Confederacy and the Shays Rebellion," 57.

53. Humphreys to Washington, 1 November 1786, in Abbot, ed., *Papers of George Washington*, IV, 325.

54. Humphreys to Washington, 9 November 1786, ibid., 351.

55. Vernon Parrington, *The Connecticut Wits* (Hamden, CT: Archon Books, 1963 [1926]), xxvii.

56. Humphreys to Washington, 24 September 1786, *PGW*, IV, 264.

57. Ibid.

58. Luther G. Riggs, ed., *The Anarchiad: A New England Poem, 1786-1787* (New Haven: Thomas H. Pease, 1861), 9.

59. Quoted in Myers, *Liberty Without Anarchy*, 80–81, 87.

60. Mercy Otis Warren to John Adams, December 1786, in Jeffrey Richards and Sharon Harris eds., *Mercy Otis Warren: Selected Letters* (Athens: University of Georgia Press, 2011), 211.

61. Benjamin Lincoln to George Washington, 4 December 1786, Founders Online, National Archive, http://founders.archives.gov/documents/Washington/04-04-02-0374-0002.

62. Ibid.

63. Ibid.

64. Knox to Washington, 19 March 1787, *PGW*, V, 97.

65. Richard Szatmary, *Shays' Rebellion: The Making of an Agrarian Insurrection* (Amherst: University of Massachusetts Press, 1980), 115.

66. Polishook, *Rhode Island*, 145-153.

67. Brown, *Redeeming the Republic*, 96.

68. James Varnum to Samuel Ward, Jr., 2 April 1787, in Smith, *Letters of the Delegates*, XXIV, 198.

69. William Ellery to Nathaniel Appleton, 2 October 1786, quoted in Polishook, *Rhode Island*, 144.

70. James Varnum to Samuel Ward, Jr., 2 April 1787, in Smith, *Letters of the Delegates*, XXIV, 198.

71. Knox to Washington, 29 May 1787, Founders Online, National Archive, http://founders.archives.gov/documents/Washington/04-05-02-0185.

72. James Madison to Thomas Jefferson, 27 March 1780, Founders Online, National Archive, http://founders.archives.gov/documents/Madison/01-02-02-0004.

73. E. James Ferguson, *Papers of Robert Morris*, xxxii.

74. See Adrienne Koch, *Jefferson and Madison: The Great Collaboration* (New York: Oxford University Press, 1964); and Leibiger, *Founding Friendship*, chap. 2.

75. For Virginia politics, see Norman Risjord, *Chesapeake Politics, 1781–1800* (New York: Columbia University Press, 1978).

76. James Madison to Thomas Jefferson, 12 August 1786, Founders Online, National Archive, http://founders.archives.gov/documents/Madison/01-09-02-0026.

77. Ibid.

78. For the Jay-Gardoqui negotiations and the crisis they precipitated in Congress, see Frederick Marks, *Independence on Trial: Foreign Affairs and the Making of the Constitution* (Baton Rouge: Louisiana State University Press, 1973), 25–34; John Kaminski, "Honor and Interest: John Jay's Diplomacy During the Confederation," *New York History* 83.3 (2002): 293–327.

79. Address of the Annapolis Convention, in Syrett, ed., *Papers of Alexander Hamilton*, III, 687–688.

80. Notes for Speech Opposing Paper Money [ca. 1 November 1786], Founders Online, National Archive, http://founders.archives.gov/documents/Madison/01-09-02-0066.

81. James Madison to George Washington, 1 November 1786, Founders Online, National Archive, http://founders.archives.gov/documents/Madison/01-09-02-0064.

82. James Madison to James Madison, Sr., 1 November 1786, Founders Online, National Archive, http://founders.archives.gov/documents/Madison/01-09-02-0063.

83. Washington to Madison, 5 November 1786, Founders Online, National Archive, http://founders.archives.gov/documents/Madison/01-09-02-0070.

84. Madison to Washington, 8 November 1786, Founders Online, National Archive, http://founders.archives.gov/documents/Madison/01-09-02-0074.

85. Madison to Edmund Pendleton, 24 February 1787, Founders Online, National Archive, http://founders.archives.gov/documents/Madison/01-09-02-0151.

86. Henry Knox to George Washington, 9 April 1787, Founders Online, National Archive, http://founders.archives.gov/documents/Washington/04-05-02-0129.

87. Humphreys to Washington, 9 April 1787, Founders Online, National Archive, http://founders.archives.gov/documents/Washington/04-05-02-0128.

88. Riggs, ed., *The Anarchiad*, 67–69.

89. Rhode Island Delegates to John Collins, 28 September 1786, in Smith, *Letters of the Delegates*, XXIII, 571. These delegates, of course, had been appointed before the new, radical regime was elected in 1785.

90. Madison to Pendleton, 22 April 1787, ibid., 395.

91. Madison to Edmund Randolph, 2 April 1787, ibid., 362.

92. Madison to Pendleton, 22 April 1787, ibid., 395.

93. Vices of the Political System of the United States, in Rakove, *James Madison*, 75.

94. Madison to Thomas Jefferson, 19 March 1787

95. Richard B. Morris, *The Forging of the Union, 1781–1789 (New York, Harper & Row, 1987)*, 265.

96. Thomas Jefferson to John Adams, 30 August 1787, in *The Papers of Thomas Jefferson*, ed. Julian Boyd (Princeton: Princeton University Press, 1955), xii, 69.

97. Beeman, *Plain, Honest Men*, 82–84.

Conclusion

1. James Madison to Thomas Jefferson, 24 September 1787, Founders Online, National Archive, http://founders.archives.gov/documents/Jefferson/01-12-02-0274.

2. James Wilson, speech to the Pennsylvania ratifying convention, 24 November 1787, in Colleen A. Sheehan and Gary L. McDowell, eds., *Friends of the Constitution: Writings of the "Other" Federalists, 1787–1788* (Indianapolis, IN: Liberty Fund, 1998), 73.

3. George Washington to the Marquis de Lafayette, 18 September 1787, Founders Online, National Archive, http://founders.archives.gov/documents/Washington/04-05-02-0309.

4. Washington to Benjamin Harrison, 24 September 1787, Founders Online, National Archive, http://founders.archives.gov/documents/Washington/04-05-02-0316.

5. David Humphreys to Washington, 28 September 1787, Founders Online, National Archive, http://founders.archives.gov/documents/Washington/04-05-02-0320.

6. Henry Knox to Unknown (Draft), September 1787, in John Kaminski et al. eds., *Documentary History of the Ratification of the Constitution*, 27 vols., (Madison: University of Wisconsin Press, 1976–), IV.

7. Edmund Pendleton to James Madison, 8 October 1787. See Woody Holton, *Unruly Americans*.

8. James Wilson, speech to the Pennsylvania ratifying convention, 4 December 1787, in Sheehan and McDowell, eds., *Friends of the Constitution*, 216.

9. Civis [David Ramsay], "An Address to the Freemen of South Carolina on the Subject of the Federal Constitution," 4 February 1788, in ibid., 456.

10. Henry Knox to Unknown (Draft), September 1787, in Documentary History of the Ratification.

11. James Madison to Thomas Jefferson, 24 September 1787, Founders Online, National Archive, http://founders.archives.gov/documents/Jefferson/01-12-02-0274.

12. James Wilson, speech to the Pennsylvania ratifying convention, 24 November 1787, in Sheehan and McDowell, eds., *Friends of the Constitution*, 83.

13. Fabius [John Dickinson], "Letter VII," in ibid., 487.

14. A Landholder [Oliver Ellsworth], "To the Holders and Tillers of Land, III," in ibid., 292.

15. A Citizen of New York [John Jay], "Address," 1788, in ibid., 153, 150.

16. Saul Cornell, *The Other Founders: Anti-Federalism and the Dissenting Tradition in America, 1788–1828* (Chapel Hill: University of North Carolina Press, 1999), chap. 2.

17. Patrick Henry in Herbert J. Storing ed., *The Complete Anti-Federalist, 7 vols.* (Chicago: University of Chicago Press, 1981), V, 229.

18. Ibid., III, 13.

19. "The Address and Reasons of Dissent of the Minority of the Convention of Pennsylvania to their Constituents," in ibid., III, 145–165, esp. 148.

20. Cornell, *The Other Founders*, chap. 3.

21. America [Noah Webster], in the *Daily Advertiser*, New York, 31 December 1787; in Sheehan and McDowell, eds., *Friends of the Constitution*, 169, 176, 178.

22. A Citizen of America [Noah Webster], "An Examination into the Leading Principles of the Federal Constitution," Philadelphia, 17 October 1787, in ibid., 373–405, esp. 400.

23. Ibid., 400–401.

24. "Dissent of the Minority of Pennsylvania," in Storing, ed., *Complete Anti-Federalist*, 148.

25. Jonathan Elliot, ed., *The Debates in the Several State Conventions on the Adoption of the Federal Constitution* (Washington, 1836), II, 426.

26. Peter Lindert and Jeffrey Williamson, *Unequal Gains: American Growth and Inequality Since 1700* (Princeton: Princeton University Press, 2016); Branko Milanovic, *Global Inequality: A New Approach for the Age of Globalization* (Cambridge: Harvard University Press, 2016); Thomas Picketty, *Capital in the Twenty-First Century* (Cambridge: Harvard University Press, 2013).

27. Those changes continued, of course, after the ratification of the constitution. As Richard Bushman shows, the allure of gentility did not diminish. "By the middle of the nineteenth century," he writes, "vernacular gentility had become the possession of the American middle class." Bushman, *Refinement of America*, xiii.

A NOTE ON THE TYPE

THIS BOOK has been composed in Miller, a Scotch Roman typeface designed by Matthew Carter and first released by Font Bureau in 1997. It resembles Monticello, the typeface developed for The Papers of Thomas Jefferson in the 1940s by C. H. Griffith and P. J. Conkwright and reinterpreted in digital form by Carter in 2003.

Pleasant Jefferson ("P. J.") Conkwright (1905–1986) was Typographer at Princeton University Press from 1939 to 1970. He was an acclaimed book designer and AIGA Medalist.

The ornament used throughout this book was designed by Pierre Simon Fournier (1712–1768) and was a favorite of Conkwright's, used in his design of the *Princeton University Library Chronicle*.